Pious Passion

Comparative Studies in Religion and Society
Mark Juergensmeyer, editor

Pious Passion

The Emergence of Modern
Fundamentalism in the
United States and Iran

Martin Riesèbrodt

Translated from the German by
Don Reneau

UNIVERSITY OF CALIFORNIA PRESS
Berkeley · Los Angeles · London

Originally published in German as
*Fundamentalismus als patriarchalische
Protestbewegung.* © 1990 J. C. B. Mohr, Tübingen.

University of California Press
Berkeley and Los Angeles, California

University of California Press, Ltd.
London, England

First Paperback Printing 1998

Library of Congress Cataloging-in-Publication Data

Riesebrodt, Martin.
[Fundamentalismus als patriarchalische Protestbewegung. English]
Pious passion : the emergence of modern fundamentalism in the
United States and Iran / Martin Riesebrodt ; translated from the
German by Don Reneau.
p.   cm. — (Comparative studies in religion and society : 6)
Includes bibliographical references and index.
ISBN 0-520-07464-5 (pbk : alk. paper)
1. Fundamentalism.   2. Shi'ites—Iran.   3. Islamic fundamentalism.
4. Islamic fundamentalism—Iran.   I. Title.   II. Series.
BT82.2.R5413   1993
299.3'0821—dc20   92-32233
                                                                        CIP

Printed in the United States of America

9   8   7   6   5   4   3   2   1

To M. Rainer Lepsius

Contents

Preface

As of 1990, when this book was first published in German, there had been no comparative sociological treatment of fundamentalist movements. The present work, therefore, can neither offer a synthesis of previous work nor attempt to conclude a debate, but must first clear the way for such a scholarly discussion. The goal of the book is accordingly modest. It seeks, through its definition of the subject, methodology, and results, to lay a basis, offer hypotheses, and stimulate questions for further universal historical, comparative research on fundamentalism.

Even if the preparation of the present work was a rather lonely affair on the whole, numerous institutions and individuals nevertheless contributed to it through their encouragement and discussions. But for a one-year stay at the Center for European Studies at Harvard University, I would never have selected the topic. I thank Abby Collins, Guido Goldman, and Stanley Hoffman for their hospitality at the Center, and Harvey Goldman for his active efforts on my behalf. My further thanks are due the Deutsche Forschungsgemeinschaft for a two-year *Habilitation* fellowship, Harvard's Sociology Department for six months of hospitality, the Research Institute of the Humanities at Dartmouth College for a three-month stay, and the Fundamentalism Project of the American Academy of Arts and Sciences, organized in Chicago by Martin Marty and Scott Appleby, for the opportunity to present and discuss my results in public.

Walter Bühl provided me the opportunity to complete my *Habilitation* in unsettled times. His openness, fairness, and enormous scholarly competence created the environment that enabled me to complete this book. For all of this, my special thanks. I had fruitful discussions at Harvard with Orlando Patterson and in Stony Brook with Said Arjomand, whose works on the sociology of Shi'ism have also provided me with theoretical enrichment. Albert Hourani, Miriam Cooke, Gene Garthwaite, and Kevin Reinhart were important discussion partners at Dartmouth. But I profited there above all from my intellectual exchange with Bruce Lawrence as I have from my discussions with Gail Kligman over many years. Above all, the works of M. Rainer Lepsius have had an enormous influence on me. To him, the teacher of many who never studied with him, this American edition is dedicated on the occasion of his sixty-fifth birthday.

Thanks also to Naomi Schneider, Valeurie Friedman, and Mark Pentecost from the University of California Press and to the translator, Don Reneau. I am particularly grateful to Stephanie Fowler for editing the text and improving its readability considerably.

I thank my wife for her generosity in putting her own interests aside for several years. That she did so consistently without reproach was of particular help to me. The manuscript was read in part or in whole by Walter Bühl, Friedrich Graf, Horst Jürgen Helle, Gangolf Hübinger, Mark Juergensmeyer, Hans Kippenberg, Bruce Lawrence, and Bernd Ostendorf. I am grateful to all of them for their critical assistance. They are responsible for all of the errors and weaknesses in the work; the good insights came from me. Or do I have this backward?

CHAPTER 1

Fundamentalism as a Sociological Problem

Since the end of the 1970s, "fundamentalism" has rapidly become a catchword in academic and journalistic discourse. The term is used primarily to designate the religious protest movements and militant groups whose radical demands and spectacular actions have dramatically altered political relations, above all in Islamic countries, but also in Israel, the United States, and South and East Asia.

Inside the revolutionary coalition in Iran that toppled the shah in 1979, Shi'ite clergy and its followers proved the strongest force, establishing an Islamic republic under the leadership of Ayatollah Khomeini. In the same year Sunni fundamentalists occupied the Great Mosque in Mecca. In 1981 a terrorist fundamentalist group assassinated the Egyptian president Anwar Sadat. Among the factors contributing to the political deterioration of Lebanon, not least was the increased power of the Iranian-oriented Hizb Allah, whose hostage taking and use of suicide commandos against Israeli, French, and American soldiers brought it international attention. The resistance against the Soviet occupation of Afghanistan was maintained to a critical degree by fundamentalist Sunni and Shi'ite guerrillas. In the Sudan fundamentalist tendencies in the Islamic north increased in strength and sharpened the conflict with the non-Muslim south. And even Turkey, with its decades of secularization policy, has been experiencing a resurgence of Islamic fervor for some years.[1]

Fundamentalism, however, is in no way limited to the "backward Orient." On the contrary, since the late 1970s fundamentalism has once

1

again become a prominent topic in the leading Western industrial societies, with unabashed parallels drawn to developments in Iran: "The fanatical mullahs have been let loose in the land, *this* land," writes Peter Berger, referring to the United States.[2] Prominent fundamentalist television preachers, like Jerry Falwell and Pat Robertson, joined forces with conservative politicians and enjoyed some success influencing the U.S. presidential and congressional elections of 1980. Particularly among liberals, their resurgence spurred reminiscences of Prohibition and the Scopes trial, of the McCarthy era and the resistance to the civil rights movement.

Fundamentalist movements have emerged in other countries as well. Gush Emunim in Israel represents a militant variety of Jewish fundamentalism. Radical-traditionalist Catholic movements of the twentieth century have had close connections with fascist movements, especially in Eastern and Southern Europe. More recently, traditionalist and integralist subcurrents within the Catholic church have strengthened. Fundamentalism among the Sikhs in India and the Sinhalese Buddhists in Sri Lanka suggests that such movements are possible in all religions of salvation and redemption.

Fundamentalism is therefore neither an exclusively Shi'ite, Islamic, or Iranian phenomenon, nor a specifically Protestant, Christian, or North American one. It is found worldwide.[3]

FUNDAMENTALISM AND SOCIOLOGY

In view of the political significance and universal distribution of fundamentalism, we might expect that, in addition to political journalism and the regionally, nationally, or culturally oriented academic disciplines, the theoretically oriented, empirical social sciences would have taken pains to interpret and explain the phenomenon. That, however, is by no means the case.

Although there are many studies of individual fundamentalist movements, a theoretically oriented—that is, an intercultural and historically comparative—treatment of this topic is only in its infancy.[4] The lack of a unified terminology, a clear definition, and a differentiated typology makes it difficult to compare the results of the various studies. The assumption that concepts of fundamentalism refer to even remotely similar and meaningfully comparable phenomena cannot be taken for granted. Are there significant points in common among the various "fundamentalisms"? If so, what are they?

This lack of clarity leads to the classification of fundamentalisms under other movements. The most frequent comparison, and probably the most appropriate as well, is between fundamentalist and fascist movements. In the absence of careful comparative analyses, however, it is difficult to ground this classification scientifically. Fundamentalism has also been interpreted as populism and, Islamic fundamentalism in particular, as a Third World anti-imperialist movement.[5]

How can we explain this discrepancy between the enormous political significance of fundamentalism and its insufficient sociological treatment? The simplest, and to some the easiest, explanation is that no unifying theory is possible, because at issue are completely heterogeneous phenomena that can only dubiously be designated by the same concept. This argument is not to be dismissed out of hand, since an undifferentiated subsumption of, for example, the pacifist Amish and the militant Hizb Allah under the same category illuminates nothing. Frequently expressed in such rejections, however, is a lack of understanding in principle of intercultural comparisons unless they emphasize the respective distinctions. Comparisons that seek to generalize, especially in the case of such culturally specific phenomena as religious movements, meet considerable skepticism. After all, our perception is widely preformed by the dramatization of cultural differences, for example of those between the Orient and the Occident.

The lack of a comparative sociology of fundamentalism is further reinforced by a range of factors coincident with the rise and development of the discipline: its bias against religious phenomena, its Enlightenment historical teleology, its Eurocentric limitations.

Sociology stems from the same social processes of urbanization and industrialization that engendered fundamentalist protest, but makes its appearance as an adversary to the traditionalist camp. Representative of the new secular academic elites, sociologists consider themselves agents of enlightenment, committed to a rational implementation of progress that they often equate with secularization. As a result, they tend to underestimate the significance of religious phenomena. Religion is regarded as the relic of a past epoch, destined either to disappear entirely or to be forced into the private sphere. When religious phenomena, especially of an ultraconservative or reactionary nature, contrary to those expectations have figured significantly in historical events, they have often been so fervently opposed that sober analysis of their origins and self-definition has not been possible.[6]

A worldwide revitalization of religion for the orientation and legitimation of social action has accompanied the rise of fundamentalist movements. Liberation theology in Latin America, the peace movement in the Federal Republic of Germany, the role of Catholicism in Poland and the public positions adopted by the Catholic bishops in the United States on economic, social, and military policies, and the renaissance of Russian Orthodoxy compel a revision of basic assumptions concerning the inevitability and irreversibility of secularization and institutional differentiation. Sociology, if it wants to retain its status as an empirical social science, must give religious movements a place in the discipline that befits their actual historical significance.

This means that sociology must acknowledge fundamentalism and take it seriously as a potentially universal religious and political phenomenon. Fundamentalist movements raise problems central to our times, not questions of bygone eras. Forcing fundamentalism into the spheres of the exotic, the ridiculous, or the diabolical or using Manichean polarizations to stigmatize its adherents as antienlightenment or antimodern interferes with our recognition of fundamentalism's structural problems and thereby reduces our chances of limiting damage and suffering.

The task of sociology is to soberly elucidate why such movements are presently booming in nearly all world religions; what experiences mobilize people politically; in which interpretive models these experiences are transformed; what fears, hopes, and goals the carriers of such movements have; and what processes of structural change lie behind them. This, however, can be achieved only through systematic comparisons of fundamentalist movements in various religions and cultures, from which we can attempt to arrive at a theoretical explanation.

Beyond this, sociology must also ask how fundamentalism compares with other social (and political) movements. In addition to its differences, fundamentalism manifests distinct parallels and overlappings with other movements, in particular, populism and fascism. Here, too, there is no advantage to strategies that hastily subsume fundamentalism under other categories, labeling it, for example, "religiously colored" populism or fascism in "religious garb." Until we have carefully analyzed its similarities and differences, we should appropriately treat fundamentalism as a distinct type of social phenomenon. We must therefore clarify the effects of the central role that religious intellectual traditions, categories, symbols, and often religious intellectuals, have in fundamentalism. Do fundamentalism, populism, and fascism arise under similar or different conditions? How do they distinguish themselves in the social composition of their elites and adherents and in the content and structure of their ideologies? Premature subsumptions or superficial analogies are not helpful.

Such a comprehensive program cannot, of course, be fulfilled within the compass of this book. But the questions addressed provide a context and indicate the long-term research interests from which this study can be put in perspective. My object here was to take a step in the designated direction. In view of the relatively scant sociological research, it is first necessary to attempt a comparison of the fundamentalist movements of different cultures. We can then question the sense and fruitfulness of such an undertaking and next develop hypotheses for further research.

An essential precondition of such a comparative sociology is the establishment of definitional and typological terms that on the one hand clearly delimit fundamentalism from other social and religious movements and on the other differentiate and structure the abundance of fundamentalist phenomena. Given such a basis, aimed at maximal precision and clarity, we can then elaborate the structural features of fundamentalist movements that transcend their respective cultures. I do this here in a comparison between Protestant fundamentalism in the United States from 1910 to 1928 and Shi'ite fundamentalism in Iran from 1961 to 1979. Why am I investigating only two movements? Why did I choose precisely these two? What aspects did I choose to analyze?

The existing literature on fundamentalism is limited largely to investigations of only one movement, from which parallels to other fundamentalist movements, fascism, or populism are occasionally drawn. These unsystematically associated similarities can indeed be illuminating in individual cases, but they offer no methodologically reliable basis for a theoretical explanation. A better approach to an elaboration of a sociological theory of fundamentalist movements would be to investigate many cases with the same thoroughness and with the same questions and conceptions. Such an undertaking, however, would require unlimited amounts of work, time, and knowledge.[7] Therefore, I decided to test first the fruitfulness of such a comparison using only two fundamentalist movements. If this type of analysis is not useful, it is meaningless to add more cases. If it is successful, then at least a foundation has been laid on which we can critically build further investigations.

My specific choice of Protestant fundamentalism in the early twentieth century in the United States and prerevolutionary fundamentalism in Iran is not only a product of personal interest but is also based on

scientific criteria. Since the popularization of the term "fundamentalism" is associated with these two movements, it makes sense to use
these cases to test the possibility and fruitfulness of a generalizing intercultural comparison.

In the periods investigated, both movements can be classified under
the same type of fundamentalism. They are organized as protest movements, are led in a decisive sense by religious intellectuals, and arise
from comparable conditions, primarily those associated with rapid urbanization. The temporal limitation permits the most extensive comparison of the participants in different fundamentalist movements. The economic and demographic transformations change the social structures of
both societies in similar directions. Thereby they create generations that
are shaped by comparable sociohistorical experiences. The comparabil-
ity has, however, obvious limits. Therefore the new structures created
by the Iranian revolution and the seizure of power by the clergy exceed
the bounds of this study, and in the United States the formation of
Protestant fundamentalism as a theological doctrine is of less interest
than its transformation into political demands and actions.

The comparison between Protestant fundamentalism in the United
States and Shi'ite fundamentalism in Iran is not, of course, based on
assumed similarities between the social structures or the economic, political, and legal institutions of the two countries. Nor did I assume that
no significant differences existed between ascetic Protestantism and
Shi'ite Islam. Reference to such obvious differences, however, in no way
renders such a comparison absurd or undermines its results. Instead, the
real question is how, under such distinct social, economic, and political
conditions, such similar movements can appear. The apparent contradiction between the dissimilar social conditions and the obvious parallels
in ideology, carriers, and the causes of mobilization should in fact stimulate scientific curiosity and call into question established habits of
thought and perspectives.

Peter Berger has formulated an objection to the comparison undertaken here that must be taken seriously. He represents the view that,
despite a few parallels, an unbridgeable gap yawns between Protestant
and Islamic fundamentalism. The ideal order of Protestant fundamentalism is found in the nineteenth century; it is a part of Western modernism.
The ideal order of Islamic fundamentalism, in contrast, is in the seventh
century; it is premodern and antimodern.[8] I do not regard this objection
as ultimately valid. The ideas of order in both fundamentalisms possess
both a legitimating and a pragmatic side. The legitimating model refers to

the orders of the original communities of the respective religious founders. The pragmatic model derives in both cases from the more recent past. Thus, Islamic fundamentalism in no sense strives to do away with the petroleum industry, the modern mass communications media, the automobile, or modern weapons systems in order to restore the original community in technological or economic terms. The mobilizing and legitimating functions of a statutory ethical literalism should not be confused with the actually envisioned social order, which is neither in Protestantism nor in Islam the original community of the founder.

Finally, one could raise political and moral objections to a comparison of Shi'ite and Protestant fundamentalism, primarily in view of postrevolutionary practices in Iran and the militance of most Islamic fundamentalist groups in the Near and Middle East since the end of the 1970s. A comparison of the two movements, however, in no way implies their moral or political identification. More accurately, in that sense, no parallel is drawn between the two movements and no comparative evaluation undertaken.

To prevent misunderstandings, however, it must be explicitly stated that Shi'ite fundamentalism in Iran was by no means particularly militant prior to the revolution, even though the Pahlavi regime brutally repressed and humiliated the entire religious opposition. In contrast, there was some measure of cooperation among the leaders of Protestant fundamentalist groups and the Ku Klux Klan, and members of one organization often belonged to the other. The moral-political dimension, therefore, cannot simply be bound to the allegedly peaceful character of Protestantism or the militancy of Islam. Those who are interested in this dimension need to analyze the structural conditions that either incline a movement to violence or make such an inclination improbable. In the event, Christian varieties of fundamentalism are no less capable of militancy than Islamic ones.[9]

The comparison of two fundamentalist movements as conceived here opens up several avenues for sociological theory. On the one hand, one could aim at a universal theory of fundamentalist movements, which would have to rest in principle on a comparison of all fundamental movements within all cultures and—insofar as this is not excluded by definition—all epochs.[10] On the other, one could strive to elaborate a historically and structurally limited theory, although on a global scale, which takes as its object religious-fundamentalist movements in the context of modernization, especially rapid urbanization and industrialization.

As I have suggested above, however, what interests me is a theory based on the idea of *radical-traditionalist* movements, departing from Said Arjomand's concept of *revolutionary traditionalism*.[11] Religious fundamentalism, accordingly, is a variant of the type of movement that conjures up a mythical past to mobilize traditionalists politically. Fundamentalism is thus placed in a larger context, and we can attempt to compare its ideologies, adherents, or causes of mobilization with those of secular movements while at the same time recognizing that the movements also have inherent differences.

My comparison of Shi'ite and Protestant fundamentalism consciously abandons the perspective internalized by many since Max Weber's *The Economic Ethic of the World Religions,* that is, the drawing of historical comparisons from the point of view of the particular development of the West. As legitimate and illuminating as this perspective was and remains for research into the endogenous development of modern capitalism and modern democracy, its application to other phenomena and problems may not be advancing our knowledge of them. Moreover, this perspective has contributed to an interpretation of the Western path of development as the "normal" one and other historical developments as "deviations," although such was not Weber's intention.

My approach here assumes that all societies are equally "normal" or "exotic." Our often antiquated notions of "civilization," and the value judgments implicit in them, lead others besides sociologists astray. This, naturally, does not mean that I ignore culturally specific distinctions, but they provide neither the premise nor the explanatory goal of my approach. Culturally specific distinctions must also be qualified at the outset by an empirical demonstration of their actual effects. It is quite possible, for example, that the millenarian and messianic components of the sectarian past common to both Shi'ite Islam and ascetic Protestantism are more significant for the development of fundamentalism than the distinguishing aspects of the Protestant Christian and Shi'ite Islamic religious traditions.

Generalizing and individualizing methods are by no means mutually exclusive over the longer run.[12] At the outset, however, and in view of the current state of research, it seems to me to make sense to pursue a generalizing perspective. Only in this way, in my judgment, can a theoretically oriented foundation be laid for comparative research into fundamentalism. Later on this generalizing approach can be further developed to emphasize more strongly the particularities of the various fundamentalist movements, paying attention not only to their distinct cultural traditions but also to their specific institutional structures.

Max Weber's concept of the relative autonomy of the various social spheres, not the least of which is religion, is important here. To uphold this concept, however, both the inner laws of religion and its dependencies and interdependencies with other social factors must always be defined anew for each case.

This work represents a contribution to comparative sociology. Its ambition therefore is not to add to the body of empirical historical academic research but to establish a theoretically oriented sociological conceptualization, an intellectual reordering of material according to a new vantage point. The book's central thesis is that fundamentalism refers to an urban movement directed primarily against the dissolution of personalistic, patriarchal notions of order and social relations and their replacement by depersonalized principles. It therefore concerns a social transformation of epochal proportions, a qualitative change in virtually all social relations, interactions, and institutions.

Because, however, the effects of this transformation stretch over many decades, they do not by themselves explain the phases of fundamentalist mass mobilization. The phases, in my view, are prompted by the interaction of structural causes and immediate circumstances. I argue that the most important structural cause is the dramatic reduction in the chances of the traditionalist milieu to reproduce itself culturally under conditions of rapid urbanization, industrialization, and secularization. In these circumstances the milieu not only is threatened from without but it also begins, often in the form of a generational conflict, to disintegrate from within. Also present as an additional immediate occasion for mobilization are public and frequently provocative attacks against traditional values and symbols by other social groups or the state.

As will become evident in later, empirical chapters, the interpretation only briefly sketched here rests on an attempt to reconstruct the fate of those mobilized, based on a systematic interrelationship between transformation processes, their religious interpretation, and protest actions. My interpretation in no way claims to establish a broad model encompassing all fundamentalist movements. I claim validity only for the two cases investigated, in the hope, however, that I have presented some hypotheses that will stimulate further the comparative study of fundamentalism.

FUNDAMENTALISM: A DISPUTED CONCEPT

The concept of fundamentalism still lacks a commonly accepted definition or application, indicating the nascent state of comparative research on fundamentalism. The same label is used to designate, for example, the militant Hizb Allah and the pacifist Amish. Therefore, for better or worse, I begin my investigation by presenting a definition of fundamentalism that attempts to transform it into a sociologically meaningful concept. Because this construction is determined by theoretically informed perspectives and fundamental assumptions, I draw them also into the discussion.

Before I present and justify my own definition, however, I would like to relate briefly the history of the concept of fundamentalism, its historical origins and diffusion in American Protestantism, and its subsequent application to Islamic movements. For the question naturally arises of whether the fundamentalism concept is generalizable in the first place or whether alternatives are available, such as the concept of integralism stemming from francophone Catholicism. Or should one simply introduce historically neutral terminology, as, for example, that of radical neotraditionalism?[13]

Fundamentalism was coined in 1920 by Curtis Lee Laws, the editor of a Baptist periodical called the *Watchman-Examiner*. He used the term to designate a broad conservative movement made up of various groups within American Protestantism. It stated its position in a series of brochures, "The Fundamentals: A Testimony to the Truth," which appeared between 1910 and 1915. Published by leading conservative theologians of the time, approximately three million of these tracts were disseminated. Sixty-four authors—theologians, preachers, and missionaries—contributed ninety articles, which discussed contested points of dogma primarily in the defense of biblical literalism.

This new movement represented a minimal consensus among various conservative positions rather than an independent, closed theological system. Unanimity was founded on five *fundamentals* of faith. The most important point was the infallibility of the Bible, which was considered the verbally inspired word of God and consequently was to be interpreted literally, not symbolically. The other four principles of faith—the Virgin Birth, the Resurrection, Christ's proxy atonement of sin, and the Second Coming—were concerned with making precise the claims of biblical literalism. The selection of these elements was in no way accidental; theologically, they represented fundamentalism's unified opposition to the modern biblical criticism of liberal theology and the social reformist theology of the Social Gospel. Beyond that, the fundamentalist camp unified opposing currents, postmillenarian as well as premillenarian, religious nationalist as well as pacifist.

The concept of fundamentalism at the time, however, was meant to designate less a religious and theological coalition than a social movement developing after the First World War, one which successfully exerted political influence. Thus were fundamentalists critically involved in enacting Prohibition, and they achieved their greatest success in forbidding the teaching of the Darwinian theory of evolution in the public schools of several American states.

In view of this transformation of fundamentalism from a theological position into first a religious and then a social movement, it is not surprising that it is subject to more than one designation or classification. Depending on the academic focus and theological or political position, it can be characterized on the one hand as religious-theological traditionalism or on the other as a radical right-wing movement. In one light fundamentalism is the passive victim of modernization, seeking only to defend "old-time religion"; in another it is the narrow-minded and intolerant activist, confronting the promoters of progress, freedom, and enlightenment. Some images of fundamentalism are derived primarily from the controversies of the 1920s, but others are based on its theological texts and their continuity with currents of the nineteenth century.[14] Common to most of these interpretations is the identification of fundamentalism with a concrete movement in the United States in the early twentieth century.

William McLoughlin, in contrast, represents a more strongly theoretical perspective. He interprets fundamentalism in the context of a general explanation of the great movements of "awakening" in the United States. In his view these awakenings were the occasions for an adjustment of worldviews to changed social, economic, psychological, and ecological conditions through recourse to one's cultural heritage. The progressives ("New Lights") succeeded in giving shape to this adjustment in opposition to the reactionaries or traditionalists ("Old Lights"), who, however, over time joined in the new consensus. McLoughlin sees fundamentalism as essentially a reactionary movement or, formulated differently, as the nativist phase within this period of adjustment.[15]

Admittedly, this bifurcation between progressive and reactionary forces may be a dubious abridgement, and the functionalist belief in integration ignores the continuity of religious currents with opposed value orientations. Nevertheless, this approach has two advantages in comparison with its predecessors. First, it attempts to bring political, economic, social structural, psychological, and cultural factors into systematic interrelation. Second, it manifests, if somewhat timidly, the beginnings of a generalization beyond the American context. Fundamentalism appears here as part of a complex social process of transformation and cultural reorientation that in principle could be found in any society.

Another generalization about fundamentalism has gradually made its way into some of the academic literature on religion and into the American vernacular in general. Here, all groups espousing biblical literalism are subsumed under the category. Thus some speak of a fundamentalism within black churches, and Bryan Wilson in his definition of fundamentalism encompasses, among others, the Salvation Army, Pentecostals, Amish Mennonites, and "snake handlers."[16]

This broadening of the concept has advantages and disadvantages. One advantage is the introduction of a theoretical perspective resulting from a more general characterization of fundamentalism that transcends the actual "fundamentalist" movement. The subsumption under the same category of heterogeneous phenomena in religious-theological and sociological terms, however, is problematic. Black churches are thus lumped together with those of the traditionalist, Anglo-Saxon middle class; charismatic groups centered around religious experience and emotion and rationalistic moralists, the proponents of the "electronic church" and the antitechnological Amish, and world-fleeing sects and religious-political mass movements are all included. Such an overly broad understanding of fundamentalism fails to supply a suitable foundation for sociological comparisons.

Theoretical approaches to the interpretation of fundamentalism also integrate it into wholly distinct contexts, thereby sketching quite diverging pictures of it. It has been characterized as an antimodernist movement of uneducated yokels; a right-wing radicalism with religious coloration; the nativist phase within periods of cultural adaptation to prior socioeconomic transformations; a primarily religious movement with political, social, and cultural implications; and finally a purely religious phenomenon.[17]

The application of the concept of fundamentalism to Islam is not in fact more recent but has gained much wider currency since the Iranian revolution of 1979. Nor in this case has a consistent usage emerged. The concept is generally either implicitly avoided or explicitly rejected. Journalistic language has tended to associate fundamentalism with the more violent aspects of militant or radical Islam.

Various arguments justify the explicit rejection of the fundamentalism concept. Many experts on Islam object to the adoption of a concept from an alien cultural and historical context or they assume in principle the uniqueness and incomparability of such phenomena. In all cases they accept concepts, such as Islamism, that generalize within the Islamic cultural sphere, but this is obviously unsuited to our purposes.

Others argue that *all* Islamic positions represent a literalist interpretation of the Koran and are therefore fundamentalist. Thus the concept is not transferable, because literalism does not distinguish fundamentalists from other Muslims.[18] This position, however, is clearly based on an incomplete understanding of Protestant fundamentalism, which as we will see is in no way reducible to a conflict between biblical criticism and biblical literalism or between the theory of evolution and the doctrine of creation.

In the academic literature interested in theoretically oriented concept formation, the fundamentalism concept competes primarily with that of integralism. Integralism is used most frequently in francophone literature and represents the Catholic variant to the Protestant concept of fundamentalism in the anglophone world. Integralism originally designated an antimodernist movement within the Catholic church around the turn of the century. Since it is in many basic features thoroughly comparable to Protestant fundamentalism, which appeared at the same time, it would be no less legitimate to select the Catholic model instead of the Protestant as the conceptual foundation for comparable Islamic movements.[19] Nevertheless, the integralism concept is more limited by its strong association with Catholic antimodernism and the hierocratic power interests of the Catholic church than is the fundamentalism concept with its point of historical origination.[20]

Theoretical approaches to the interpretation of Islamic fundamentalism also sketch quite various images of the phenomenon. Some consider it a typical Third World response to the neocolonialism of the great powers, with the single difference that in distinction to other movements it incorporates religious ideology and symbolism. Some characterize it primarily as antimodernism, antipluralism, or a movement directed against the Enlightenment. A few interpret Shi'ite fundamentalism as petit-bourgeois chiliasm in reaction to capitalist disintegration of the traditional economy.[21] Yet again, others emphasize the lack of cultural orientation and the disappointed social expectations

on the part of younger, often poorly educated migrants to the city
from rural or provincial milieus.[22] Even if all of these explanations
were partially correct, how they fit together would remain an open
question.

The most convincing definition of fundamentalism within Islam
comes from Stephen Humphreys.[23] He delimits fundamentalism from
both traditionalism and conservatism as well as from modernism. Islamic modernism and fundamentalism represent reactions to secularization. Both are therefore new phenomena, the responses to a changed
social milieu, but with mutually distinct recourses to religious tradition.
Fundamentalism is, consequently, by no means undifferentiatedly antimodern or anti-intellectual. Humphreys characterizes Islamic fundamentalism primarily by its insistence on the validity of the Koran's statutory
and ritual stipulations. He identifies its most important transmitters in
general as groups pushed to the side of or made anxious by modern
developments, primarily artisans, traders, and the clergy. Its ideology
and symbolism also appeal to groups that do not belong among its
adherents in the narrower sense, such as members of the lower urban
classes and even frustrated intellectuals with a modern education.[24]

Until now few attempts have been made to make the fundamentalism
concept fruitful for cross-cultural comparisons. There is naturally no
lack of parallels drawn polemically, between, for example, Protestant
fundamentalists of the present and Shi'ite mullahs.[25] Serious conceptual-
izations are, in contrast, rare. Primarily notable among them, in my
view, are the attempts by Lionel Caplan, Martin Marty, and Bruce
Lawrence to approach fundamentalism in cross-culturally comparative
terms.[26]

Caplan's attempt, nevertheless, seems to me to fall considerably short
of success. In his introduction to the anthology published under his
editorship, *Studies in Religious Fundamentalism,* Caplan analyzes a few
aspects of fundamentalism without reference to a specific definition,
typology, or model. Thus the criteria according to which various phenomena have been subsumed under a single category ultimately remain
unclear. The empirical multiplicity of fundamentalism becomes for Caplan an occasion not for developing a clear terminology but for increasing confusion: he states, for example, that we are all "to a certain
degree" and "in a certain sense" fundamentalists.[27]

In contrast, Martin Marty, the organizer of the universal comparative Fundamentalism Project of the American Academy of Arts and
Sciences, identifies a few of the significant characteristics of fundamen-

talism, such as its reactive character, separatism, Manichaeism, claim to absolutism, antipluralism, moral absolutism, and anti-evolutionary mentality, for which history is interpretable not as progress but as degeneration.[28] This provisional compilation of essential features of fundamentalist thinking is helpful, although its systematic unification is yet to be accomplished.

A somewhat different accent is put on the matter by Bruce Lawrence, who largely takes up Humphrey's suggestions on Islamic fundamentalism and generalizes them further.[29] Lawrence emphasizes above all the novel character of fundamentalism. He defines it as a religious ideology formed in conflict with modernism and characterizable by five features: its status as the view of a sectarian minority; its oppositional attitude; its male-dominated, charismatic leadership by subordinated elites; its polished technical vocabulary; and its historical novelty deriving from its antimodernist, reactive impetus. The strength of Lawrence's approach lies mainly in its understanding of fundamentalism as a product of the tension between tradition and modernity in the world religions of Judaism, Islam, and Christianity. His interest here is rather of an intellectual-historical or social-philosophical sort. Nevertheless, his study has laid a cornerstone on which a sociological work can also build, because here for the first time fundamentalism, as a transcultural phenomenon, has been located in a developmental historical framework.

FUNDAMENTALISM: TOWARD DEFINITION AND TYPOLOGY

Because "fundamentalism" has become established, it makes little sense to replace it by another term. Nor would anything be gained by its replacement. The problem lies not in the concept itself but in its capacity to generate necessary distinctions. We need a clear definition of relevant criteria, not more neologisms, which proliferate in the literature.

An attempt to make the conception of fundamentalism more precise confronts the immediate problem of integrating academic and colloquial usage. If we define the fundamentalism concept too narrowly, to make it operable sociologically, there is the danger that everyone will formulate their own definitions that no one else will follow. Conceived broadly, in correspondence with colloquial usage, it remains sociologically amorphous. For that reason my definition encompasses a typological differentiation that refers to the broad understanding of the concept as it has become widely established in the academic literature on religion. This path seems to me preferable both for pragmatic reasons and from a theoretical point of view.

As a first step I would like to take up the identification of fundamentalism with biblical or koranic literalism. Fundamentalist thinking is marked by a profound experience of crisis. The cause of the crisis is society's desertion of eternally valid, divinely revealed, and textually literal received principles of order, which had once been realized in an ideal community—the "Golden Age" of original Christian, Islamic, or other communities.[30] Overcoming the crisis is possible only by a return to these divine statutory prescriptions. Fundamentalism thereby distinguishes itself both from traditionalism and from utopian strategies, both of which likewise lay claim to an authentic realization of the revealed principles of order. Yet literalism and authenticity in the given cases have different functions.

Traditionalistic literalism represents an aid to orientation to and affirmation of a certain sanctioned way of life. As a rule it also creates an inner, and possibly outer, world of imaginary idols and saints, to whom the faithful analogously relate themselves. Fundamentalist literalism, in contrast, reflects an ideology fighting a cultural struggle, one in which literalism, or the way of life associated with it, is disputed. In this sense fundamentalism is—if not *revolutionary traditionalism*—then at least *mobilized and radicalized traditionalism*.[31]

Fundamentalist literalism also distinguishes itself from social revolutionary or reformist projections of the future that likewise seek legitimacy through an appeal to divine law, revelation, or an ideal original community. This identification with an ideal original order can be effected in either *mythical* or *utopian* terms. As myth it has the function of a restorative surmounting of a crisis. The "Golden Age" is to be recreated through a return to its principles of order as handed down verbatim. As utopia, in contrast, the ideal order serves the purposes of a "progressive" social reformist or social revolutionary surmounting of the crisis. Not the letter but the "spirit" of the ideal order as it was once in the past is to be realized under new conditions.[32] Consequently, "mythical" thinking is characterized tendentially by a statutory ethic; "utopian" thinking, in contrast, is supported by a radical ethic of conviction. As with all typological distinctions, borderline cases and other variations are conceivable. I apply the fundamentalism concept to those positions that can be categorized, however roughly, as "mythical." Those choosing not to adopt this terminology should nevertheless retain the distinction between these two forms of religious revitalization.

DEVELOPMENT AND TYPES OF RELIGIOUS REVITALIZATION

Rapid social change
|
Crisis consciousness
|
Religious revitalization and
search for authenticity
|
Regress to the revealed and realized ideal order

Utopian regress   Mythical regress
| |
"Analogous" authenticity   "Identical" authenticity
|
"Spirit" of the ideal order   Literalist   Experiential
                                     (sacred text)   (gift of grace)
                                     | |
                                     "Rational"   Charismatic
                                     fundamentalism   fundamentalism

Historical-evolutionary thinking   Antievolutionary thinking
| |
Social reform or revolution   Fundamentalism
(Ethic of conviction)   (Statutory ethic)

Further, fundamentalism refers to a social phenomenon, not only in the banal sense that its origins are somehow social and its intellectual posture represents a mass phenomenon but also in the sense that it promotes above all new processes of socialization and community formation.[33] In contrast to most of the definitions mentioned above, mine does not limit fundamentalism to religious-political movements but encompasses a number of distinct organizational forms and attitudes toward the world. Consequently, fundamentalism contains a multiplicity of types that should be kept distinct from one another because they are often difficult to compare sociologically.

Following Max Weber, if we distinguish between affirmation of the world and rejection of the world on the one hand, and between mastery of the world, adaptation to the world, and flight from the world on the other, then fundamentalism can be generally characterized by a world-rejecting attitude. Insofar as this attitude does not derive from religious tradition, its origins lie in dissatisfaction with current social conditions.

This rejection of the world can have either flight from the world or mastery of the world as its consequence. In the first case adherents seek to establish an ideal community by withdrawing from the world. In the second they seek to force their ideal of a just social order onto the world. This distinction between fundamentalisms of flight and mastery allows us to differentiate between nonpolitical sects and social movements with political agendas. It is possible also for a fundamentalist group, depending on historical circumstances and the composition of its membership, to swing between the two ideal types within a given time period. My comparison of Iranian Shi'ite and American Protestant fundamentalism focuses on two cases of world mastery.

The fundamentalism of world mastery can present itself either as reformist or revolutionary. As a reformist movement it respects political institutions and the constitution. It attempts to achieve its substantive demands, at least partially, through public protest and pressure on political bodies. Revolutionary fundamentalism, in contrast, seeks an institutional transformation of society, regards the existing regime as illegitimate, and wants power for itself. Faced with failure, reformism can be transformed, either into a revolutionary movement or into a quietism or separatism that spurns the world.

Moreover, relying on Max Weber's distinction between orthodoxy and heterodoxy and Ernest Gellner's juxtaposition of scholar and saint, it seems to me expedient to differentiate between a book-centered ("rational") and an experience-centered ("charismatic") fundamentalism.[34] "Rational" fundamentalism demands solely a rationalization of the daily conduct of life in accord with religious principles or prescriptions, the success of which amounts to a certainty of salvation. At its core is a strict moralism, and its representatives are interpreters of scripture and preachers of morality. Rational fundamentalism corresponds to the "puritan" pattern.[35] Charismatic fundamentalism lends full recognition to ethical prescriptions but in addition demands the ability to experience extraordinary gifts of grace as confirmation of the state of religious salvation. Its practice is accordingly centered more around religious experience, miracles, and the extraordinary. It is therefore typically embodied in the saint and miracle worker, the hero and martyr.

"Rational" fundamentalism is more likely to be associated with the ideals of the established, traditionalist, urban middle classes, and charismatic fundamentalism is more suited to the ecstatic and magical needs

TYPOLOGY OF FUNDAMENTALIST
ORGANIZATIONAL FORMS

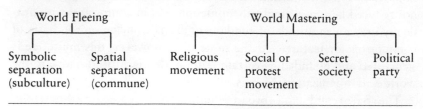

World Fleeing		World Mastering			
Symbolic separation (subculture)	Spatial separation (commune)	Religious movement	Social or protest movement	Secret society	Political party

of the urban lower classes. As a rule it incorporates popular, heterodox religious ideas and practices, frequently of rural provenance. As mass phenomena both types of fundamentalism can often be found as parallel reactions to rapid social transformation. In the American case, because of denominationalism, they are more differentiated institutionally. In Shi'ism they are combined through hierocratic power interests and the parallel traditions of interpretative scholarship and the charisma of suffering, just as they are ideally embodied in the person of Khomeini.

This ideal-typical differentiation in practice frequently encounters hybrids and movements undergoing transition. Particularly in charismatic fundamentalism it is easy for the extraordinary aspects to become overemphasized or reified. The rationalization of life conduct then becomes overlaid by the experience of the gifts of grace and in some cases is repressed. Charismatic experience and the technique by which it is brought about move to the center. At that point transitions to the magical coercion of God or mysticism suggest themselves, with the adherents sometimes feeling relieved of their obligations toward a statutory ethical regulation of their life conduct. As soon as this aspect becomes dominant, I no longer classify the group as fundamentalist.

Finally, it is possible to distinguish fundamentalism according to its organizational forms and the composition of its elite. Fundamentalism thus appears both as a public protest movement and as a secret society. Correspondingly, either collective mass actions, like strikes and demonstrations, or acts of terror undertaken by small groups, like assassinations and kidnappings, assume center stage in its activities. We find in the leadership elites of fundamentalism both lay persons and members of the clergy. In both the American Protestant and the Iranian Shi'ite cases the clergy has a more dominant role than in most Sunni fundamentalist movements. Under what conditions that becomes possible is the subject of later discussions.

What is new in this definition of fundamentalism and what does it accomplish in comparison to the alternatives? I consider two aspects important. First, this definition avoids decisionism. Fundamentalism is not reduced here to a single phenomenon, but in conformity with academic usage a multitude of fundamentalisms coincide on the basis of common major features. At the same time, however, this multitude is structured and bounded by certain criteria, that is, attitudes toward the world and organizational forms.

The goal of combining a broad definition with a typological differentiation has been to provide a foundation for a historical and comparative sociology of fundamentalism. Thus it will be possible to represent processes of transformation within fundamentalist groupings in historical-sociological terms as transformations of type, for example, from a world-fleeing subculture to a terrorist secret society, from a religious movement to a social movement to a political party or separatist commune. A continuity of meaning, corresponding to the self-understanding of adherents, is thereby appropriately maintained, and the beginnings of a theory of fundamentalist development over lengthy periods of time is established.

It will also be possible to designate criteria for cross-cultural sociological comparisons. Of course, a comparative sociology of fundamentalism must first undertake a comparative analysis of the same type of fundamentalism in different cultures. For there is little sense in beginning the preparatory work for a theory of fundamentalism with a comparison, for example, of an Islamic fundamentalist party and a Protestant fundamentalist commune. Accordingly, my study concentrates on two fundamentalist protest movements.

CONCEPTS AND THEORETICAL PERSPECTIVES

Charles Tilly distinguishes four theoretical traditions under which we can classify most interpretations of collective behavior and social movements: those of John Stuart Mill, Karl Marx, Emile Durkheim, and Max Weber.[36] The tradition of Mill has obvious difficulties with "irrational" movements, and that of Marx tends to reduce them to expressions of alienated social conditions, class ideologies, or false consciousness.[37] Obviously, my definition and typology of fundamentalism, which assign a central role to questions of worldview, do not have precedent in their work. Thus it is not surprising that primarily authors oriented toward Durkheim and Weber have concerned themselves with "radical-traditionalist" or right-wing extremist movements. In the sociological literature the Durkheimian theoretical emphasis on integration is clearly dominant; here, on the contrary, Weber's theoretical perspective on conflict is more evident. This influence affects all three levels of the investigation, manifesting itself in the emphasis on and extensive usage of fundamentalist ideology as a source for interpreting the movement, in the analysis of the movement's carriers, and in the discussion of the causes of mobilization.

In the sociological treatment of fundamentalist or comparable right-wing radical movements, four approaches continue to be prominent and may better be classed in the Durkheimian tradition: the theory of mass society and the connected theory of totalitarianism; the concept of the status movement; its further development into a "dramatistic theory of status politics"; and structural functionalism.[38] The Weberian tradition primarily includes theories of the development of Western modernity, such as that of Peter Berger, and theories of social movements. I draw on these approaches in the following discussion.

ANALYSIS AND SIGNIFICANCE OF IDEOLOGY

Of the three aspects of fundamentalism that I analyze, ideology is the most dependent upon theoretical premises. The majority of roughly Durkheimian approaches attribute no great significance to ideology, following their basic assumptions about extremist movements. Theories of mass society and of totalitarianism are concerned with movements of alienated, uprooted individuals who, because of industrialization, urbanization, and the disintegration of intermediate institutions, find themselves isolated and thus, as an atomized mass, vulnerable to the irrational appeal of authoritarian leaders.[39]

Theories of political radicalism and the status movement, such as those of Seymour Martin Lipset and Richard Hofstadter, note in fundamentalism primarily a phenomenon of irrationalism. In a clear analogy to Durkheim's explanations of anomic suicide, they distinguish between class and status politics.[40] Class politics is characterized by the competition for economic interests, and status politics by that for public recognition and prestige. Class politics appears in times of economic downturn, status politics in growth periods. Class politics is rational and therefore subject to regulation; status politics is based on irrational fears and is scarcely or not at all subject to governmental control. Status politics is typified by the anxiety created in a group threatened by a perceived or actual decline of status, which finds expression in nativism, anti-Semitism, conspiracy theories, and so forth. Reading ideology according to psychopathological categories therefore seems more appropriate to Durkheimian analysts than interpreting its content.

The structural functionalist interpretation of fundamentalism by Talcott Parsons is related to that of Lipset and Hofstadter. Nevertheless, his analysis stresses the secular processes of social transformation, referring less to the economic cycles motivating class and status politics. Parsons sees in bureaucratization, industrialization, and secularization the cause of the social tensions to which fundamentalism reacts. In this context fundamentalism, for Parsons, denotes a type of irrational reaction on the part of traditionalists made insecure by change that can result not only in a religious movement but also in a patriotic, secular political movement. Thus this approach also neglects fundamentalist ideology in favor of a psychologizing interpretation of the phenomenon.[41]

Such an underestimation of ideology is likewise characteristic of Joseph Gusfield's noteworthy variant of a "dramatistic theory of status politics." He does not, indeed, qualify status politics as irrational but attributes to status interests the same justification as class interests. Nevertheless, the content of ideology is less important in his analysis than ideology's function as a symbol of self-identification in a struggle for prestige and influence. Gusfield emphasizes above all the role of the state in the distribution of public prestige. Through legislation the state can continually assess the symbols of social groups, in that it defines norms and deviations.[42]

An alternative perspective on the content of ideologies is offered by theories of social movements that include in their analyses the social projections and values contained in the ideologies. Because of their limitation to "progressive" movements, however, such theories have not yet borne much fruit for the analysis of radical-traditionalist movements.[43]

The roles of ideology and cultural factors in the formation of "antimodernist" movements are given the most extensive consideration by Peter Berger and, following him, James Hunter.[44] They regard modernism, in the sense of Western development, as a threefold process of economic, political, and cognitive rationalization. The functional rationalization of politics in the form of bureaucratization and of the economy in technological production as well as their symbolic institutionalization in utilitarian values lead to a transformation of central social structures and thereby of the role of religion.

Modern development is taken to have, above all, three problematic consequences for religion: the disintegration of the supernatural view of life by modern science; cultural pluralism in the sense of the contiguous existence of various subcultures, particularly in large, modern cities; and structural pluralism in that life is divided into private and public spheres, whereby religion becomes a personal matter.[45] Religion can react by adapting, withdrawing, or resisting. Fundamentalism would be understood in these terms as a protest against the three forces of modernization, not so much as an irrational position but as an interest-guided assertion of values in a group conflict. In contrast to Gusfield's interpretation, Berger and Hunter would represent fundamentalism not only as a "symbolic crusade" but also as a cultural struggle to be interpreted on the level of content.[46]

My theoretical approach is relatively close to Peter Berger's conception. Because the conflict between fundamentalism and modernism concerns not only the distribution of public prestige but also the proper conduct of life, social relationships, and institutionalized values, I emphasize the analysis of ideology. This is evident in my definition and typology of fundamentalism, in which specifically substantive cognitive figurations and attitudes toward the world make up the critical categories. How, then, do I apply the ideology concept and how do I justify its emphasis?

With Edward Shils, I reserve the concept of ideology for those systems of thought that selectively accentuate and dramatize their interpretations of the world and that possess a pronounced legitimating function.[47] If one adopts this characterization, fundamentalist ideology and action based on it can be understood as a reinterpretation of religious tradition, formulated and practiced during a process of social transformation that is experienced as dramatic. New experiences are understood in traditional terms and concepts and transformed with the aid of religious symbols and rituals into social action. One can thus characterize fundamentalism, with reference to Karl Mannheim, as a *traditionalism that has become reflexive*.[48] In the process of reflection, traditionalism is broken; it undergoes reinterpretations, shifts of emphasis, and radicalizations and even generates innovations. Thus the ideology of fundamentalism is not identical with that of traditionalism but amounts to in certain cases an even revolutionary refounding of tradition.[49] To me the concept of radical—in the sense of radicalized—traditionalism is therefore the most accurate one to apply to fundamentalism.

The significance of ideology becomes immediately evident when we attempt to identify fundamentalists. We observe people acting together in public, demonstrating, striking, or participating in rallies. What enables us to identify them is the fact that they explain, legitimize, and symbolically express their actions in a way that as a rule is a part or condensation of their comprehensive ideology. This ideology defines not only their central interests and values but also their perception of the past and expectations for the future.

Within fundamentalist ideology it is possible to distinguish two levels, which, admittedly, are nearly inseparably interwoven in practice: a salvation history and a social critique. The social critique addresses actual grievances, considered clear and particularly dramatic symptoms of the social crisis. Governmental measures, the behavior of social groups, and cultural, economic, political, and legal circumstances are directly identified. The guilty are named, images of the enemy created, and demands for policy changes posed.

The salvational dimension of the ideology locates the meaning of the contemporary crisis between the ideal order of the past and eschatological expectations of the future. With its nativism, messianism, and millenarianism, it lends the fundamentalist protest its Manichaean dramaturgy and metaphysical legitimation. Insofar as fundamentalism actively promotes a design for a just social order, it is equally fed by the interpretation of the present crisis in terms of the salvation history. Fundamentalist thinking is thereby characterized by an interpenetration of present experience and salvation history, wherein this experience is interpreted in the light of religious tradition, symbolism, and drama. Neither of the elements can be reduced to the other. Both are of great significance for an interpretive understanding and causal explanation of fundamentalist action.

The course and rhythm characteristic of fundamentalist protest can be understood and made subject to prognosis only through a consideration of the dimension of fundamentalist thinking deriving from the salvation history. Without a knowledge of its symbols and gestures, its idols and myths, the religious logic underlying public action is invisible. Those who examine such movements solely in terms of psychopathological categories can neither understand nor explain the dramaturgy of collective protest actions and revolutionary overthrows. Hans Kippenberg provides a brilliant example of the significance of decoding the dimension of the salvation history in his analysis of street fighting during the Iranian revolution.[50]

Ultimately, only an analysis of ideology can determine whether fundamentalist movements in different cultural and religious traditions share major cognitive figurations. If they do, this would indicate that comparable social groups, despite divergent cultural traditions, interpret comparable historical experiences in similar ways. The elaboration of cognitive patterns that transcend particular cultures would convey important insights as to the universality of fundamentalist movements.

Moreover, methodological considerations also favor an adequate treatment of ideology. In the analysis of the causes of fundamentalist mobilization, as of those of other social movements, one confronts a difficult methodological problem, which, from my perspective, cannot be solved without recourse to ideology. As a rule it is possible to discover political, economic, legal, cultural, and social transformations occurring simultaneously, all of which are equally plausible for an explanation of mobilization. Some interpreters simply figure that the more factors they name, the better their explanations. Others decide for themselves which causes of mobilization are plausible and which are not. Obviously, it is necessary to define one's selection criteria.

I do not, for example, consider it persuasively explanatory to name processes of social transformation that have a demonstrably negative impact on the carriers of fundamentalism if these processes, or phenomena derived from them, are not thematized either directly or indirectly by those affected. How would one establish, for example, whether a protest against homosexuality or prostitution was actually aimed at the economic monopoly of supermarkets or the political power of multinational corporations? Such an interpretation rests on problematic anthropological and behavioral theories that can lead to speculation and interpretive caprice. From my perspective the ideology of a social movement offers an important source of the relevant factors of mobilization.

These statements must not be misunderstood as an apologia for a naive treatment of ideology. Though ideology does indeed thematize the causes of mobilization, it does not simply reflect them. As a rule it names not only processes of structural transformation but also phenomena that are implicit in them or, as the case may be, caused by them. Frequently, individual themes achieve an exaggerated symbolic significance, as, for example, the theory of evolution in Protestant fundamentalism or the veiling of women in Islamic. A single point of conflict becomes surrogate for the whole collection of oppositions in the cultural struggle.

Furthermore, ideology possesses a multitude of functions that prohibit a naive interpretation. Thus it integrates the segments of various classes, strata, and groups; creates a salvation history in which the past and future can be ideologically interpreted; and legitimates action undertaken by the social movement. It is therefore not sufficient to analyze ideology in order to select among the possible causes of mobilization those that are actually relevant. On the other hand those who ignore ideology and fail to draw on it critically to formulate or, at least, scrutinize their interpretation become speculative. Only a systematic linkage of ideology, practice, and processes of structural transformation will, in my view, provide an empirically well-founded explanation.

ANALYSIS OF THE MOVEMENT'S CARRIERS

The investigation of the carriers of fundamentalist movements is a complicated undertaking. Depending on one's theoretical approach, the carriers of fundamentalism can be identified as social classes or strata, as the "uprooted" or "alienated," or as individuals sharing common values. Not the least effect of such reductionist explanations is that they have led to a general rejection of sociological categories for the investigation of "purely religious" phenomena.[51]

An interpretation of fundamentalism as a class movement is ill founded and therefore rare.[52] In essence, two interpretations of the carriers of fundamentalism compete. In the theory of the status movement, social strata—usually a rural, lower-middle stratum—are identified as the carriers;[53] in the theory of mass society, in contrast, it is the "dislocated."[54]

An interesting further development of the conception of mass society is found in the work of Said Arjomand.[55] Although the anomie thesis is at the center of his interpretation of fundamentalism, he also takes into account newer investigations of the social integration resulting from voluntary associations of people who have migrated from the countryside to the city. Carriers of the movement are primarily "uprooted" elements from a traditionalistic, predominantly rural milieu. Fundamentalism is based not on an amorphous mass mobilized by declassed intellectuals, in Arjomand's view, but on a mobilization of religious associations through which dislocated urban migrants have already overcome anomie and marginality. These religious associations are marked by the intensification of orthodoxy and orthopraxy typical of urban religiosity. Fundamentalism does not represent a rural religiosity imported into the city but an urban one into which rural members are socialized. They thereby become the most important source of followers for fundamentalist leaders.[56]

Nevertheless, Arjomand's interpretation, too, remains problematic. He underestimates the important role of established city dwellers, primarily of the lower-middle class. He does acknowledge the undoubted overrepresentation of the petite bourgeoisie in the Islamic movement in Iran. But he maintains that this is in no way characteristic of fundamentalism because merchants and artisans make up an essential part of all radical movements.[57] Because of the large numbers of these traditional middle-class participants, their symbolic embodiment of a pious way of life, and their financial contributions, however, Arjomand's distinction between characteristic and uncharacteristic carriers is weak. Moreover, the "uprooted" may possibly be more precisely characterized in terms of class or social stratum. Arjomand's interpretation demonstrates that the avoidance of a concept of class or stratum does not represent a solution either.

Describing the carriers of a movement by class or stratum, however, has two main problems. First, one does not usually find just a single class represented within a movement but various classes. Second, in social movements commonly identified with a certain class, only a portion of the members of that class are represented, even though, as a rule, in a significantly higher percentage than would correspond to their population share. There is, therefore, always a considerable share of the same class that is not mobilized. Taken together, any analysis of the composition of social movements must thus take into account both social diversity and the only partial representation of the predominant class. Sociology must face this problem and draw the appropriate conceptual consequences from it.

It would certainly be unwise to reject altogether categories of class and stratum and return to the amorphous concept of the "masses." Nor do the concepts "alienated" and "uprooted" offer much further assistance, since they do nothing but turn the anomie thesis into a claim concerning the movement's carriers. The probability of suffering a specific fate in the process of urbanization and industrialization, however, is by no means the same for different strata (or status groups) or classes (or class segments). In this case class categories remain quite illuminating, if only partially, needing supplementation by additional categories. In many social movements specific social classes dominate quantitatively or qualitatively (or both). For example, one group may take over key functions or stamp the movement with their particular material interests or values.

In the investigation of the carriers of a movement, therefore, one confronts two sets of problems. First, the integration of portions of various classes requires explanation as does, second, the absence of integration of parts of the same class. If one assumes everyday experience and its interpretation to be the stimulus for collective social action, then segments of different classes could unite under two conditions. First, integration could occur if individuals have undergone the same or at least comparable experiences, for example, defeat in war, colonialism, social decline, economic crisis, political repression, and they express these experiences in a common language and symbols. Or, second, they have had different experiences, for example, a decline in status, a decline in income, or unfulfilled expectations of upward mobility, but are able to transform and generalize these differences through a common language and symbols into a collective protest against the injustice suffered.

The absence of integration of all members of the same class is, accordingly, explained by the absence either of a common experience or a common interpretive model. Thus, despite membership in the same class, different trades (for example, the steel versus the automotive industry), religious-cultural ties (the Protestant versus the Catholic "established" middle class), regional affiliation (Northerners versus Southerners), or ethnic heritage (Persians versus Arabs) could hinder the acquisition of common experiences or the use of a common language and symbolism. Also, trade-specific or regional economic structural differences (like the automotive industry in the northern United States as opposed to the petroleum industry in the South) could have caused comparable experiences of crisis but at different times, thus impeding simultaneous action. To be sure, a third interpretive possibility is added by Mancur Olson's theory of collective goods, the explanatory power of which, however, is limited to cases in which ethnic, regional, cultural, religious, or other differentiating qualities have not already made collective action difficult or impossible in the first place.[58]

These examples of factors contributing to or impeding integration or participation suggest four methodological consequences. The first is that one should investigate a number of qualities shared by people engaged in a social movement, avoiding a premature reduction of their association to socioeconomic factors. Second, it is advisable to investigate separately the causes of mobilization for all the segments of classes, strata, or groups significantly involved, that is, not to assume from the outset a common cause for everyone in the movement. Third, the mechanisms of integration into the movement, such as networks, ideologies, or symbols, and the groups which predominate have to be identified.

This implies, fourth, that the nonmobilization of other segments of participating classes must be investigated for purposes of verification and control.

The sociological category best suited to an analysis of the carriers of social movements that also satisfies these conditions is that of the *sociomoral milieu,* which M. Rainer Lepsius defines as "social units formed by the coincidence of several structural dimensions, such as religion, regional tradition, economic position, cultural orientation, and class-specific composition of intermediary groups."[59] Depending on the empirical case, further structural characteristics, such as ethnicity, language, gender, and above all sociohistoric generation, could prove useful.

The concept of sociomoral milieu also acknowledges that social movements are not the sum of isolated individuals but are founded on preexisting community or societal groupings. Accordingly, the center of fundamentalism as a social movement is understood here as the political mobilization of a preexisting traditionalist sociomoral milieu, organized chiefly as voluntary religious associations. Whether newly organized groups of "dislocated" traditionalists or longer-term associations of established city dwellers or a mix of the two predominate is an empirical problem.

This conceptual framework appears to me to offer the best combination of a broad perspective with an analytically clear definition of the object. The investigation of movement carriers is not predefined by narrow sociological concepts; rather, many possible elements in the constitution of the carriers can be applied hypothetically to the empirical data. This is the best way to avoid reductionist interpretations and at the same time to represent more easily the historical-cultural differences between Iranian Shi'ite and American Protestant fundamentalism.

This study supplements the sociomoral milieu with two additional concepts: first, a distinction between a movement's core and peripheral carriers and, second, between its actual and potential carriers. The differentiation between core and periphery serves to identify dominant groups that emerge as the typical organizers and members, thereby distinguishing them from other groups that are significant neither in numbers nor in other attributes. The distinction between actual and potential carriers serves to elucidate the nonsimultaneous nature of mobilization. It differentiates between those members of a sociomoral milieu at any one point in time who are already fundamentalist and those who yet remain traditionalist.

ANALYSIS OF THE CAUSES OF MOBILIZATION

We must clarify initially what we mean by "causes" of mobilization. What relationships pertain between them and ideology and carriers? How can these interconnections best be investigated systematically? It seems sensible at the outset to distinguish between the occasions and the causes of mobilization. There exist, of course, protest movements concerned with the thematization of a specific issue that disappear once the problem has been dealt with. In such movements the occasion and the cause of mobilization coincide. However, once the protest has taken aim against a number of processes of social transformation and social grievances, which, in addition, are lent internal ideological coherence by those affected, the immediate occasion and more deeply embedded causes are no longer identical. There can be no doubt that fundamentalist movements are to be ascribed to this more complex type of protest movement.

What, then, are the logical and empirical relations between occasions and causes? It seems to me that essentially two strategies are conceivable. For an identification of the causes of mobilization, one could resort, on the one hand, to a systematization of the occasions or, on the other, to an analysis of the specific experiences of deprivation on the part of those mobilized. The distinction lies primarily in the degree to which one draws the self-interpretation of those affected into the analysis. In both cases the data thus established must be embedded in a conception of the processes of social transformation. My preference is for a combination of both procedures. The occasions of mobilization and the subjective self-interpretation and objective fate of those mobilized are to be brought together systematically and related logically and empirically to processes of structural transformation.

Under investigation, then, is which transformation processes have a negative impact on the carriers of fundamentalism, including those by which the carriers feel themselves to be negatively affected and to which they are manifestly reacting. To determine this, it is necessary to analyze the occasions of protest and ideology. For, as inadequate as an analysis of occasions and ideology might be for the determination of the causes of mobilization, it is just as implausible to assume that the occasions of protest behavior have nothing to do with the deeper causes of discontent and that the "genuine" causes make no appearance whatever in the formulation of the protest by those involved.

The relationship between the causes of mobilization and the carriers of the movement is likewise complex. As has been shown, the carriers of fundamentalism cannot be adequately described by class or social stratum, which is why the milieu concept has been given preference. Because, however, different classes are represented in fundamentalism, one must reckon with the possibility of different causes of mobilization. It is possible here to depart from the historical experience that the primary target of the protest will be those processes, or their carriers or symbols, that lead to a reduction in market opportunities, political influence, significance of educational knowledge and value orientation, legal privileges, or the general esteem accorded the life conduct of the carriers of fundamentalism.

It seems advisable here to take up Theodor Geiger's investigations of the established middle class (*Mittelstand*) and Robert Merton's reference group theory and concept of relative deprivation in order to encompass the interaction of the processes of social transformation.[60] Social change on a larger scale does indeed signify considerable interference in the distribution of economic opportunities; the potential to enjoy earnings and power; chances for education and prestige; status gains and losses; competition among strata, classes, and milieus; processes of vertical demarcation; processes of horizontal marginalization; and the orientation of behavior, claims, and expectations among competing social units. Only the reconstruction of the shifts in social stratification, of the symbols and consumption habits of social groups rising or falling or expanding or being pushed to the margins, offers a suitable framework for the interpretation of fundamentalist movements. Drawing on Gusfield, the role of the state must be accorded great significance in these transformative processes and in the mobilization of the traditionalist camp.[61] Generally, the state emerges not as a neutral mediator but as a partisan and provocative force.

The delimitation of fundamentalism as an urban protest movement does not so much represent a pragmatic reduction of variables as it implies that fundamentalism represents a primarily urban phenomenon. This applies in a twofold sense. First, rationalistic, literalist-orthodox interpretations of religion are generally urban forms of religiosity, as is amply demonstrated in the scholarly literature on comparative religions.[62] Second, this conclusion simply corresponds to the empirical evidence. The centers of both Shi'ite and—despite widespread prejudices to the contrary—Protestant fundamentalism of the 1920s are to be found in large cities.

In view of this fact there is every reason to believe that urbanization represents the process of structural transformation of the greatest relevance to the interpretation of both Shi'ite and Protestant fundamentalism. Nevertheless, urbanization alone explains nothing, because it can equally be invoked for the rise of the labor movement, the Progressive movement, the German Youth Movement, or the women's movement. Moreover, fundamentalist movements have not arisen everywhere urbanization has occurred. That is why in the following analysis of the causes of mobilization I do not depart from modernization processes such as industrialization, urbanization, or secularization. Rather, I ask: Which processes of transformation threatened or damaged the status of the various fundamentalist carrier groups? Which other groups made social gains as a result of these processes? And how are these experiences expressed in the ideology and behavior of fundamentalism?

CHAPTER 2

Protestant Fundamentalism in the United States, 1910–1928

Radical-traditionalist reactions to rapid social change are found in all religions of salvation and redemption. In societies predominantly influenced by Christianity, however, different reactions occur depending on whether the dominant faith is Catholicism, Lutheranism, or ascetic Protestantism. Catholic countries have produced mainly right-wing radical movements with anti-Christian to clerical leanings; in Lutheran countries we find mainly secular right-wing radical movements. Fundamentalist mass movements, in contrast, have formed primarily in societies strongly stamped by *ascetic Protestantism,* that is, by Calvinism and the Baptist sects.

How are these different developments to be explained? Certainly, religious doctrines, ethics, and ideologies have roles. But I give other structural factors greater weight: the institutional autonomy of religion in relation to the state, religious pluralism, the absence of hierocratic domination, and the dependence of individual clerics on their clientele. These characteristics predispose the religious tradition, on the one hand, to a formulation of felt injustice and the religious elite, on the other, to become spokespersons and organizers of protest movements. Given these structural conditions, religion does not become an instrument of state domination and control over society but a medium of social self-organization and social control.[1]

These structural conditions are largely absent in the Lutheran tradition; the nationalization of religion considerably neutralized its socially critical potential. In Catholic countries the autonomy of the clergy is often overlaid by hierocratic centralism as well as by concordats between the Vatican and the state powers. Fundamentalist currents are either hierocratically instrumentalized and channeled or they are marginalized, in some cases even excommunicated. The structural conditions listed above favoring the rise of fundamentalism are found most clearly in the countries of ascetic Protestantism, above all in the United States. These characteristics helped to determine the specifically democratic populist formation of fundamentalism.

These peculiarities of American Protestantism—separation of church and state, religious pluralism, absence of hierocratic domination, dependence of the clergy on their clientele—are the products of a long historical development, from the colonial period through independence up to the First World War. The following briefly outlines the genesis of these structural characteristics and their qualitative evolution to the beginning of the present century.[2]

ASCETIC PROTESTANTISM AND POLITICS

Protestantism in colonial North America began with the establishment of the Anglican church in Virginia in 1607, but it was shaped primarily by its development in the New England states. There it assumed the form of ascetic Protestantism as it evolved amid the tension of Calvinist-Puritan conceptions of election and order, on the one hand, and Baptist-Pietist hopes for individual redemption and salvation, on the other.

The Calvinist traditions of integration into an objective order and the inscrutable caprice of a transcendent God were embodied most markedly in the Massachusetts Bay Colony, founded in 1630. As Congregationalists the settlers there understood themselves as a reformist movement inside a corrupt Anglican church. They rejected its practice of having bishops appointed by the crown and instead members handled the administration of the congregations. Only congregation members enjoyed the rights of citizenship, and the criterion for membership was proof of the experience of a complete spiritual renewal. In the Massachusetts colony of 1640, therefore, only about 8 percent of the population had political rights.[3]

The colony was governed both by a governor and his council and by elected representatives of the towns. Members of the clergy were barred from the magistracy. The political order was understood not as the realization of a divine order but as a human contrivance with no claim to reverence. Nor did John Cotton's proposal to base Massachusetts law directly on the The Commandments find any support. In practice the colony was governed according to English common law.[4]

The Puritan Massachusetts colony tolerated no deviation from its theological positions and conceptions of sociomoral order. Both internal opponents and adherents of Baptist sects, who questioned the Puritans' monopoly of both political power and spiritual election, were persecuted with unabating strictness. Thus was Anne Hutchinson, a member of the Boston congregation, banned in 1637 on account of her antinomian attitudes. Hutchinson emphasized the independence of individual redemption from the observance of church and state laws and its dependence solely on the grace and love of God. In 1644 the Baptists suffered the same fate, and between 1659 and 1661 four Quakers were publicly hanged in Boston following repeated bannings and floggings.

As early as the seventeenth century the significance of church membership led to heated controversy over admittance to the congregation. The extremely elitist procedure for the conveyance of religious qualifications was first mitigated through the Half-Way Covenant (in 1657) and ultimately, by order of the motherland, transformed into an extra-religious criterion by the Act of Toleration (1693), which tied the right to vote to the possession of property and not to membership in the church.[5]

The Baptist emphasis on rejecting the world, the personal nature of the relationship between God and the faithful, and the associated individualistic, anti-institutional (both antichurch and antistate) understanding of religious practice and the attainment of salvation first spread primarily outside the Puritan colonies. But there, too, in the course of the awakenings a stronger emotional, pietist transformation of religion ultimately occurred. Nevertheless, it bore less a world-rejecting, not to mention world-fleeing, character, but, in the theology of Jonathan Edwards, adopted a cautious historical optimism and a religious interpretation of the tasks and destiny of the colonies.

Edwards believed that the kingdom of God on earth would not be realized instantaneously, like a miracle, but would develop gradually. The millennium, therefore, was not to be founded in a historical catastrophe but in the divine plan for continuous progress, in which America was presumed to have been allotted a prominent position. This post-millenarian optimism gave shape to a religious-political evangelicalism that represented a broad social consensus, especially in the open frontier regions to the west, for more than one hundred years.

Religious pluralism, which is defined by the equal status and rights of all faiths before the law, can be traced conceptually to the early colonial era, particularly among the Baptists and Quakers. Despite occasional exceptions, however, governing bodies in practice accorded special privileges to certain religions. Thus were either the Congregationalists or the Anglican church established in all the colonies or states with the exception of Rhode Island, Pennsylvania, and Delaware.

Even the constitution of 1789 and the amendments adopted in 1791 introduced no legal changes into this situation. They did, however, establish religious pluralism at the federal level through the First Amendment, which held that Congress could make no laws signifying the establishment of religion or infringing upon the free practice of religion. This principle, gradually adopted voluntarily by the individual states (Massachusetts being the last to act, in 1833), gave a legal basis to religious pluralism throughout the United States.[6]

With this development, strict demarcations became less necessary, and the distinction between churches and sects was largely replaced by the concept of denominations. The growth of the frontier confessions of the Baptists, Methodists, and Disciples of Christ further advanced an evangelical consensus, leading to the decline of Puritanism. The new evangelicalism was rooted in, first, a historically optimistic religious nationalism; second, the theological shift from Calvinist predestination to an Arminian freedom of will; third, a religious affirmation of capitalism and democracy; and, finally, the spread of an enthusiastic, emotional religious style.[7]

The religious-political conceptions of the colonial period increasingly lost their specifically Puritan character upon American independence. In combination with religious pluralism they were transformed into a "civic" religion, an ideology of integration for the new nation. This transformation gave the political and economic foundations of American society, democracy and capitalism, an added religious legitimation. They became the signs of the election of America and the content of its divine mission in the world.

At the same time, however, the concept of a civic religion contains the potential for criticisms of society. The ideas of citizenship and an ideal social order can serve as standards by which it becomes clear how far society has strayed from religious ideals or the extent to which it still falls short of them.

A further characteristic of evangelicalism is the steady recurrence of waves of awakenings in which America's populist-democratic individualism achieves particularly strong expression. As the awakenings of the eighteenth century already show, there was a major thrust against the establishment of religious authorities and hierarchies and their control over the religious or political tutelage of the individual. Religious hierarchies were thus repeatedly leveled and the personal connection to God through immediate divine experience established anew. Mediation of heavenly blessings and professional interpreters of the Bible were unnecessary, for God's commandments and their meaning were considered directly accessible to every believer.

With this fundamentally individualistic, antiauthoritarian, populist-democratic attitude, broad strata of the population were repeatedly mobilized religiously. This attitude also explains a tendency toward "anti-intellectualism," the disdain of theological problems in favor of religious practice. Thus the evangelical consensus of the nineteenth century combined a marked emphasis on the public significance of religion with a simultaneous separation of religious and state institutions.

In the second half of the nineteenth century the evangelical consensus began to break apart. The main disruptions were the conflict over slavery and urbanization and industrialization. The pluralistic character of religion in America was intensified by the rapid growth of African-American churches, by the waves of Irish Catholic and German Lutheran immigration, and by newly established sects such as the Mormons. The problem of slavery led to intraconfessional splits, which were further consolidated by the Civil War. Nevertheless, the United States remained in this period a strongly Protestant, predominantly agrarian society.

With the end of the Civil War came the rapid transformation of the United States into an industrial society. Industrialization, the tremendous growth of the cities, new waves of immigration of non-Protestant groups from Eastern and Southern Europe, and the transformation of the worldview through biblical criticism and Darwin's theory of evolution changed Protestantism and confessional pluralism altogether. New kinds and areas of religious conflict arose, from which fundamentalism emerged as one among many currents.[8]

Industrialization led to sharp regional differentiation within the United States. The new industrial centers stimulated heavy migration, causing industrial cities to expand explosively and dramatically changing their character. Large parts of the United States, however, particularly in the South, remained agrarian, and the gap between city and countryside widened. Industrialization, urbanization, and mass immigration were concentrated principally in the roughly rectangular area marked by Boston, Chicago, Saint Louis, and Baltimore. In this area especially, the Protestant confessions were challenged by the new conditions.

They were called upon not only to take a theological stance but also to take action on the conflict between entrepreneurs and labor, on social disruption and moral decay in the cities, on mass immigration of religiously and ethnically alien groups, on changes in values, and on challenges to the prevailing worldview. The markedly heartless character of newly arising industrial society introduced a dramatic degree of tension into the Christian commandment on brotherly love. Yet the strategies for overcoming this tension were multiple, and the increasing differentiation of modes of life resulted in a multitude of new religious answers, changing the quality of pluralism.

Within the Protestant denominations the question of the proper theological and practical resolution of the crisis created conflicts, spawning new factions and leading over the longer term to actual splits. More than anything else the elaboration of the theology of the "Social Gospel" and its influence on the structure of religious institutions prompted a mobilization of traditionalists. I return to these issues later in more detail.

In addition, a great many new religious movements were founded that burst the theological bounds of Protestantism. And an equal number of new religious currents challenged traditional religious interpretations. Intense conflicts erupted within the Protestant church over historical and philological biblical criticism. Some theologians and clerics conformed to the new scholarly discoveries and standards, but many held to traditional thought. This split naturally had a particularly powerful impact on educational institutions and their curricula, which were also being forced to adapt to other challenges brought on by changing times.[9]

Darwinism revolutionized traditional ways of viewing the world. It called into question the biblical story of creation and thus the literal interpretability of the Bible. Recast in the ideological terms of Social Darwinism, it also served to justify misery and exploitation. Moreover, Protestantism was losing its influence over considerable segments of the urban lower classes, which were composed to a large extent of Catholic and Jewish immigrants from Southern and Eastern Europe. At the same time, atheistic ideologies, such as anarchism and socialism, were also gaining adherents in the labor force.

All of these developments exerted far-reaching effects on American Protestantism and its structural elements. Religious pluralism, despite several divergences, united in a general consensus on essential issues. It now not only began to lose its Protestant character but also was forced to meet the competition of secular ideologies. This development changed the significance of the institutional separation between church and state. For political institutions had been, up to this point, borne along by a Protestant spirit. That was now by no means guaranteed. The democratic character of religious confessions as well as political institutions were, or appeared to be, threatened by authoritarian structures and ideologies, such as the influence of the Catholic hierocracy, political bossism, the power of the new captains of industry, and the organized labor movement.

All of these developments came to fruition during the period from the Civil War to World War I. They were discharged of their potential for conflict, however, only through the upheaval brought on by the First World War and its effects on American society. It was no accident that the transformation of fundamentalism from a theological position and religious movement inside the confessions into an interdenominational political protest movement ensued only after the war.

PROFILE AND BOUNDARIES OF THE FUNDAMENTALIST MOVEMENT

The reasons for various characterizations and delimitations of Protestant fundamentalism thus become clear. It can be treated as a theological position, as a multiplicity of religious movements within various confessions, as an interdenominational religious umbrella movement, or as a political protest movement of the "radical center." Moreover, many authors have reduced it explicitly or implicitly to the campaign against the dissemination of evolutionary theory in public schools. Other definitions are possible as well.[10]

Fundamentalism is investigated here as a protest movement or a social movement, concepts that are not exactly characterized by precision. They are often casually used to summarize spreading social moods and opinions as well as any resulting action. In contrast, my definition of a social movement requires that at least the beginnings of institutionalization, as given by group formation, ideology, and coordination, be apparent, providing a basis for mass mobilization. A social movement differs from other types of collective action in that the motives, the ideological foundation, and the legitimation of action are made explicit. The contours of a social movement are shaped not by diffuse agreements in thought or feeling but by shared action. I treat various currents related by ideologies and carriers, but which, however, are neither co-ordinated nor cooperating, as individual social movements.[11]

Into the 1960s the prevailing view of fundamentalism blended the flag-waving evangelist Billy Sunday, the Prohibition movement, cross burning and Ku Klux Klan terror, and the Scopes trial (with an intellectually overtaxed William Jennings Bryan in the lead role) into a single representation of extreme nationalism, intolerance, insidious nativism, and backwards ignorance.[12] Fundamentalism, in this view, is presented less as a social movement than as an apparently homogeneous intellectual attitude. In this mosaic it is naturally overlooked that Bryan was a pacifist, that Sunday had no role in the fundamentalist movement of the 1920s, that leading fundamentalists publicly distanced themselves from the Ku Klux Klan, and that conservatives and liberals worked together for a lengthy period to win passage of Prohibition legislation.

Religious historical and theological interpretations of fundamentalism have greatly contributed to a revision of this caricature. But they have confined fundamentalism so narrowly within a religious framework that they have ignored or devoted insufficient attention to the social conditions surrounding its rise and its relationships with charismatic groups and the Ku Klux Klan. Thus next I will begin to define fundamentalism as a social movement by investigating the interconnections between evangelical premillenarianism, postmillenarian-evangelical Presbyterian orthodoxy, the Ku Klux Klan, and the Pentecostals.

Fundamentalism and Premillenarianism   The contemporary application of the fundamentalism concept was by no means uniform. Although no doctrine concerning the millennium was definitively established as biblically literal in *The Fundamentals* (1910–1915), with the foundation of the World's Christian Fundamentals Association (1918) and its definition of premillenarianism as a tenet of faith, the identification of fundamentalism with premillenarianism was confirmed.[13] At the beginning of the 1920s both opponents and postmillenarian sympathizers identified fundamentalism with premillenarianism. More recently, Ernest Sandeen has reestablished this association, making it the basis of his conception of fundamentalism.[14]

Nevertheless, for a variety of reasons this theology-based identification of fundamentalism with premillenarianism should not be maintained. For one, the actual orthodox coalition of the early twenties was cast much more broadly and in no way confined to premillenarians. Thus, for example, one of the leaders of the postmillenarian Presbyterian orthodoxy, Clarence E. Macartney, was pictured on the title page of the leading premillenarian periodical, *The King's Business,* in 1926, above the caption "Eminent Leader Fundamentalist Forces of Presbyterianism."[15]

For the premillenarians, biblical literalism, not the issue of the millennium, set them apart from other movements. This was made clear in the principles of faith set down in the *Baptist Bible Union,* in which premillenarianism was not even mentioned, primarily in order not to exclude the Southern Baptists.[16] Not only the inclusion of postmillenarians but also the exclusion of specific segments of the premillenarian camp make it clear that an identification of the fundamentalism movement with organized premillenarianism would be misleading.

The premillenarians can be roughly divided into three groupings: quietist-prophetic, activist-prophetic, and charismatic, whereby both prophetic groups are rational literalists. The quietist faction was represented by clerics such as Arno C. Gaebelein and Isaac Haldeman. They were "world rejecters," concerned exclusively with theologically interpreting the "signs of the time"; they regarded all politically reformist action as temptation by Satan.[17] This group kept considerable distance between itself and fundamentalism as a protest movement, although they occasionally collaborated on lectures and prophecy conferences.

The activist-prophetic faction contained premillenarians motivated by postwar changes in religious institutions and in society at large to form an alliance in the World's Christian Fundamentals Association and to adopt an activist orientation. They organized themselves in centers, such as the Bible Institute of Los Angeles, the Northwestern Bible School in Minneapolis, and the Moody Bible Institute in Chicago, and around certain personalities, such as William B. Riley in Minneapolis, John R. Straton in New York, Reuben Torrey in Los Angeles, J. Frank Norris in Fort Worth, James M. Gray in Chicago, and J. C. Massee in Boston. These institutions represent the core of the premillenarian wing of fundamentalism in the 1920s.[18]

Most of these premillenarians belonged to the Northern Baptists, and they founded the Baptist Bible Union, under the chairmanship of Thomas T. Shields, to mount a more effective opposition to liberal influences within their denomination. They did not declare premillenarianism among their articles of faith, however, primarily to encourage cooperation with the extremely conservative, but postmillenarian, Southern Baptists. But this goal turned out to be unfounded, partly because the traditional homogeneity of the South had been scarcely disturbed by "modernists" and partly because the mistrust held by the South for the North hindered any such alliance.

The charismatic faction, the "Pentecostals," was fragmented into numerous subgroups. Although many sections of the Pentecostals, for example, the Assemblies of God, espoused biblical literalism as well as premillenarian expectations, and sought collaboration with fundamentalist organizations, they were rejected by the latter as charismatic sectarians because of their practice of glossolalia, or speaking in tongues. The extent to which this rejection was theologically driven, or motivated by competition for adherents among the lower classes in both city and countryside, remains for the moment undecided.

This fragmentation of the premillenarians into three major factions plus a multitude of subgroups demonstrates that the doctrine of premillenarianism alone was not sufficient to prompt organizational coalescence and cooperation. Likewise, no noteworthy collaboration occurred between the Baptists of the North and those of the South. Thus there were indeed a host of campaigns against the teaching of evolutionary theory in the public schools, but they were not part of the fundamentalist movement organized on the national level. The single prominent exception was the "tiger of the South," J. Frank Norris of Fort Worth, an important element within the fundamentalist movement nationwide. Norris, however, was considered an outsider and a troublemaker by Southern Baptists; a common Baptist foundation was thus also insufficient to make common action possible. The South had simply not yet been mobilized by industrialization and urbanization, though because of its extreme traditionalism, it had enormous potential for later fundamentalist activation. The possibility of unification into a fundamentalist protest movement came, on the contrary, from the conservative wing of the postmillenarian Presbyterians.

Fundamentalism and Presbyterian Orthodoxy   Alongside the predominantly Northern Baptist premillenarians, the orthodox Presbyterians provided the second pillar of the fundamentalist movement. Its theological headquarters was in Princeton. It was represented intellectually by J. Gresham Machen, respected by friends and enemies alike, but the movement's most famous representatives were Clarence E. Macartney and Mark Matthews. Unified in their biblical literalism, they battled Protestant liberalism and modernism wherever they found it, both inside and outside their denomination.

Presbyterian orthodoxy, however, clearly diverged theologically from the views held by premillenarian Baptists. Orthodox Presbyterianism stood in the tradition of historically optimistic evangelicalism, as it prevailed in the United States up to the Civil War. To premillenarian Christians, conversion primarily signified the salvation of an individual soul from a world destined for ruin; for the traditionally Calvinist Presbyterians it possessed a further, political-cultural function in that it represented the precondition of Christian citizenship and thus of the maintenance, or establishment, of a Christian republic. The premillenarian Baptists were proponents of a strict separation of church and state, but Presbyterian orthodoxy retained strong remnants of the Calvinist fusion of the two.

Despite such wide differences in theological and political thought, Baptist premillenarians and orthodox Presbyterians did collaborate. This cooperation took place primarily in the opposition to evolutionary theory and its teaching in public schools. The exaggerated symbolic significance of Darwinism is perhaps explained by the deficit of common points of view on other theological, political, and economic issues. With this symbol, however, common action could be inspired, and the integration of the two camps of fundamentalism occurred chiefly on that ground.

On the basis of opposition to evolutionary theory, articles written for periodicals by one side were taken over by those in the other, speakers were exchanged, organizations founded, and campaigns initiated. William Jennings Bryan was an important force in integrating the two groups and was respected by all sides. He was a Presbyterian, but his democratic populism put him close sociopolitically to the Baptists.[19] His function as a bridge between the groups cannot be overestimated.

Fundamentalism and the Ku Klux Klan   On the collaboration between fundamentalists and the Klan there has been more speculation and insinuation than proof. Liberal critics in particular, finding both equally unsympathetic, like to identify the two movements with each other.[20] Conservative authors, in contrast, avoid discussing the subject, presumably because it is either embarrassing or it seems beside the point.[21] Neither approach furthers our understanding, and we need to clarify the facts concerning the alignment of the two movements.

Generally, arguments that support the identification of fundamentalism with the Ku Klux Klan are based on cooperation between the Ku Klux Klan and individual clerics and shared ideology. Between 1922 and 1928, 16 of 102 Klan offices (about 16 percent) were filled by Protestant clerics. And among the thirty-nine "national lecturers" of the

Ku Klux Klan, twenty-six, or two-thirds, were Protestant pastors.[22] Moreover, there are reports that members of the Ku Klux Klan visited fundamentalist churches during Sunday sermons, made offerings to the pastors, and frequently spoke a few words themselves. Ideological agreement is found in the Klan's practice of accepting only white Protestants as members, embracing the Americanism of the Pilgrim fathers, supervising the enforcement of Prohibition, advocating biblical literalism, and opposing evolutionary theory.[23]

The chief argument against the association of the Ku Klux Klan and fundamentalism is that no statements supporting the Klan were made, either in the leading ecclesiastical press or in the protocols of the national conventions of the larger denominations. More commonly, the topic was avoided, although in a few instances opinions against the Klan were expressed, some even by leading fundamentalists such as John R. Straton.[24]

Much of religiously motivated fundamentalism was quite ideologically distinct from the Klan, however, as is apparent from the writings and periodicals of leading clerics. In many of these, instead of racism and anti-Catholicism, one finds a call to moral education and missionary work; instead of nativism and "100 percent Americanism," they promote the preaching of Biblicism and Christian universalism. Such views, to be sure, were not held by all fundamentalists, and certainly least of all by the leading fundamentalist of the South.

J. Frank Norris, pastor of the First Baptist Church in Fort Worth, Texas, stood undeniably close politically and ideologically to the local Ku Klux Klan in his extreme anti-Catholicism. Moreover, he put meeting halls at the Klan's disposal and printed its advertisements in his periodical, *Searchlight*.[25] But John R. Straton, who did distance himself from the Ku Klux Klan, was likewise extremely anti-Catholic. The central aspects of Klan ideology—racism and anti-Catholicism—were not shared by fundamentalists in general nor did they have a dominant role in their campaigns before the presidential candidacy of Al Smith. Even though there were instances of local cooperation and coordination between the Ku Klux Klan and fundamentalists, they are clearly isolated cases that do not support any generalization.

Perhaps the assumption of an "elective affinity" best reflects actual recruitment patterns. Traditionalists mobilized primarily as a response to foreign religious or ethnic immigration (or internal migration) would tend to be attracted to the Ku Klux Klan; those who were mobilized more by the social, religious, and cultural fissures within the white middle class would be more likely to turn to fundamentalism. As Goldberg, for example, has reported in Colorado, it is also possible that individuals, including local pastors, belonged to both organizations at the same time.[26] But the two organizations competed for essentially the same adherents and material resources, and the intellectuals of the two movements competed for ideological leadership. The regional spread of fundamentalism and the Ku Klux Klan, as insufficiently researched as it is, does not necessarily suggest an affiliation of the two organizations.[27] In any case, the evidence for dual membership and the coordination of leadership between the Ku Klux Klan and fundamentalism is too slight to justify treatment of the two organizations as a unified social movement.

Fundamentalism and Charismatic Groups   It has already been mentioned that cooperation was not achieved between premillenarian Baptists and charismatic groups, despite their considerable theological agreement. This development is noteworthy in that both the premillenarian interpretation of the return of Christ and biblical literalism would have made collaboration possible. Cooperation appears to have foundered primarily on the conscious exclusion of charismatic "sectarians" by the established churches.[28]

This split between experience-centered and book- or ethics-centered fundamentalism grew from differences in theology, religious practices, and demographic and social characteristics. Theologically, the charismatic groups emphasized signs of salvation, that is, divine gifts of grace, which confirmed to individual believers their status among the elect or their sinlessness. They engaged in an extreme religious practice, glossolalia, the repetition of the apostles' experience of the pentecost. Here an elitist claim is combined with a strongly emotional religious practice. Charismatic groups were generally made up of people from lower socioeconomic classes in both rural and urban areas, primarily in the Midwest, the South, and the Southwest. And, at least in the early phase of the movement at the beginning of the century, the charismatic groups broke down racial and ethnic or cultural barriers.

Thus several explanations are available for the exclusion of charismatic groups by "rational" fundamentalism. In my view the rejection was primarily theologically grounded, but was no doubt intensified by social, ethnic, and demographic characteristics. The critical theological question was whether the sign of election lies primarily in conducting one's life according to the Bible or in having an additional emotional-ecstatic experience of God's grace. This question had important social as well as religious implications: charismatism undermines the claim that only the Anglo-Saxon middle class's way of life represents a sign of election. For rational fundamentalism, therefore, the charismatic movement was both a threat and a challenge. The most important factor shaping the fundamentalist movement was acceptance of the primacy of an ethically rational way of life. Accordingly, the fundamentalist movement excluded the charismatics despite broad agreement in theology, but was able to bridge the much wider theological gaps between Baptists and Presbyterians.

The Core of the Fundamentalist Movement   My analysis of the ideology, the carriers, and the causes of mobilization of Protestant fundamentalism as an urban protest movement is confined to those groups that actually did cooperate on the basis of common convictions and interests. Accordingly, I do not consider in this context either the extreme, apolitical premillenarians, the charismatic movements of Pentecostals and Holiness groups, or the Ku Klux Klan. I limit my analysis of the fundamentalist movement to its three most important, partially crosscutting currents.

One of these groupings is exemplified by Presbyterian orthodoxy, represented by theologians and clerics like Clarence E. Macartney, Mark Matthews, and J. Gresham Machen, by lay preachers like William Jennings Bryan, and by periodicals like the *Princeton Theological Review* and the *Presbyterian*. Regionally, orthodox Presbyterians are concentrated in the mid-Atlantic states, especially in big cities like Philadelphia. The (mostly premillenarian) Baptists compose a second grouping, represented by clerics like William B. Riley, J. Frank Norris, Thomas T. Shields, and John R. Straton. They were organized in the Baptist Bible Union, published journals like the *Fundamentalist*, the *Baptist Beacon*, the *Searchlight*, and the *Christian Fundamentalist in School and Church*, and were institutionally represented by educational centers like the Northwestern Bible and Missionary School in Minneapolis. Their point of regional concentration is in the Midwest and Southern California.

That is also the home of the third current to be treated here, the interdenominational premillenarians, represented by such institutions as the Moody Bible Institute in Chicago and the Bible Institute of Los Angeles, by clerics like Reuben A. Torrey, James M. Gray, Thomas C. Horton, and by journals such as the *King's Business*, the *Moody Monthly*, and the *Sunday School Times*. A large part of them were also organized in the World's Christian Fundamentals Association.

THE IDEOLOGY OF PROTESTANT FUNDAMENTALISM

I characterized fundamentalism at the beginning of this study as a specific intellectual construction of social reality. In the fundamentalist interpretation, society is in severe crisis, for which there is but one solution: a return to the principles of the divine order once practiced in the original community, whose laws have been handed down in writing. The only thing to do is put them literally and consistently into practice. But which social conditions call forth the protest, lead to a mobilization of segments of the traditionalist camp, and to the formation of a fundamentalist movement? Against which persons and institutions, against which groups, classes, or milieus, is the fundamentalist social critique aimed? How are these problematic social relations and developmental tendencies interpreted in the light of salvational expectations? And what are the characteristics of the mentality discernible in these interpretations?[29]

THE FUNDAMENTALIST SOCIAL CRITIQUE

The point of departure for the fundamentalist critique of society was the erosion of faith and values in the world and, especially, in the United States, which had already lost or was threatened with losing its original identity as a Christian nation and civilization. This fall from the divine principles of order was taking place not only outside but also within the Protestant church.

For fundamentalism three institutions had previously guaranteed the Christian character of the American nation: the family; the Protestant denominations and their congregations, Sunday schools, and educational centers; and the public schools. All three pillars rested on the Bible as the authentic word of God. All three were being shaken by the spread of unbelief and erroneous doctrines disseminated by "false teachers": the denominations by biblical criticism, the public schools by the spread of evolutionary theory, and, finally, the family by adultery, prostitution, divorce, alcoholism, and gambling.

The fundamentalist critique was addressed primarily to Protestant denominations; to non-Protestant confessions, new sects and cults, and those infected by secular ideologies; and, finally, to those responsible for the condition of public institutions. The order in which the above are listed also corresponds to the historical development of fundamentalism from a theological position to a religious movement and then to a social movement.[30]

Critique of the Protestant Confessions   Fundamentalism initially
arose within various Protestant denominations, predominantly the Baptists and Presbyterians of the North. The mobilization of traditionalists
and the organization of fundamentalism as a religious-theological movement was centered on the questioning of basic convictions of faith, first,
by the revolutionizing effect of Darwinian evolutionary theory on the
prevailing worldview and the value relativism of Nietzsche; second, by
historical-philological biblical criticism; and, finally, by the emphasis
being placed by some on the social dimension of the Christian message
and the necessity for social reforms in the theology of the Social Gospel,
which was a reaction to mass social suffering in the course of industrialization and urbanization.

The fundamentalist critique was aimed broadly at all signs of modernism or liberalism. Its assault on Protestant denominations concentrated
primarily on four interrelated tendencies: processes of transformation
of dogmatic principles; the definition of Christian tasks; the organizational structure of religious institutions; and the values proclaimed by
those institutions. The people or institutions that best symbolized these
"heretical" tendencies to fundamentalism were the Chicago theologian
Shailer Mathews, the New York Baptist pastor Harry Emerson Fosdick,
and the University of Chicago and its patron John D. Rockefeller, who,
moreover, worked closely with Fosdick and, particularly, Fosdick's
brother.[31]

For the fundamentalists, "higher criticism's" transformation of the
significance of the Bible from the verbally inspired word of God into
the work of pious authors subject to contradiction and error called
their worldview into question. From their perspective, modern tendencies were historicizing and relativizing timeless divine revelation, causing its loss as the eternal truth for all people. The eager adoption of the
vocabulary of evolutionary theory by some modernist or liberal theologians confirmed and intensified the fundamentalists' conviction that
they preached not (Protestant) Christianity but modernistic, secular
ideology.[32]

From a fundamentalist perspective the renunciation of biblical literalism and, especially, the doctrine of creation, necessarily led to a belief
system no longer grounded in Christianity. That is why J. Gresham
Machen titled his break with modernist currents *Christianity and Liberalism,* rather than speak, for example, of a "liberal Christianity."[33]
Biblical criticism changed an entire religious worldview: cosmology,
anthropology, Christology, and eschatology. Furthermore, it caused the

Bible to lose its central role as a concrete guide to and legitimation of pious conduct.

The conscious creation of the world by God was being replaced, in the view of fundamentalists, by an unconscious, biologically determined process of evolution. The conscious creation of man by God and the Fall were being repressed in favor of the accidental development of humanity from the animal realm and the idea of a higher social development of humanity. In this anthropological change fundamentalists also saw the collapse of their traditional Christology. Without the Fall the mission of the Son of God, namely, Christ's self-sacrifice for the sins of humanity, made no sense at all. And, finally, eschatology, with its post- or premillenarian return of Christ, the final judgment, and the eternal salvation of believers (as well as the damnation of unbelievers), was founded on the anthropology and the Christology. The renunciation of dogma allowed unbelievers into the churches, which in the fundamentalist view were no longer facing opposition from without but being undermined from within. The bastions responsible for the spread of the heretical views of biblical criticism were, above all, the Bible schools, colleges, and universities.

The conflict over the alleged subversion of the faith by biblical criticism and evolutionism, however, was by no means confined to theological debates. It extended to the definition of tasks, organizational structure, and moral standards of the Protestant denominations, affecting not only religious practitioners but also ordinary church members. Fundamentalists criticized the liberals in general and the Social Gospel in particular for its broadening of the church's mission. Their critique of the Social Gospel primarily questioned how caritative or socially or politically active the church should be. This problem, too, was founded on divergent theological assumptions concerning the origin of sin. The Social Gospel interpreted sinful behavior primarily as the outcome of social conditions, which therefore had to be changed. Fundamentalism understood sociomoral departures as the result of not having been saved. The chief function of the church, from the fundamentalist perspective, accordingly, should not be social amelioration but individual conversion. Social measures were justified exclusively as a means to the end of saving individual souls and were not to become an end in themselves.

For similar reasons fundamentalists also rejected the broadening of church functions proposed and pursued by liberals primarily for reasons of market strategy. Academic educational institutions or leisure organizations were not appropriate means to save souls or win members for the church. They were actually a distraction from the true mission and task of the church and an opportunistic conformance to social tendencies, which were to be reformed, not imitated.[34]

Fundamentalists criticized and fought their liberal opponents not only on account of the latter's alleged subversion of dogmas and their new definition of the church's tasks. They also clearly recognized that liberal innovations implied a structural change in the churches, which, in their eyes, threatened the reformist achievements of Protestantism and would create bureaucratic and centralized institutions comparable to those of the Catholic church.

Fundamentalists and liberals were united, however, on the point that the chaotic competition among the various denominations and congregations was ruinous and had to be overcome. Their strategies in response were, naturally, quite different. Fundamentalists represented voluntarism and autonomy. They promoted voluntary association, decentralized organization, and interdenominational cooperation on the basis of customary (orthodox) convictions.[35] These basic principles were upheld by such organizations as the World's Christian Fundamentals Association and the Baptist Bible Union.

Liberals, in contrast (at least from the perspective of fundamentalists), favored a bureaucratically centralized organizational model corresponding to the trusts that had been prohibited in industry and destructive of the autonomy of congregations and denominations. Moreover, this liberal solution to the problem of competition was based not on religious principles but on a completely unprincipled market approach that trivialized religion's claims to truth in favor of economic considerations. The future, accordingly, seemed to belong to large churches, with their diverse offerings and versatile clergy and staff.

For fundamentalists, alliances like the "Interchurch Movement" represented such an attempt to destroy autonomy, voluntarism, and orthodoxy through the establishment of a bureaucratically centralized hierarchy. Their fears were intensified by the frightful vision of a "League of Churches," a union of all Christian churches, including the Catholic and Orthodox, which some Protestants proposed as an analogue to the League of Nations.[36]

Fundamentalists also opposed the liberals' tolerance of phenomena that represented symptoms of moral decay, such as dance, popular music (jazz in particular), or provocative dress, all of which served to stimulate people sexually and thus lead them into temptation. Liberal churches not only did not condemn such things but to some extent even embraced them. Thus, in the fundamentalist claim, young women dressed as men had played jazz in church, degrading Christianity into "rag-time religion." Church services were held earlier, so that members would have more time on Sunday afternoons to engage in sports. Such moral decadence appeared to fundamentalists as the logical consequence of the erosion of the dogmatic principles of the faith. For it was upon such principles that the foundations of morality and conscience were set.[37]

An illustration in the *King's Business* exemplifies this fundamentalist perspective. Below the title "The Unbelieving Preacher-Professor at the Bar of Justice," readers saw a judge pointing at the accused. Above the judge was the question: "Who is responsible? For the destruction of faith in the Bible as the word of God. For the tidal wave of crime and vice. For the flaunting disregard of moral standards." And the judge cries out: "Thou art the man." At the same time it was insinuated that this "preacher-professor" was also an enemy of the Constitution. Below the book on the judge's bench appeared the caption: "The Bible is the rock foundation of our Constitutional Government."[38]

Critique of Foreign Cultural Influences and New Religious Currents
Particularly representative to fundamentalists of the carriers of unbelief were new religious movements and cults spreading around the turn of the century; Catholicism, which was growing from the wave of Southern European immigrants; German "Kultur"; and bolshevism. Among the new religious movements and cults those that fundamentalism considered the most subversive of the Christian foundations of American society were Mary Baker Eddy's Christian Science; the Jehovah's Witnesses, or "Russelites," as they were called after their founder; theosophy; and spiritualism. They were regarded either as pure superstitions or dangerous falsifications of the Christian faith. Fundamentalists particularly attacked minimizations or denials of the sinfulness of humanity and promises of salvation not based on individual conversion and a belief in Christ.[39]

Above all, Christian Science, which replaced the concept of sin with one of "false consciousness," was regarded as sowing dangerous illusions among people as to the seriousness of their predicament in the world and the decisions they made accordingly. A central criterion of the delimitation of fundamentalism from other religious currents can be identified in its strict theocentrism, that is, Christocentrism, which was either denied altogether by the new trends or gradually revised in the direction of a more anthropocentric worldview. The conflicts between fundamentalism and the new religions were therefore primarily religious, although from a fundamentalist perspective unbelief led inevitably to immorality, manifested in social behavior.

The attitude of fundamentalism toward the Catholic church was more strongly political. Although, naturally, there were unbridgeable religious-theological barriers here as well, two aspects in particular figured in the actual conflict: one, the old fear of "papal ambitions for world dominance" and the conspiracies allegedly instigated by Rome to this end; and two, the association between "rum and Romanism," that is, the resistance to Prohibition by Catholic immigrants from Ireland and Southern and Eastern Europe.[40]

The third great spoiler of Christian civilization in the United States was German *Kultur*. The essence and ruinous influence of German Kultur was seen, first, in German rationalism in the form of historical-philological biblical criticism, which allegedly sought to undermine the foundations of the faith from within, and, second, in the evolutionist ("Social Darwinian") philosophy of Friedrich Nietzsche, which attacked Christianity from without. Fundamentalism found the direct effect of these two currents in the German initiation of the barbaric First World War. Moreover, there was "German beer," which also undermined the foundations of Christian morality.

The anti-Germanism of fundamentalism first arose under the impression of World War I and was then intensified through the attacks of the liberal Chicago theologian Shirley Jackson Case, who accused the pacifistic premillenarian fundamentalists of being in the pay of the Germans.[41] To fundamentalists the horrors of war and its deleterious impact on social morality, which reached to the United States as well, represented a warning of the potential effects of the intellectual destruction of the Christian foundations of society. They found further confirmation of this view in the circumstance that many of the representatives of Nietzschean philosophy and biblical criticism in the German professoriat had championed and glorified the war.[42]

Bolshevism represented the fourth deleterious current to fundamentalists. Bolshevism, which increasingly predominated over the German threat with the end of the war, was not, as a rule, distinguished from socialism or anarchism. The danger of bolshevism lay, according to the fundamentalist critique, in its combination of atheism and desire for world dominance: "Bolshevism, a force as ambitious, as tyrannical and menacing as Prussianism, has set out to conquer and enslave the world."[43] The effects of bolshevism were seen by fundamentalists, and by no means only by fundamentalists, in changes in America's political landscape: anarchist bombings, an upsurge in intellectual radicalism on the left, the Communist Party and the labor union movement, the spread and radicalization of strikes. In all of these developments immigrants from Russia were prominent.[44]

The subversion of Christian civilization in the United States was exemplified, from a fundamentalist perspective (in contrast to domestic religious currents), by alien phenomena pressing in from the outside: the Roman church's ambitions for world domination, German Kultur, and Russian Bolsheviks aided by their accomplices inside the country. In distinction to nativist movements of the time, however, scarcely any anti-Semitic tendencies can be identified among fundamentalists. They were much more inclined to interpret the return of Jews to Palestine as a "sign of the times," as the fulfillment of prophecy, as a signal of the return of Christ and the early onset of the millennium. Because of this positive interpretation of the Jews in the Christian salvation history, fundamentalists were substantially immune to anti-Semitism.

Nevertheless, passages in fundamentalist publications made it clear that this attitude was tied to the expectation that the Jews—the American Jews included—would "fulfill the prophecy." This had chiefly a twofold meaning. Initially, they were to return to the "Promised Land," in order, later, to convert to Christianity. From that one can conclude that Jews were less welcome as fellow American citizens than as emigrants to Palestine. The attitude of fundamentalists toward Jews who simply wanted to be and remain American citizens was evident in a critical commentary to a declaration of the Central Conference of American Rabbis, which rejected a Jewish state in Palestine and characterized the Jews in the United States as a part of the American nation. Of such Jews it was said: "As faithless Israelites even in Moses' day, lured by the leeks and onions and garlic of Egypt, wished to turn their backs upon the fair land that a loving God had appointed for them, so they, captivated by the pro[s]perity that they have enjoyed in America and England, have no longing for the land God has given them by an irrevocable covenant."[45]

Beyond this, fundamentalists expected Jews also to fulfill the second part of the prophecy and convert to Christianity.[46] Even if no anti-Semitism in the traditional sense is found in fundamentalist thought in the period 1910–1928, and Jews were not ascribed a destructive role comparable to that of Catholics, German Kultur, or bolshevism, it is by no means true that the Jewish religion and culture was respected for their own sakes nor, certainly, can there be any talk of "philo-Semitism."[47]

Critique of the Sociomoral Crisis   After having identified, from a fundamentalist perspective, the most important agents of the destruction of Christian civilization, we now turn to their methods and objectives. How was the loss of Christian faith manifested? Which institutions were destroyed? What norms and values declined in significance in the regulation of behavior and motivation of action?

For fundamentalists the crisis of American society consisted above all in the decline of the Bible as a guide, subject to a literal understanding, to pious conduct. The crisis was most evident to them in the weakening of the family, churches, and public schools as the guarantors of a Christian upbringing. The loss of faith also explained the symptoms of moral decline in society, such as the higher divorce rate, adolescent criminality, the consumption of alcohol and tobacco, uninhibited pleasure seeking and sexual deviations, the unbridled drive for profit, and extravagance.

The central sign of crisis for fundamentalists was the change in sexual morality. Their publications and pamphlets were filled with complaints about prostitution and venereal disease, about dance halls and indecent dress on women, about music and dance, about the cinema and theater. John R. Straton, the pastor of the Calvary Baptist Church in New York, became the most prominent of the commentators on these subjects in such tracts as *The Dance of Death, Church versus Stage, The Menace of Immorality in Church and State,* and *Fighting the Devil in Modern Babylon.*[48]

Equally condemned were the changes in personal habits and leisure-time pursuits. Most important here, of course, was alcohol consumption, which led to sexual licentiousness, crime, and poverty. That is why the fundamentalists' first line of attack was the passage and then the continuation of Prohibition. Alongside alcohol consumption, fundamentalists criticized the use of tobacco products. Even the distribution of tobacco to soldiers raised a cry of protest. An even stronger condemnation was leveled at women who smoked, sometimes even in public![49]

Pilloried in addition were the extravagance and ostentation of the wealthy, who adorned their house pets with gold and jewelry or hosted elaborate public dinner parties in times of privation. The threat to salvation by the accumulation of riches was also emphasized.[50] The premillenarians, but also the Presbyterian William Jennings Bryan, frequently expressed a populism, founded in a sympathy for the "little people."

Thus a cartoon depicted how "the people" had fallen figuratively into the clutches of the "present evil age" of "false teachers" and "profiteers."[51]

Fundamentalists also criticized the increasing focus on consumption, above all in the context of Christmas celebrations: "Far more is heard of Santa Claus than of Jesus on this day in the average home. Then it is a day of prodigal waste of our money, which is not really ours but His. We bestow all manner of useless toys and gifts on children and grown-up people, who already have more than is good for them."[52] The mentality of consumption and leisure, fundamentalists charged, led not only to the adulteration of Christmas festivities but also to the profanation of the Christian Sabbath, which, like in Europe, was being degraded into a holiday: "On the Lord's Day, the house of God is deserted, while the parks, beaches, and mountains, and movies are crowded."[53]

Fundamentalists found further symptoms of decay in the decline of political and economic morality. Universities seemed less to provide a true education than to supply students with methods for making money. Patriotism was being commercialized: the flag was used to overcharge customers, and the tobacco industry exploited popular sentiment for the soldiers at the front.[54] And sin and immorality provided economic gain to those who made money off of dance halls, prostitution, alcoholic drinks, and tobacco.

The decline in political morality was evident in the apparent acceptance and even promotion of the threat to, or gradual disappearance of, the United States as a Christian (that is, Protestant) nation.[55] In the area of foreign policy this applied at least for some fundamentalists to the American entry into the world war and, above all, plans to join the League of Nations. In domestic policy political decline was evident in the corruption of urban party apparatuses, in the circumvention or planned repeal of Prohibition, and in efforts to shed the public schools of their Christian character.

Considerable segments of the fundamentalist camp initially opposed the United States' entry into the war. They modified this position only after America had become a participant, and after they had been heavily attacked for their pacifism by liberal theologians, who even insinuated that the fundamentalists were paid by the Germans. It is important to keep in mind, however, that most of the early fundamentalists were neither nationalistic nor militaristic. Thus did the *King's Business* publish articles with such titles as "The Demoralizing Effects of War," "The World War Mad," and "The Moral Wreckage of the War." The articles not only listed the demoralizing effects of the war on both soldiers and the civilian population but also regarded the fact of the war itself as a sign of the failure of modern civilization.[56]

Not only premillenarian fundamentalists considered war and rearmament unchristian. The postmillenarian Presbyterian William Jennings Bryan wrote as late as 1922: "The devil never won a greater victory than when he persuaded statesmen to make the absurd experiment of trying to prevent war by getting ready for it."[57] Fundamentalists, in particular premillenarians, rejected the euphemistic interpretation of the American entry into the war as a mission "to make the world safe for democracy." War remained for the majority of them a crime. Yet in this case participation in the war was also thought a necessary, albeit painful, consequence of barbaric German policy.

Criticism was leveled not only at the glorification of war but also at the idolization of the nation. A soldier's sacrifice of his life for his fatherland did not lead to redemption, as misguided clerics announced, but solely a belief in Christ's sacrifice of Himself for the sins of mankind.[58] Egotistical and degenerate men who had performed acts of heroism and sacrifice in the war were still subject to eternal damnation. With this critique fundamentalists clearly distinguished themselves from the fusion and increasing identification of patriotism and religion, to be found above all among their liberal contemporaries. While fundamentalists sought to Christianize the nation, the liberals were nationalizing Christianity.

A broad consensus within fundamentalism existed, however, concerning the League of Nations, which was regarded as a part of the general deterioration of political morality. Opposition increased over time. At first the League of Nations was seen as superfluous, then as offering deceptive hope. For lasting peace was to be gained not through the devices of sinful man but only through the return of Christ. Increasingly, fundamentalists saw in the League of Nations the danger that it would not be based on the Bible and Christian principles and—because Catholic nations were in the majority—that it would become a tool of Rome for achieving world domination.[59]

In domestic developments two tendencies, among others, prompted an assessment of political-moral decline: resistance to Prohibition and efforts to shed the public schools of their Christian character. The rejection—or circumvention—of Prohibition legislation was in particular strongly identified with Catholics and the "urban machine" of the Democratic party. Fundamentalists initially saw the trend away from Christianity in the schools in sometimes successful efforts to do away

with Bible instruction. In twelve of the forty-eight states at the end of
the 1920s, reading the Bible was regarded as "sectarian" and therefore
forbidden in public schools.[60] Such a development could not but have
had a deeply unsettling effect on people who saw America as a Christian
nation based on the Bible.

Nevertheless, much greater publicity and symbolic value were given
to another issue: whether the theory of evolution, which contradicted
the biblical story of creation, was to be allowed to be taught in the
public schools. Fundamentalists initiated campaigns in several states in
favor of legislation banning the Darwinian teaching from the schools.
From this protest came the famous 1925 case against Scopes, a biology
teacher in Dayton, Tennessee. To this day the Scopes trial defines the
image of fundamentalism in the 1920s in the public consciousness and
much of the literature.[61] Teachers and professors had already seemed a
suspect group to fundamentalists, one that bore a considerable share of
the responsibility for the corruption of the younger generation and,
therefore, the whole of society. The Scopes trial only confirmed and
intensified this prior judgment.[62]

Fundamentalists suffered extreme anxiety, finally, over the functional decline of the family as the guarantor of a Christian upbringing
for children and thereby a foundation of a Christian society. Several
factors coincide here. First of all, fundamentalists claimed that the decline of the churches, public schools, colleges, and universities ham-
pered Christian education in a fundamentalist sense or, to the extent
that their influence extended to the family, called it into question. To
that was added the general sociomoral decadence in society, expressed,
for example, in prostitution, gambling, and drinking. Social decay contributed to the destruction of the family by promoting divorce and
exercising a damaging influence on children. More than anything else,
however, women's emancipation encouraged this development: "There
is a full-fledged rebellion under way, not only against the headship of
man in government and church but in the home. . . . The cultivation of
the modern woman's idea of 'my individuality' is bound to be a de-
stroyer of the home life and a breeder of divorces."[63]

Not the least of the threats to Christian upbringing was the abandonment of the "family altar," the reading of the Bible in the home, and the
practice of prayer in the family circle, under the direction of the father.
This ideal of family piety, depicted in an illustration on a title page of
the *King's Business,* seemed according to the picture caption to have
basically become a thing of the past. For it was not to be preserved but

recreated altogether: "Honoring God in the home. Re-establish the old-fashioned family worship and let the word of God settle all our problems."[64] Elsewhere the resignation was equally apparent: "The old-fashioned home has disappeared; the old family Bible, thumbed by father and mother, is gone; a thousand things have come into the home and into daily life that leave but slight opportunity for the Old Book and for prayer."[65]

This subversion of the patriarchal family undoubtedly represented the core of the fundamentalist critique of society. Nearly all of the symptoms of crisis were viewed and evaluated according to their effects upon the family. Belief, Bible, morality, and family were regarded as an indissoluble unity, from which, for better or worse, other social institutions were essentially derived.

THE DRAMA OF SALVATION HISTORY

Fundamentalism's critique of the decline in faith and, consequently, in the central institutions of Christianity and general social morality mirrors the usual traditionalist or conservative complaints about changing times. Nothing is any longer as it once was: churches, schools, universities, young people, morality. What is specific to fundamentalist thinking, however, are the ideas derived from its "salvation history," which include the election of America, the struggle between the forces of God and Satan, and the approaching millennium.

To define these salvational ideas uniformly for the whole of Protestant fundamentalism in the 1920s may not seem legitimate at first glance. Doctrines among the various factions diverged sharply. For example, the salvational dimension among Presbyterians, who stood more in the Calvinist tradition, was more closely tied to ideas of political order than it was among premillenarian Baptists, who were consistent defenders of the separation of church and state and emphasized individual salvation from a world destined for decline.

However, with the transformation of fundamentalism from a conservative, religious-theological umbrella movement into a social movement with increasing cooperation among its various wings, we can confirm a politicization of even the premillenarians. To be sure, the latter neither fully addressed nor settled the implicit contradiction between quietistic theory and political activism. Premillenarianism, despite its religious individualism, obviously could not escape the insight that the chances of individual salvation were to some extent determined by a reproduction of the fundamentalist milieu and thus dependent on the condition of the central institutions of the family, church, and public schools.

An external pretext used by segments of the premillenarians to legitimate their politicization was America's need for public repentance of its sins and request for God's help in the war. Such a demand was raised by premillenarians as early as January 1918, with unmistakable reference to the Old Testament prophets: "The war would be brought to a very sudden and very satisfactory close if the different allied nations would humble themselves before God, confess their sins, acknowledge God's rights in national, commercial, political, and individual life, and then cry to God for His help."[66]

Fundamentalists regularly repeated this summons. In April 1918 the Senate passed a resolution initiated by the House of Representatives calling for a day of public repentance, public prayer, and fasting. President Wilson accepted the proposal and designated May 30 the appointed day. The turn in the war and the victory of the allies were subsequently interpreted as a result of this public act of submission to God.[67] This whole process obviously helped persuade premillenarians of the acceptability of action that was more directly political. In any case, the gap between the two wings of fundamentalism narrowed, which may not have leveled all their differences but did allow for an elaboration of the aspects of the salvation history the various wings held in common.

For the following discussion I distinguish the salvation history in fundamentalism temporally as the mythologized past, the crisis-ridden present, and the eschatological future. The significance of the conflicts in the present and the rationale of fundamentalism's mission make sense only given a consideration of the tension deriving from fundamentalism's relationship with the mythical past and the eschatological future. Fundamentalist thought and action in the present obtain their specific legitimation from this salvational dramaturgy.

Divine Revelation and Its Carriers   Protestant fundamentalism regarded itself as the most recent link in a long historical chain of religious thought, the most important instance of which was represented by first-century Christianity. This chain ran from the renewal of the Reformation to the realization of the American colonies and the founding of the United States of America.

With the rejection of Christ by the Jews, the status of a chosen people was transferred onto the congregation of Christians. The latter's development, however, was adulterated by the establishment of the papal church of Rome, which represented a fall from original Christianity. Only with the Reformation, which, through the Bible, once again made divine revelation accessible to humanity, was the autocracy overcome and the true church reestablished.

With the emigration of the Pilgrim fathers to America and the founding of colonies there, a new union was created and a new people chosen as the carriers of divine providence. The pious colonists of the Plymouth Plantation and the Massachusetts Bay Colony established a New Jerusalem, a new Israel, based on their own beliefs. Thus the foundations were laid for the realization of a Christian society based on the Bible, and Christian principles were written into the American constitution upon the new nation's independence. In the fundamentalist reconstruction of the traditional Christian salvation history, a direct line ran from the leaders of the early Christian congregations to the Pilgrim fathers to the founding fathers, that is, from Paul to John Winthrop to George Washington and from there on to Abraham Lincoln.

The Conflict in the Present   This view of the past gave the present conflict between fundamentalism and the various forms of "unbelief" its religious significance. Fundamentalists saw themselves as the defenders of the word of God and as the executors of His commission in a world increasingly falling prey to unbelief and thereby to Satan and sin. Their struggle against modernism, liberalism, Germanism, Catholicism, and bolshevism, therefore, was not merely based on a difference of opinion or a matter of taste but was also in their eyes an episode in a world-historical drama in which the forces of light were cast against the forces of darkness.

For fundamentalists, immorality was founded upon unbelief. That was the source of the dramatic intensity lent to questions of sexual morality, dress, dancing, and leisure-time and consumer behavior. Those who behaved indecently, those who danced, gambled, drank alcohol, or failed to respect the Sabbath, did not simply have other habits or characteristics but demonstrated in their behavior their unbelief, their decision against God and in favor of Satan. Tolerance, a virtue for fundamentalists when applied, for example, to the question of the millennium, became a sin when applied to this moral decay.

The Return of the Messiah and the Millennium   As unified as the fundamentalists were in principle in their view of the salvational past and present, so were the majority of Presbyterians and Baptists divided over their eschatological expectations. The postmillenarian Presbyterians optimistically held that the establishment of the millennium through Christianity was possible and anticipated the return of Christ at the end of the millennium. The premillenarian Baptists, in contrast, believing in the increasing decadence of the world and seeing the onset of the millennium in the impending return of the Messiah, were more pessimistic about the possibilities of human endeavors.

Nevertheless, the two wings were successful in pushing their differences into the background and in defining problems to allow for common action and thus for the establishment of a social movement within fundamentalism. The front was defined by a line running between biblical literalists and everyone else: "The split will not be over the question of the manner in which the millennium is to come, but it will be between those who repudiate the Bible as the Word of God and want social service and German Kultur in its place—and those who believe . . . that the Bible is the very Word of God and that its program is to be followed."[68] What was important, then, was the struggle against unbelief, even though the chances of success in this struggle remained undecided. Moreover, the two groups were united behind their divinely ordained mission to preach evangelism to the entire world. Above all, however, they both believed in the physical return of Christ to earth and the Last Judgment and recognized that one chose between eternal salvation and eternal damnation, which were understood in quite realistic terms.[69]

BASIC PATTERNS OF FUNDAMENTALIST THOUGHT

The combination of social criticism and of the salvation history reveals the basic patterns of fundamentalist thought. Five aspects of fundamentalist thought are particularly characteristic: Manichaeism, xenophobia, religious nativism, a conspiracy mentality, and a specific view of female sexuality.

The Manichaeism in fundamentalist thinking is, of course, already present in Christian thought in its distinctions between God and Satan, the forces of light and darkness, good and evil, and God's commandments and sin. These expressed dualisms rarely find application and largely disappear in pragmatic compromises in the everyday lives of most religious people, but they stand in the center of fundamentalist thought and are subject to continual actualization and dramatization. The effects of this dramatized Manichaeism are evident primarily in the representation of the enemy, in the self-perception of the movement, and in the categorical perception of society's crisis.

The enemies of Protestant fundamentalism, whether liberal theologians or German beer brewers, proponents of the Social Gospel or bootleggers, Bolsheviks or gamblers, prostitutes or atheists, all were agents of Satan and thus themselves Satanic powers. Thus, for example, the University of Chicago evoked the following comments as the perceived stronghold of liberal theology: "There should be a combined attack of real evangelical forces against the Satanic powers entrenched in the fortress of Chicago," and "Mr. Rockefeller endowed with millions a university, professedly for the Lord's cause, and the devil took possession and installed his representatives to see that his devilish, deceptive work was carried on in this high place."[70]

The fundamentalist self-perception derived unavoidably from its characterization of the enemy. Fundamentalists saw themselves as agents of God, as orthodox and pious. The crisis in American society at the turn of the century was perceived not as a structural crisis caused by industrialization, urbanization, and mass immigration but as a moral crisis brought forth by unbelief.

The second characteristic of the fundamentalist mentality is its marked xenophobia. Nearly all of the Satanic forces buffeting society had not originated in the United States but had been brought in by foreigners or imported from foreign places: liberal theology, atheistic philosophy, war, as well as beer and evolutionary theory from Germany; rum from the Catholics; bolshevism from Russia; the profanation of the Sabbath from Europe; the tango from South America.

Even if their view was not always explicitly stated, it was nonetheless clear to fundamentalists that the reviled moral abuses, such as prostitution, alcoholism, and crime, were in the main brought in by European immigrants, that foreign workers were especially eager to go on strike and be politically radical, and that the political culture was being destroyed by the bossism of the Irish and Italians. Fundamentalism thus regarded the sociomoral crisis in the United States as an epidemic brought into the country by a foreign contagion. The natives were, perhaps, vulnerable to its spread, but the causes of the crisis lay elsewhere. A comment on biblical criticism nicely illustrates this way of thinking: "Not an original theory in biblical criticism has been propounded by an American critic; every conclusion is borrowed, and every argument is kidnapped from foreign lands."[71] The basically xenophobic character of fundamentalism was also evident in its rejection of all forms of international cooperation. Whether in reference to the

League of Nations or ecumenicalism, fundamentalism was constantly fearful of having to relinquish its autonomy and basic religious position and of falling under the domination of foreign powers.

The other side of xenophobia was exemplified by nativism. Foreign influence was to be pushed back, and an indigenous tradition and strength, and an indigenous "essence" and "identity," were to be cultivated. This element of fundamentalist thinking is interesting in that fundamentalist nativism differed from that of secular right-wing radical movements and ideologies. Fundamentalist nativism of the 1920s was almost exclusively of a religious-cultural type and strongly eschewed— at least explicitly—ethnic or racist elements, as were prevalent, for example, in the parallel nativism of the Ku Klux Klan.

The return to the indigenous religious-cultural roots of the Pilgrim ancestors and founding fathers, and not, for example, to the Anglo-Saxon heritage, found its most impressive expression in the attitude of fundamentalists toward immigrants. To fundamentalists the "Americanization" of immigrants meant in the first instance their conversion to Christianity based on the Bible: "The Bible is the best book for making real, true American citizens out of foreigners, or natives either."[72] What this meant concretely from a Presbyterian perspective was the glorification of work as a sure means of resisting the temptations of Satan. The following passage reads like a parody of the Weberian thesis: "This is the only way America will solve the problem of bringing the foreigner to Christ. Work!—then work some more, and after you are tired, get up and still work."[73]

The fourth characteristic of the fundamentalist mentality was its paranoid certainty that ominous powers were conspiring against true Christianity, that is, fundamentalist Protestantism, and its most important homeland, the United States of America. The chief conspirator was Rome. The Catholic church, in this view, had plotted the world war, was in bed with the Germans, and was using the Kaiser as a means to achieve world domination.[74]

Even during the war, Rome, and not Germany, had been designated as posing the greatest danger: "Apparently Rome has her eye upon the triumph of the Kaiser and upon an alliance with him for the domination of the world. The greatest danger to our Republic is not from the Kaiser, but from Rome." The Catholic church was equally allied with bootleggers, who gave it considerable financial support: "There has been a long understanding, if not formal alliance, between Rum and Romanism."[75]

Moreover, fundamentalists argued that the Catholic church had worked to remove the Bible from the public schools in the United States in a plan to cause their decline and then set up its own parochial schools. And it promoted the idea of the League of Nations in order, in view of the majority of Catholic nations, also to further its plans for world domination.[76]

A further characteristic of fundamentalist thinking concerns male-female relationships and female sexuality. At issue here is an extremely dualistic view of the inborn tendencies and nature of men and women, based on the myth of Eve. Woman was seen as a threat to man, as a temptress to sin, as the "typical Eve," of whom Satan made use to corrupt man. This basic pattern was expressed with particular clarity in the writings of the leading New York fundamentalist, John R. Straton, who discussed questions of sexual morality in nearly all of his books. His *Slaves of Fashion* included chapters on "The Connection Between Women's Dress and Social Vice" and "The Scarlet Stain of Sexual Impurity."[77]

Even when the case of (usually) rich men seducing (usually) poor, inexperienced girls was sometimes addressed, the seductive role of women remained generally in the foreground. Straton noted in a report of a "carnival performance": "The lewd women in that show performed vile 'oriental' dances . . . intended to arouse the lower passions of young men present."[78] In the *King's Business* he wrote, "The modern dances . . . are designed to kindle the passions of young men," and commented on "the power a girl has either to lift men up or pull them down."[79] Straton described the morally degenerate, man-seducing woman as follows:

> The most sinister and menacing figure of our modern life is the cigarette smoking, cocktail drinking, pug dog nursing, half-dressed, painted woman, who frequents the theaters, giggles at the cabarets, gambles in our drawing-rooms or sits around our hotels, with her dress cut "C" in front and "V" behind! She is a living invitation to lust, and a walking advertisement of the fact that many of our modern women have lowered their standards of life![80]

Of particular interest in comparison with Iran is Straton's proposal of a "national costume" for women, designed to preserve propriety.[81] Obviously a central concern of both Protestant and Islamic fundamentalism is to desexualize women in public through dress.

THE IDEAL ORDER

At bottom, Protestant fundamentalism's notion of order can be best expressed by the following: "The ideal form of government from the

Bible standpoint is the Theocracy, that is, the world ruled by the Creator, and every man a loyal loving obedient subject."[82] This rule of God could be established by consistently enforcing the laws revealed to man by God, an idea that contains a universal ethical monism in a twofold sense. First, there is only a single "correct" ethics for all times, for all people, societies, and cultures: namely, the Christian ethics revealed by God. Second, this ethics composes a closed unity. It comprehends all social spheres equally. Modern ethical pluralism, allowing distinct, partial ethics in politics and economics, for example, is rejected. Christian ethics, in the fundamentalist claim, is capable in principle of ordering all human relationships on biblical foundations.

Yet, how does one interpret these laws? How can they be realized under the conditions of a developing industrial society? Who are the legitimate interpreters of divine will? And what governmental form corresponds to it? Most of these questions cannot be answered by simple reference to concepts but characterize the tension that exists between two polar alternatives.

It is possible to identify areas of ambivalence within fundamentalist thinking, which derive, in part, from the historical circumstances accompanying them. In many cases, however, these can be traced back to the distinct traditions of the two most important camps: the individualistic, apolitical tradition of the premillenarian Baptists and the tradition of Presbyterian orthodoxy bound up with Calvinist religious-political conceptions of order.

Between Universalism and Nationalism   Premillenarian thought in its ideal typical form represents the idea of Christian universalism. Accordingly, there exists an invisible community of truly converted Christians who follow the commandments of God. A nation cannot be Christian in itself; not collectives but individuals are the carriers of the faith. The Calvinist-Presbyterian tradition, in contrast, more strongly represents a religious nationalism according to which the United States was attributed the role of a commonwealth chosen by God. This elevated status included the mission of being a model for the world.

In actuality, many fundamentalist concerns did not reflect this distinction. The premillenarian camp, in particular, was internally divided, oscillating between apolitical pacifism and unreflected religious nationalism. This tension was especially evident during the world war and with the increasing involvement of the United States. On the one hand, all religious justifications of the American entry into the war were disputed, and it was repeatedly emphasized that there were no truly Christian nations. On the other hand, the United States was extolled as a "Protestant nation" and "the greatest nation in history." And "our God" became the American God without qualification once He had decided the war in favor of the United States.[83]

Aside from the war, it was primarily the transformation of fundamentalism into a politicized social movement that increasingly displaced Christian universalism with religious nationalism. It was a nationalism that understood itself as in the vanguard and sought, both as a model and through its mission, to Christianize the world. It can thus be characterized as an exemplary, expansive religious nationalism with a universal claim to validity.

Between Republicanism and Democracy   A second tension arose over the concepts of republicanism and democracy. Here as well, the divergence between premillenarian Baptists and Presbyterian orthodoxy had an essential role. The premillenarians were unambiguously antidemocratic, associating democracy with lawlessness, socialism, and mob rule. This corresponded to its anthropology, its skepticism of a just order on earth achieved by humanity's own devices. Presbyterians, in contrast, assessed democracy positively, which, again, corresponded to their optimistic judgment concerning humanity's potential on earth.

Both groups represented the ideal of a religious republicanism. But the Presbyterians believed in the attainment of republicanism by way of democracy, and the premillenarian camp tended to conceive the two ideas of order as antagonistic. The well-known premillenarian cleric Isaac Haldeman thus characterized democracy as dangerous because it led to autocracy and revolution, and, moreover, it increasingly approximated socialism.[84] Such opponents regularly presented the League of Nations as a (frightening) example of democracy: "We are informed that the League of Nations will have much to do with 'Making the world safe for Democracy.' . . . What the world needs is to be made safe for the Lord Jesus Christ!"[85]

In a few cases democracy was identified with lawlessness and vigilantism. Racial unrest, which broke out in Tulsa, Oklahoma, after whites had attempted to lynch a black, inspired extensive commentary: "Democracy—the rule of the people—is here. . . . The tide of democratic lawlessness is rising higher every year, defying all authority. The socialist spirit of revolution gains strength in every land since the world war."[86]

Among premillenarians the idea of democratization was so laden with anxiety that it was directly tied to eschatological images of the prophetic rule of the anti-Christ. Unimpeded democracy led, in this view, to anarchy, to a "red republic," from which world dictatorship necessarily ensued: "Godless democracy is bound to develop the most devilish rule this world has ever seen."[87]

The subject of democracy appeared in completely different guise in the publications of Presbyterian orthodoxy. While the premillenarian Haldeman spoke of the "peril of democracy," the Presbyterian Harry Vogelsonger was more concerned with the "perils to democracy."[88] To the Presbyterians, democracy was valued as an achievement of Calvinism, which was founded solely on the sovereignty of God. Without divine sovereignty democracy could not exist at all, but only autocracy, the authority of the strong over the weak. Democracy was based on the idea of equality before God.[89]

The Presbyterian William Jennings Bryan, finally, added a populist component: an unshakeable faith in the rectitude of the people.

> Our nation can, by its example, teach the world the true meaning of that democracy which was to be made safe throughout the world. The essence of democracy is found in the right of the people to have what they want, and experience shows that the best way to find out what people want is to ask them. There is more virtue in the people themselves than can be found anywhere else; the faults of popular government result chiefly from the embezzlement of power by representatives of the people—the people themselves are not often at fault. But, suppose they make mistakes occasionally: have they not the right to make their own mistakes?[90]

Democracy demanded engagement of the Christian citizen, who, in association with others, would prohibit sinful behavior through appropriate legislation. Bryan placed his faith in the power of Christianity to persuade, which, under democratic conditions, would be capable of establishing a Christian republic.[91]

Fundamentalism and Capitalism   How, then, do the concrete ideas of an economic order appear from the perspective of Christian principles? And what positions did fundamentalism take in response to modern industrial capitalism, large-scale modern enterprises, trade unions, strikes, lockouts, and class conflicts?

Like those treated above, there were sometimes fundamentally different answers to those questions by premillenarians and orthodox Presbyterians. In a thoroughly informative article, "Protestantism and Property," in the *Princeton Theological Review,* Presbyterian Earnest E. Eells remarked that the premillenarians took a nearly pre-Protestant position on the question of property, standing in the tradition of medieval mysticism and asceticism: "Renouncing the world and its goods in the hope that the promises of the Scriptures will be fulfilled in the millennial age to come, seeing in the underpaid minister or missionary, who is 'supported by faith,' the modern saint, and looking on poverty and misery as a sign of the imminent return of the Lord—this is not far from the pre-Protestant views on property."[92]

Eells's depiction is accurate insofar as the premillenarians perceived economic relations largely through the categories of poverty and wealth. They directed their critique at extravagant wealth but also at poverty to the extent that it led to immoral behavior. Although some did trace the conflict between capital and labor to mutual greed, the premillenarians nevertheless frequently expressed sympathy for the "little people," particularly contrasting their plight with the extravagance and ostentation of the rich.[93] They felt that wealth posed an especially great spiritual danger.[94]

Premillenarians tended to depict themselves as "little people," in line with the tradition of Baptist populism. Thus, for example, someone wrote in the *King's Business*: "The great bulk of the members of our evangelical churches are from the *common people*." And, elsewhere, the solemn remark: "show us a church, poor, illiterate, obscure and unknown, but composed of praying people. They may be men of neither power nor wealth nor influence. They may be families that do not know one week where they are to get their bread for the next. . . . They are His chosen vessels of salvation and His luminaries to reflect His light."[95]

Among premillenarians the leading fundamentalist of the South, J. Frank Norris, was exceptional in taking a resolute prolabor stand. He accused the churches of having concerned themselves far too little with the working people. Large donations from millionaires were always being celebrated in public, rather than the small contributions scratched together by ordinary people. Norris even attacked the economic system that produced such millionaires: "We are glad for the benefactions of a Rockefeller, a Carnegie and a J. Ogden Armour, but I will tell you something that is ten thousand times better and that is a system of justice that will prevent the making of the Rockefellers, the Carnegies and the J. Ogden Armours."[96]

Moreover, Norris stepped in for higher wages. In his view the low wages of the time (1919) led to the destruction of families. Higher wages, in contrast, would have a positive effect on the economy by elevating purchasing power and on the church, education, the family, and the nation. Nor did Norris attempt to play the workers off against the unions but defended union members against the charges that they were anarchistic bomb-throwers.[97] It was much more the case, in his view, that the best security against anarchy would be precisely an organized labor force. Capital and labor had, at bottom, the same interests, for underpaying the workers would not be profitable over the long run for entrepreneurs.[98]

All fundamentalists believed that work was an effective prophylactic against sin. Thus they were particularly fond of quoting such principles as "He who does not work shall not eat," and "One should eat one's bread by the sweat of one's brow." The most significant distinction between premillenarian and postmillenarian fundamentalism was Presbyterian orthodoxy's explicit, theologically grounded defense of capitalism and private property: "There is no greater need in the present state of Sociological discussion than a reasoned *apologia* for the Capitalist order of society."[99] Alongside historical and economic arguments, of primary interest here is the theological justification of capitalism. To Presbyterians the highest values were individualism and freedom, the freedom to work or not work (and in that case to starve), to accept or reject working conditions, to strike or undertake a lockout.[100] The critique of socialism rested chiefly on its atheism and anti-individualism.

Socialism and the unions represented a collectivist counterimage to Presbyterians. Strikes, which were organized by the unions, ruled out any question of individual freedom: "In a great miner's strike in England, organized by men who seem to be utterly ignorant of economics, there were thousands of men compelled to strike, because they did not dare to disobey the command of a Junta who controlled their actions."[101] Presbyterians repudiated the socialist principles of collective property, the international solidarity of the working class, class struggle, and the social revolution for material reasons and considered them opposed to the Christian principles of individualism, private property, patriotism, brotherly love, and moralism. Fundamentalists often saw an application of the Christian commandment on brotherly love in the introduction of arbitration into conflicts between capital and labor.[102]

If, despite the differences between pre- and postmillenarian fundamentalists, one were to set forth the characteristics of a Christian economy, it would be best to begin with the principle of "stewardship," which was accepted by both.[103] God, in this view, is the owner of all property, which he has only entrusted to individuals. Those so blessed,

however, are charged with using these goods not selfishly but in conformance with the commandments and in God's spirit.

From the fundamentalist perspective this ideal best corresponded to a
capitalism restrained by the ethics of Christian brotherhood and based
on an ascetic work ethic. On one side was the pious entrepreneur who
increased prosperity but lived modestly himself, giving money to the
church to raise God's glory; on the other was the God-fearing worker,
who labored hard but received in return a just wage, with which he
could feed his family. Entrepreneurs and workers did not represent
opposing classes but confronted each other as individuals charged with
fulfilling the earthly tasks assigned to them by God conscientiously and
in the spirit of brotherhood.

These economic ideals alone demonstrate that fundamentalism was
not an interested party in a modern class conflict. In its basic characteristics the blend of asceticism and compassion is more like eighteenth-
century Scottish moral philosophy. Its economic model substantially
reflects the ideal of a preindustrial, petit bourgeois, patriarchal capitalism. This order, as it existed extensively in the nineteenth-century
United States, was interpreted by fundamentalists as the realization of
Christian principles, and they therefore demanded that the latter be
applied to modern industrial society as well.

Family Structure and Social Morality   Despite the significance of the
nation, politics, and economics, the family was particularly prominent
in the fundamentalist conception of order, providing the foundation for
all other institutions. The ideal was the traditional patriarchal nuclear
family with a clear, gender-based division of labor. The mother was
responsible for the household and raising the children; the father, as
head of the family, saw to its livelihood and, when necessary, was
responsible for politics, in the sense of protecting the interests of his
family. The family was the guarantor of a Christian upbringing and way
of life, whereby the "family altar," praying together, and Bible readings
by the father were allotted central significance.[104]

Moreover, the family was embedded in the local congregation of the
church, which was simultaneously the most important site for spending
one's leisure time. One's behavior was to be characterized by thrift and
modesty. Alcohol and tobacco consumption were generally repudiated
and were especially morally objectionable for women. Clothing, above
all the dress of girls and women, was supposed to be respectable and

decent, without any intimation of sexual allure. Sexual relations outside marriage were strictly forbidden and taboo.

Underlying all fundamentalist ideas of order was the personalistic-patriarchal structure. Authority rested on the piety of women and children toward the father and the *pietas* of the father toward God. The patriarchal family based on the Bible was the foundation of political community and the basic model according to which economic and political relations were to be conceived.

THE CARRIERS OF PROTESTANT FUNDAMENTALISM

As early as the 1920s a preconception concerning the carriers of fundamentalism was already current, and it persists in the literature of today. It is that fundamentalism recruited its members from among the uneducated population in small towns and rural areas of the American Midwest and South. One of the first to formulate this stereotype was John Mecklin. Since that time it has not only been presented as fact in regard to fundamentalists but has also been applied to the extreme right-wing movements that arose later.[105]

This naive Enlightenment interpretation of fundamentalism and related movements, which regards them as the result of a lack of modern education and consequently localizes it in rural areas, has been disputed by several authors since the mid-1960s. Thus did Michael Rogin refute the identification of the McCarthy movement with agrarian populism, documenting the involvement of the Republican party establishment. Kenneth Jackson has persuasively argued that the Ku Klux Klan of the 1920s was essentially an urban phenomenon, with its most significant political successes in the cities. And Ernest Sandeen has shown that fundamentalism as a religious-theological movement arose chiefly in the northern cities of the United States.[106]

These arguments for the urban locale of extreme right or radical-traditionalist movements have prompted other researchers to modify the old model of rural and small-town origination. One now finds that the organizers and adherents of urban fundamentalism are identified as migrants to urban areas who had not yet conformed their values to the structural conditions of modern big cities. They were, so to speak, in the city physically but still had their minds in the country.[107] Although this identification of urban migrants as the carriers of fundamentalism has some validity, the argument as a whole is too simple. For one thing, many adherents of fundamentalism had long been resident in the cities. Second, such arguments treat belief systems like substances, categorizing them according to demographic and geographic criteria.

Urban migrants joined a variety of social movements and associations, so that their classification as carriers of a "rural consciousness" is simply not admissible. The kind of people urban migrants associated with and how they adjusted intellectually and culturally depended on social heritage, education, age and gender, reasons for migrating, first contacts in the city, the new social relations established during the search for dwellings and work, and their successes and failures.

In my analysis of the dissemination and carriers of fundamentalism, I take up the approaches of Rogin, Jackson, and Sandeen mentioned above. For I am able to demonstrate that the fundamentalism of the 1920s was also primarily an urban protest movement of the American North, Midwest, and Southern California. To avoid misunderstandings, I restate the typological differentiations discussed at the outset between traditionalism and fundamentalism, between a fundamentalism of mastering the world and one of fleeing the world, between rational and charismatic fundamentalism, and between the actual fundamentalist movement and its potential as a movement.

The subject of this work is solely the politically active fundamentalism of world mastery, that is, the protest movement of the 1920s organized and supported essentially by Baptists and Presbyterians in the North. The investigation consequently encompasses neither the broad fundamentalist *potential* of the South and rural Midwest nor the numerous charismatic fundamentalist groupings favoring flight from the world. In this analysis of the carriers of fundamentalism, therefore, one must not expect a fundamentalism of the sort described by Erskine Caldwell in *Deep South* nor the one represented in the urban milieu by the various branches of the charismatic movement.[108] None of these groupings were part of the fundamentalist protest movement, which, even in the premillenarian camp, can be identified as a *rational fundamentalism of world mastery.*

DEMOGRAPHIC DISTRIBUTION

Let us look first of all at the regional centers of those denominations in which fundamentalism formed most clearly. It quickly becomes apparent that the Old South was largely uninvolved in the struggle against modernism as it was organized on a national level, a fact that was clear to contemporaries. The two denominations in which the conflict raged most furiously were the Northern Baptists and the Presbyterian Church in the USA, that is, the Baptists and Presbyterians of the political North. Neither the Presbyterians of the South nor the extremely conservative Southern Baptists had a role inside the fundamentalist movement.[109]

What were the causes of the Old South's reserve? Three aspects seem to be of significance here: politics, dogma, and structure. First, the Baptists of the South, because of their regional self-awareness and political and historical experience, were little inclined to cooperate closely with their Northern coreligionists. Second, all the leading representatives of the Baptists in the North were adherents of premillenarianism, but Southern Baptists were postmillenarians. The primary factor behind their reserve, however, might well have been the stability and homogeneity of traditionalism in the South, so that, despite the tireless efforts of a J. Frank Norris, it was clear that not many people could be persuaded that the Southern Baptists represented a refuge of modernism.[110]

This last argument gains additional confirmation from a comparison with those denominations in the North manifesting a high degree of traditionalist homogeneity. Thus the participation of Lutherans in fundamentalism was negligible, although they, more consistently than any other denominations, represented dogmatic-orthodox positions.[111] The leading personalities of fundamentalism as an interdenominational movement also came from confessions in which the conflict between modernism and orthodoxy was strongest, the Baptists and Presbyterians of the North.[112] Observing, finally, the regional distribution of the organizational centers of fundamentalism, it is likewise evident that the Mid-Atlantic states, the central Northeast, and the Pacific states were dominant, not the American South.[113]

If one examines the urban-rural distribution of the most important leaders, the most significant congregations, the prominent educational centers, the most widely distributed journals, and the fundamentalist presses, it can be unambiguously established that the stronghold of fundamentalism was not the small town as the gathering place of the agrarian hinterland but the big city—thus the activities of William B. Riley in Minneapolis, John R. Straton in New York, J. Frank Norris in Fort Worth, and T. T. Shields in Toronto. The two most significant fundamentalist Bible colleges were the Moody Bible Institute in Chicago and the Bible Institute of Los Angeles. And Presbyterian fundamentalism was headquartered primarily in Philadelphia. The main centers of organized fundamentalism and the most successful fundamentalist congregations were therefore located in big cities, such as Philadelphia, New York, Chicago, Minneapolis, and Los Angeles.

The insignificant participation of Lutherans, despite their thoroughly homogeneous dogmatic-orthodox attitude, likewise confirms the thesis that fundamentalism was primarily an urban protest movement. The Lutherans, of all the traditional churches, were primarily based in rural areas and small towns. Thus they were affected to a much lesser degree by the sociocultural processes of transformation occurring in the rapidly growing industrial cities.[114] Here, too, as with the Southern Baptists, the distinction between traditionalism and fundamentalism pertains, between the not-yet-mobilized potential and the committed adherents of fundamentalism.

Because of the popular view of fundamentalism as a rural and small-town movement, it is necessary to examine whether fundamentalism in fact had its basis in rural areas, with its centers located in big cities for organizational or administrative reasons. Since academics have not researched rural fundamentalism per se, the situation of rural churches has to be gleaned from other sources. Studies have been carried out by the liberal Federal Council of the Churches of Christ in America (FCCC) and the Interchurch World Movement.

The first FCCC study was based on surveys conducted in Windsor County, Vermont, and Hopkins County, New York, during 1909–1910. The results offered little encouragement to liberals. Compared with the situation of the church twenty years earlier, incomes had declined, and despite a population of "nearly pure American stock" a notable portion of the clergy had been recruited from immigrants.[115] Because of falling income, the clergy was having problems regenerating itself. Moreover, church attendance, despite a rise in church membership, was falling noticeably. The educational level of the clergy was described as pitiful. The study summarized the condition of rural churches as follows: "In a word, the vitality and power of the country church in these two counties is in decline."[116]

Yet more depressing from the perspective of the churches were the results of a second FCCC study, conducted by the same authors a few years later in Ohio. There, too, the churches were described as small and weak. Conditions in the countryside were characterized by social and moral decline, although in this case as well the population consisted almost entirely of long-term American Protestants. On the increase, in contrast, were the "Holy Rollers," that is, adherents of charismatic groups.[117]

The *Indiana Survey of Religious Education* of 1923 compared urban and rural Sunday school attendance in two districts. The rural regions there also did not prove to be refuges of piety. Although 41 percent of urban youth under twenty-five years of age went to Sunday schools, in the countryside the figure was just 33 percent.[118] Similar results were evident in the statistics concerning church membership in city and countryside.[119]

Not only the liberals noticed the decline of rural churches but also the fundamentalists were aware of it. They lamented the undersupply of evangelists for the farming population and the lack of consideration for their specific circumstances on the part of local churches: "One of the most distressing things in our modern American life is the way in which so many of our farmers and their families are growing up without God."[120]

These depictions help confirm that rural areas and small towns were not the centers of fundamentalist mobilization in the period under consideration. They were in fact undergoing religious stagnation or even decline, though charismatic movements did record growth in the countryside. The centers of the fundamentalist movement were the cities of the American North, Midwest, and Southern California. This regional distribution clearly supports the correlation of urbanization and industrialization with the genesis of the fundamentalist protest movement. It was most concentrated within the area roughly bounded by Boston, Chicago, Saint Louis, and Baltimore, the core region of rapid urbanization, industrialization, and mass immigration, and in other rapidly growing cities, such as Los Angeles and Minneapolis.

Fundamentalism did spread to some extent from urban to rural regions, insofar as clerics and preachers leaving the Bible institutes to move into the countryside succeeded in mobilizing local traditionalism.[121] This activation and transformation of rural fundamentalist potential was of secondary significance, however, as were the local or regional campaigns against the teaching of evolutionary theory in the public schools. Clearly, fundamentalist protest was primarily a response to the conditions spawned by rapid urbanization.

SOCIAL COMPOSITION

Whose experiences came to be expressed in the ideology and protest behavior of fundamentalism? Let us turn first of all to the organizers and intellectuals, then to the broader membership. Institutional ties and education distinguished the leading representatives of theological modernism from those of fundamentalism. In general, there were far more theologians among modernists, but pastors, evangelists, and lay preachers predominated among fundamentalists.[122] Modernists tended to be headquartered in the theology departments of large universities; fundamentalist intellectuals were more likely to teach at Bible schools and colleges. This trend roughly reflected the education the respective figures themselves enjoyed. Robert Wenger in his comparison of forty leading representatives of each movement discovered that 40 percent of the fundamentalists, but 70 percent of the modernists, had a master's or doctoral degree. Only 25 percent of fundamentalists had received a bachelor's degree, but the share of modernists remaining at this educational level was only 2.5 percent.[123]

For the most part the literature on the conflict between modernism and fundamentalism takes the relatively low educational achievement of the fundamentalist elite as proof that the whole movement can be interpreted essentially as a product of educational deficiency. Another perspective seems more fruitful to me, one that regards fundamentalists and liberals as representatives of different educational ideals. For that reason I do not consider it appropriate to compare fundamentalists and modernists in terms of the other's educational standard but to interpret both movements as expressions of sociocultural differentiation. Both movements represented the reactions, as formulated by religious intellectuals, of broad populations to the crisis occurring simultaneously in society and the denominations. These reactions express the specific experiences, values, and interests of their respective clienteles and attempt to cope with the crisis through different reinterpretations of their religious beliefs and through different organizational models.

Even if the majority of the organizers of fundamentalism were pastors, evangelists, and lay preachers, the significance of the movement nevertheless lies in their capacity to mobilize a membership that cut across denomination and occupation. What, then, was the composition of this broad constituency?

Existing studies of the constituency of fundamentalism provide the same characterization with great frequency. Fundamentalism, it is argued, sought its recruits to a large extent among the lower social strata, workers, urban migrants, and members of a petite bourgeoisie in the grip of decline. Thus, the famous Middletown study associated all fundamentalist tenets and practices predominantly with the working and lower-middle classes,[124] thus describing the membership of a fundamentalist church as "made up of working class people and less prosperous members of the business class."[125] This affinity between fundamentalism and labor is also confirmed by other contemporary studies.[126]

Nevertheless, it does not seem appropriate to accept this characterization as a given. The studies all incorporate a relatively diffuse concept of fundamentalism, one that does not distinguish rational and charismatic fundamentalism, world mastery and world flight traditionalism and fundamentalism, and fundamentalist potential and the actual movement. Thus, when such studies refer to "fundamentalism," one never knows whether they mean charismatic-ecstatic groups, such as Holy Rollers, faith healers, or people who speak in tongues, or orthodox Presbyterians and Baptist literalists.[127]

Yet precisely this distinction—between a search for salvation or confirmation of salvation based on an ethical rationalization of the conduct of daily life and a personal salvation received by the divine gift of grace—characterizes different social carrier groups. And thus it is by no means accidental that the charismatic movements, despite their biblical literalism, remained excluded from the rational-fundamentalist movement because of the ecstatic elements in their religious practice. Moreover, the strong middle-class representation by a denomination like the Presbyterians, the generally unambiguous dominance of the values of the traditionalist middle class, and the theologically informed debates between fundamentalists and modernists raise doubts over any simple association between fundamentalism and the working class.

The constituency of the fundamentalism movement, therefore, cannot be categorically defined by scattered comments in the secondary literature. But unfortunately, no representative empirical research exists for the period under discussion. I have therefore adopted another strategy and investigated the composition of fundamentalism by drawing on the congregation of the leading organizer of the fundamentalist movement, William Riley of the First Baptist Church in Minneapolis. The development of the congregation is relatively well documented for the period 1897–1930 and can be correlated with socioeconomic data.[128]

This approach presents some methodological problems, above all the generalization of the results. Does the composition of one congregation really say anything about the fundamentalist constituency as a whole? I think it does. For one thing, the First Baptist Church exemplifies a type of a *cathedral,* a central, urban church with a membership scattered throughout the city.[129] Thus this investigation avoids the bias of many other individual studies, which have been concerned with smaller local congregations of a relatively homogeneous clientele from a more bounded residential district. Furthermore, comparative material is available that confirms the results of this study.[130]

Riley took over the First Baptist Church in Minneapolis in 1897. Within six years his fundamentalist positions led not only to an enormous expansion in membership but also to a social regrouping of the congregation and then to a split in 1903. Riley raised the membership in his church almost 85 percent, to 1,037 (1903) from 561 (1896). The new membership clearly manifested specific social characteristics. The share of professionals declined by 4.9 percent, managerial employees by 3.4 percent, and businesspeople and entrepreneurs by 24.7 percent; however, the number of white-collar workers increased by 8.1 percent, both skilled and factory workers by 6.7 percent, and temporary workers (including domestics) by 10.3 percent.[131] Primarily blue-collar workers and lower-class white-collar workers were thus attracted by Riley's fundamentalism, and, above all, important segments of the economic establishment were repelled by it.

In 1897 the congregation was made up of 69.2 percent professionals, managerial employees, entrepreneurs, and businesspeople; in 1903 these groups accounted for only 37.2 percent. The share of blue- and white-collar workers changed accordingly. Most interesting here is the increase in the number of blue-collar workers. Although the share of clerical employees rose to 28.9 percent from 20.8 percent, the share of blue-collar workers and service employees rose to 33.9 percent from 10.0 percent.

Also instructive is the composition of the faction within the congregation that withdrew from the First Baptist Church in 1903 to found the Trinity Baptist Church. Members of the upper and upper-middle classes made up 80.8 percent of its congregation: 26.0 percent were professionals; 38.4 percent, businesspeople and entrepreneurs; and 16.4 percent, managers. Labor was represented by five skilled workers, amounting to only 6.8 percent of the congregation, with not a single factory worker, temporary worker, or domestic employee. The First Baptist Church was located in the center of the city, but the new Trinity Baptist Church moved out to a suburb favored by the upwardly mobile.[132]

This social regrouping appears to support the traditional thesis that workers formed the base of fundamentalism. But the impression is misleading. The First Baptist Church by no means represented a workers' congregation in 1903. The members were distributed among three socioeconomic groups, with 37.2 percent in the upper group (businesspeople, entrepreneurs, professionals, managers), 43.1 percent in the middle group (clerical workers, skilled workers), and 19.7 percent in the lower group (factory workers, unskilled workers, domestics). Distinguishing between the independent professions, white-collar, and blue-collar workers, the shares are 24.3 percent, 41.8 percent, and 33.9 percent, respectively.

However the congregation is grouped by occupation, it is not possible to attribute a class character to its social composition. Riley, therefore, did not make of his church a class-specific congregation. In fact, he overcame its earlier identity as an upper-class church, forming a congregation with a socially mixed clientele. That this social regrouping was not an isolated case, but that the socially mixed clientele was typical and, in my view, programmatic for this type of fundamentalism, is demonstrated by the parallel development of the congregation of the leading Canadian fundamentalist, T. T. Shields in Toronto.[133] In his congregation as well a split occurred, causing a social restructuring. Table 1 shows the composition of the Jarvis Street Church in 1913, after the schism, along with its reconstructed share of liberal and fundamentalist members.[134]

A comparison of the social composition of Riley's congregation in 1903 with that of Shields's congregation in 1913 yields a similar pattern, as shown in table 2. These figures provide unambiguous evidence that, at least in its early phase, fundamentalism's appeal was by no means directed disproportionately toward the lower socioeconomic classes. Fundamentalist churches attracted a socially mixed clientele, within which, despite the social regrouping effected by splinterings in the congregations, the upper and middle classes remained overrepresented.

Did the social composition of fundamentalism change with its transformation from a religious movement into a protest movement, and, if

TABLE I.

SOCIAL COMPOSITION OF T. T. SHIELDS'S JARVIS
STREET CHURCH IN 1913

Occupation	Total	Liberal	Fundamentalist
Business, professional, managerial	47.6%	65.4%	41.9%
Clerical, skilled worker	38.6%	30.8%	41.1%
Factory worker, domestic employee	13.8%	3.7%	17.0%

SOURCE: Ellis 1974, 162, 166.

TABLE 2.

SOCIAL COMPOSITION OF THE CONGREGATIONS OF
RILEY (1903) AND SHIELDS (1913)

Class	First Baptist Church (1903)	Jarvis Street Church (1913)
Upper	37.2%	41.9%
Middle	43.1%	41.1%
Lower	19.7%	17.0%

SOURCE: Ellis 1974, 117, 162, 166.

so, in what direction? For this question as well we will refer to the development of the First Baptist Church under Riley in the 1920s, that is, after his rise to become a central figure among the premillenarian fundamentalists. By the end of the 1920s, membership had risen to 3,196, making it the largest congregation in Minneapolis. The number enrolled in its Sunday schools (2,083) and its staff of twelve made it the top church in these terms as well.[135] For the social composition of the congregation in the twenties, no detailed listing of members and their occupations is available. But there are reliable data on where church members lived. The residential data permit inferences to be drawn as to class status.

Two studies, one by Ross Sanderson and the other by Wilbur Hallenbeck, have classified city districts according to various criteria. Sanderson is primarily concerned with criteria of social transformation, investigating their effects on churches. He distinguishes four quality levels. According to this classification, of the members of the First Baptist Church, 12.8 percent came from the best district, 21.7 percent from the above-average, 37.6 percent from the below-average, and 29.6 percent from the worst.[136]

Hallenbeck classified the social quality of city districts according to eight criteria: infant mortality; juvenile delinquency; poverty; frequency of suicide; proximity to industrial plants; residential transience; family dysfunction; and incidence of tuberculosis.[137] He identified five quality levels: 18.7 percent of the members of the First Baptist Church lived in the best district; 12.0 percent in the above-average; 9.1 percent in the average; 34.8 percent in the below-average; and 31.0 percent in the worst.[138]

If one compares these data with those of other churches with a clientele distributed broadly over the city, such as the Swedish Tabernacle, the Central Lutheran Church, and the Portland Avenue Church of Christ, the considerable social diversity of the First Baptist Church is striking. The congregations of the other churches tended to be from one social class or neighborhood; however, fundamentalists were drawn from all residential areas.[139]

This tendency becomes yet more emphatic if one correlates the share of members of the First Baptist Church in the various districts with the overall percentages of Protestants living there. Twenty-six percent of Minneapolis Protestants lived in the worst, 32 percent in the below-average, 12 percent in the average, 15 percent in the above-average, and 15 percent in the best districts.[140] As can be seen in table 3, if one compares this distribution with that of the First Baptist Church, one finds an astonishingly small deviation of a maximum of 5 percent.[141] The social composition of fundamentalism substantially corresponds to that of Protestantism in general. In contrast, other, obviously more clearly class-specific congregations exhibit considerable deviations; thus 30.1 percent for the Swedish Tabernacle, 26.9 percent for Saint Mark's Episcopal Church, 17.0 percent for the Portland Avenue Church of Christ, 16.9 percent for the Hennepin Avenue Methodist Episcopal Church, 13.5 percent for the Central Lutheran Church, and 11.5 percent for the Westminster Presbyterian Church.[142]

As uncertain as the above figures might be in detail, they are just as clear in showing the tendential composition of fundamentalism in the 1920s, that is, at the time when it represented a politicized protest movement. Two aspects seem to me noteworthy. First, these figures unambigu-

TABLE 3.

SOCIAL COMPOSITION OF PROTESTANTISM AND
THE FIRST BAPTIST CHURCH IN MINNEAPOLIS IN
1926

District Quality Level	Total Protestants	First Baptist Church
1 (best)	15.8%	18.7%
2 (above average)	15.0%	12.0%
3 (average)	12.0%	9.1%
4 (below average)	32.0%	34.8%
5 (worst)	26.0%	31.0%

SOURCE: Hallenbeck 1929, 24, 81.

ously show that the carriers of fundamentalism cannot be delimited according to socioeconomic criteria. The analysis of ideology has already shown that fundamentalism was not informed by class consciousness and, therefore, did not represent a "class for itself." The composition of Riley's congregation also clearly documents that fundamentalism was not a class movement in the sense of a "class in itself." Therefore, it is obviously inappropriate to ascribe to fundamentalists a "false consciousness"; rather one has to acknowledge that the criteria according to which they socialized and associated were primarily noneconomic.

The second noteworthy result refers to the transformative processes within the fundamentalist constituency. In the prewar period the upper classes were still overrepresented, despite the splits that occurred in fundamentalist congregations. In the course of fundamentalism's development as a protest movement, however, this surplus largely disappeared, and its social composition came to approximate that of Protestantism as a whole. The share of adherents from the lower classes was indeed high, but only insignificantly higher than average; the upper class was still overrepresented. Both of these results contradict conventional expectations.

Both the liberal denominations and the charismatic groups tended to be dominated by one class, but an important characteristic of fundamentalism was precisely its socioeconomic heterogeneity. Here, my distinction between charismatic and rational fundamentalism proves fruitful. For, in contrast to the Pentecostals, rational fundamentalism of world mastery was not a relatively homogeneous movement of the lower class but a movement encompassing all socioeconomic groups.

Instead of socioeconomic characteristics (or as complements to them), other criteria must therefore be considered to define the foundations of association and community in fundamentalism. In order to interpret such complex phenomena, I have introduced the category of sociomoral milieu, in which values, norms, and ethical commitments have exactly the central roles they have in the fundamentalist social critique. In essence, one can agree with George Marsden, who wrote in reference to Minneapolis: "Fundamentalism appealed to some well-to-do, and some poor, but also and especially to the 'respectable' Protestant and northern European working class, whose aspirations and ideals were essentially middle-class Victorian."[143]

At the outset I argued that ideology, the question of the movement's carriers, and the causes of mobilization must be related systematically to each other, and I pointed out the particular significance of ideology.

Applied to our case, it becomes apparent that the social structure of the congregation and its ideology are closely interdependent. In the socially heterogeneous fundamentalist congregation the social ideal of fundamentalism is symbolically represented. The church offers a model for social integration and conflict management through religious-ethical discipline and the overcoming of individual sinfulness. Identifying the carriers of fundamentalism, therefore, involves a look at a sociomoral milieu that in ideology and social composition provides a countermodel to a modern industrial society based on conflicts over material interests.[144]

The Share of Urban Migrants   A popular and frequently documented thesis holds that radical movements in general recruit a high percentage of their adherents from among urban migrants. Behind this assumption (or, as the case may be, in explanation of this fact) are two theoretical traditions. The first is derived from Enlightenment notions that would like to represent "premodern" consciousness as a rural relic. The second is the further development of the Durkheimian anomie thesis. It regards urban migrants, in their anomic situation, as easy prey to radical organizations and leaders, which help them to overcome social isolation, loneliness, and alienation.

It is also assumed that fundamentalism recruited a not insignificant share of its adherents from among migrants from rural regions and small towns. Their number and social class have not been documented for fundamentalism in the 1920s, however. Moreover, there is some basis in the literature for the suggestion that lower-class urban migrants were attracted primarily to charismatic sects. The extent to which they were also represented in rational fundamentalism remains unknown.

In reference to the First Baptist Church in Minneapolis, Ellis speculated that a very high percentage of the new congregation members Riley won to the church consisted of young urban migrants concerned with social betterment: "the followers of Riley appear to have been young migrants of white and blue collar background for whom the Calvinistic work ethic and piety remained functional in their attempts to realize the Horatio Alger myth."[145] This assertion, to be sure, is not sufficiently supported empirically. Thus, for example, the age structure of Riley's congregation was not examined, but still the inference was drawn that urban migrants were as a rule young. And the thesis of an urban migrant following is supported primarily by the fact that, of ninety-five new members won to the congregation between April and December 1897, fifty-four, or 56.8 percent, were not listed in the Minneapolis address directory. Ellis interprets this as "a sign that they may have been recent arrivals in the city or so geographically mobile they were not recorded in the survey."[146]

This conclusion is certainly plausible. Nevertheless, one cannot deduce from these data whether the people, if new arrivals at all, came from the countryside, small towns, or other large cities. Presumably, the pastor William B. Riley himself was not listed in the address book at that time. Born in the Indiana countryside, he had just arrived from Chicago, where he had been in charge of another congregation.

Unfortunately, no information is available on the origins of the 476 new members Riley attracted to the First Baptist Church between 1896 and 1903. That urban migrants had an important role within fundamentalism has been documented repeatedly by other investigations and is by no means in dispute here. To declare them the dominant or typical carriers of fundamentalism, however, appears to me on the basis of the available and documented facts of the time neither legitimate nor helpful, particularly as the history of fundamentalism up to now has more suffered than gained from such hasty determinations.

Constituents' Educational Level   The image of the fundamentalist constituency as a group of uneducated yokels can be substantially attributed to the appearance of William Jennings Bryan at the Scopes trial in Dayton, Tennessee. The struggle against evolutionary theory has been identified since that time with a general hostility to modern scientific knowledge. And, measured in terms of a modern definition of the educational system, Clarence Darrow made a complete fool of Bryan.[147] Bryan's constituency no doubt believed otherwise.

No representative investigation exists of the educational level of the broad constituency of fundamentalism in the 1920s, but we can reasonably draw some conclusions from the educational attainment of the fundamentalist elite. Even if, for example, fundamentalists lagged behind modernists, one can by no means represent them as uneducated. Whatever else is true, 75 percent of fundamentalist preachers held college degrees.[148]

Considering the broad social distribution of the fundamentalist camp in an urban environment and in view of the marked status of reading in fundamentalist culture, that which was said above in reference to the fundamentalist elite also applies to its constituency at large. Fundamentalists and modernists differed not so much in their years of schooling as in the content of their educational ideals. Faith in science, however, is not an index of higher intelligence or education any more than is faith in revelation; it merely suggests an orientation toward different worldviews and reference groups.

Constituents' Ethnocultural Background   The fundamentalist movement in the United States was substantially a protest movement of white Anglo-Saxon Protestants (WASPs). Almost all of the movement's leaders were Anglo-Saxons, except for a few of German heritage. The Presbyterians were Scotch-Irish; the Baptists, English. This ethnocultural dimension was further evidenced by the frequent exchange of evangelists, preachers, and pastors among England, Canada, and the United States, and even, to some extent, Australia. Fundamentalist publications in the United States often accept articles by British authors. And, unlike the "barbarian" nations, England was often included in statements of the superiority of American civilization.

This predominance of WASPs within the fundamentalist movement has several causes. The main one, however, is that most Presbyterians and Baptists in the North were white Americans of Anglo-Saxon descent. As far as that goes, the same applies to the modernists. Blacks had their own denominations, and other white Protestants (Scandinavians, Germans) were predominantly Lutheran, whose rural distribution meant that they were not easily mobilized.[149] The issue of ethnic background in fundamentalism, however, in distinction to the Ku Klux Klan, was minor compared with religious and cultural concerns. The fundamentalism of the 1920s was largely nonracist.

THE CAUSES OF PROTESTANT FUNDAMENTALIST MOBILIZATION

Thus far I have shown that the carriers of Protestant fundamentalism cannot be adequately described by socioeconomic categories nor did they identify themselves or make associations according to such categories. Fundamentalism was much more representative of a societal cross section, the integration of which ensued, not on the basis of class interests, but on that of shared values and ideals of proper life conduct. Despite its heterogeneous social composition, however, it is possible to identify within fundamentalism class-specific characteristics that indicate a qualitative dominance by the traditional middle class. Nevertheless, the fundamentalist milieu was oriented not by material interests but by certain values. Many members of the lower classes, including many urban migrants, aspired to realize its ideals and way of life, which were considered exemplary, moral, and pious.

How, then, did social transformation and its effects lead to the mobilization of the fundamentalist milieu? The statements of fundamentalists show that they were primarily concerned with a general crisis of faith, which had its effects in various social spheres. It was, first of all, a crisis within the Protestant denominations, then a broader sociomoral crisis, manifested above all in the decay of the traditional patriarchal family structure. It was a political moral crisis of parties, state, and nation, and finally, a crisis in economic morality. Fundamentalism's critique thus referred to those sociomoral dimensions of institutional transformation. As we have seen from their regional and demographic distribution, the experience of crisis and the articulation of protests were concentrated in urban centers. In the analysis of the causes of mobilization, accordingly, I will investigate the specific effects of institutional transformation on the traditionalist milieu in the cities.

THE INTRACHURCH STRUCTURAL TRANSFORMATION

I begin with an analysis of the conflict within the Protestant denominations. For here is where the formation of fundamentalism as a religious movement had its beginning; here began the mobilization of the traditionalist clergy, preachers, evangelists, and missionaries, that is, the intellectual elite of fundamentalism, who ultimately multiplied its impact. They had a large share in the organization of the movement, in the mobilization of the constituency, and in the transformation of religious dissent into a politicized protest movement.

For a long time the centrifugal forces within the Protestant denominations were held in check, on the one hand, by the institutional tie of congregations and of the denomination and, on the other, by their consensual critique of the moral decay of society, both of which continued to be effective well into the Prohibition campaign. However, there came to be increasing conflict in the various denominations over how to confront the social transformations then challenging believers on their worldview and affecting social, political, and economic institutions, sociomoral ideas, and leisure-time and consumer behavior. Above all, this disagreement within the churches over the changes, whether intended or merely tolerated, occasioned by liberals and modernists, represented the core of the intrachurch causes of mobilization of the traditionalists.

The literature customarily recognizes this state of affairs but interprets it in such a way as to suggest that liberals completed the necessary processes of adaptation to "modernity" but fundamentalists, because of their backwoods ignorance, were closed to such a rational response.[150] In contrast to that perspective I affirm the thesis that the split between liberals and fundamentalists was the expression of a sociocultural process of differentiation, in which liberals adapted not to "modernity" but to a new clientele, to a "modernistic milieu" shaped by the new middle classes. Liberals reflected the latter's scientific orientation in their theology and theological education, the trend away from dogmatism and toward an interdenominational social orientation in their ecumenical endeavors, and their new leisure-time and consumer behavior in the functional expansion of their congregations. Along with this emerging milieu and its money, the liberal churches moved to the better-situated suburbs and left the rural congregations and the inner city on the sidelines.

The fundamentalist clergy, in contrast, found their reference group and clientele in the traditionalist milieu, which was shaped by other ideas of faith and morality, by other leisure-time and consumer habits. Fundamentalism and liberalism within the churches were thus less the products of reason, enlightenment, and progress on the one side and superstition, ignorance, and reaction on the other than the result of the formation of two sociomoral milieus in a society undergoing industrialization and urbanization. The conflict between them was a competition for control of church institutions, for the chances of social reproduction of the respective milieus, and, especially in the rapidly growing cities, for the exemplary status of their ways of life as well as their recognition by state institutions.

In what follows I will investigate the consequences of liberal church policy for fundamentalists as they issued from four central processes of transformation: the change in worldview; the enhanced role of science in education; the centralization and bureaucratization of the churches; and ecumenical collaboration. The conflict between liberals and fundamentalists has previously been interpreted primarily as one over beliefs, stemming from fundamentalists' inferior education and irrational anxieties. If, however, one examines the consequences of the project of modernist reform in theology, churches, seminaries, and local congregations, it becomes quite evident that not only fundamental values were at issue but also people's chances for power, advancement, and careers inside religious institutions. This makes it the more understandable why fundamentalists defended themselves so passionately against institutional restructuring.

The transformation of the religious worldview was prompted above all by Darwinian evolutionary theory in the natural sciences and research into the historical figure of Jesus and biblical criticism in Protestant theology and scholarly religious studies. Traditionalists insisted upon the direct verbal inspiration of the Bible and thus on the creation doctrine and Jesus' status as the Son of God, but liberals conformed to the fruits of modern scientific method. This resulted in a divergence between the two worldviews.[151]

Although revelation, for fundamentalists, signified a one-time, closed event transmitted through the Bible, the adoption of modern scientific standards forced liberals to assume progressive revelation. Thus the cornerstones of belief were robbed of their eternal, timeless claim on the truth and made historically relative, contemporary, and tied to social development. At the same time, received norms and values were historically relativized as well.[152]

The scientification of faith had far-reaching effects on the structure and function of religion in general. For simple believers it represented, first of all, a loss of religious autonomy. For, without recourse to expert knowledge—held only by religious intellectuals—they became increasingly incapable of defining the content of their faith, now coupled to scientific standards.

Moreover, with the blending of religion and social development, as took place in the Social Gospel or the "theology of democracy" on the "social question" and the political structure, religion underwent a functional transformation. Its autonomy, based on the definition of individual salvation, which offered room for an autonomous religious motivational and behavioral system and thus a status system as well, was called into question and rendered scarcely distinguishable from political, economic, and cultural determinants of status. Ideal models and religious election thus were no longer practicable as a statutory religious ethic but became bound to other social spheres through a political ethic. An essential function of religion, especially for the lower classes—to compensate for the pressure of hopelessness, powerlessness, and a lack of success in daily life through religious election and the certainty of salvation—was thereby destroyed.[153]

The historicization and relativization of revelation and thus of the accepted values and norms it implied also aroused the protest of those

who interpreted their own way of life as an especially exemplary fulfillment of eternal commandments. This applied with particular force to
the established middle class of businesspeople, craftsmen, and independent professionals and to those who identified themselves with the
middle-class ideal and accepted it as the goal of their social ascent.

The modern worldview thus alienated broad segments of not only the
lower social classes but also the traditional middle class as well. Liberal
Protestantism, in contrast, increasingly transformed itself into a religion
of the new middle classes, a tendency that was equally manifest in
reforms of the educational centers, church organizations, and the definition of the function of local congregations and their move to the more
affluent suburbs.

The most important sites of theological conflict, in which evolutionary theory opposed the creation doctrine and the belief in the divine
inspiration of the Bible opposed biblical criticism, were the centers of
theological education. At issue in this conflict were not only two theological doctrines but simultaneously the control, structure, and definition of tasks of these institutions.[154] Liberals stood for the scientification of theological education in order, on the one hand, to elevate
the clergy to a new intellectual standard and, on the other, to establish a
new type of church, demanding of the pastor the ability to fulfill a
multitude of new functions.

The liberal strategy also implied a liquidation of the unscientific Bible
schools and colleges, which represented the backbone of the conservative and fundamentalist camps. Thousands of believers obtained their—
frequently scanty—credentials to be pastors, preachers, evangelists, or
missionaries in those institutions. They represented the bulk of the
badly paid rural pastors, who were often unable to live from their
profession without an additional source of income. They maintained
congregations in the inner-city slums and were the essential religious
caretakers of the "little people." A scientification of education implied
the future exclusion of these less educated persons from religious careers
and thus the gradual extinction of the fundamentalist elite.

The scientification of education thus worked almost exclusively to
the benefit of the liberals, many of whom obtained positions in rich
congregations or in the expanding church bureaucracy following com-
pletion of their studies, while such careers remained closed, as a rule, to
their fundamentalist colleagues.[155] The mobilization of precisely the
more poorly educated clergy, preachers, evangelists, missionaries, and
students of the Bible schools rested to some extent on the attempt of the

liberals to liquidate their institutions through the scientification of education, which resulted for many in the impossibility of attaining the social advance they hoped for by choosing the profession of the clergy. The struggle of fundamentalists for the survival of "old-time religion" is thus simultaneously a struggle for the survival of their institutions and for professional and social advancement.

A further point of conflict between liberals and fundamentalists lay in the reaction of the urban congregations, in particular, to the crisis. The liberal strategy consisted of market agreements among denominations, whereby dogmatic distinctions were overlooked and market research for religion was put on a scientific footing and congregations adopted a demand orientation and expanded their functions.[156] Liberal churches consistently moved, along with their clientele drawn mostly from the new middle classes, to the nicer suburbs, equipping their congregations and offering them a theology corresponding to their sense of life, their worldview, and their leisure-time and consumer needs.[157] They offered, for example, a wide array of educational options, musical events, theater groups, leisure groups for girls and boys, health facilities, kindergartens, and home economics instruction.[158]

The functional expansion of congregations was interpreted and encouraged by liberal church sociologists as an adaptation of the still rural conception of the congregation to a modern urban one. Just the terminology of these analyses, which was borrowed from evolutionary theory, must have offended fundamentalists.[159] Given the functional expansion of the congregations, whether encouraged or assessed as a complete adaptation to urban relations, the following is what emerged as the liberal expectation regarding the urban church of the future.

First, the number of churches would decline dramatically, for such a wide offering of services could be achieved only through the concentration and centralization of congregations. Thus the liberals issued the call for "fewer and better churches."[160] Second, the administration of the congregations would become more complex and bureaucratic, for the delegation of authority and distribution of funds presupposed regulation. Third, the role of the pastor would be transformed from one of a preacher and clergyman into one of a manager, businessman, and organizer. He would become part of the bureaucratic apparatus extending from ecumenical through interdenominational and denominational affairs down to the local congregation.[161] Finally, the financial needs of such a multifunctional congregation would make it necessary to woo church members from among more prosperous classes.[162] For the liberal "downtown church" seeking to adapt to new conditions, that meant, for example, the integration of two sets of clientele, one rich and one poor: "The church consists of two sets of people, representing older and newer strata of the constituency respectively. The two do not always agree perfectly; but the church has to have both, one to furnish the numbers, the other to furnish the money."[163]

The consequences of this combination of liberal strategy and modernist plans for the future were precisely the fundamentalists' nightmare. All that was odious to them in modern organizational principles and what they criticized as "big government," "big business," and "big labor" can be repeated here for the church: centralization, bureaucratization, increasingly anonymous relationships, the abandonment of dogma and thus the removal of Christ from the conduct of everyday life. Fundamentalists feared the rise of a hierocratic structure, whereby Protestantism would be forced to give up the achievements of the Reformation and fall back into the authoritarian structure of the papal church.[164]

The fundamentalist strategy, accordingly, was completely different. Fundamentalists fought for the autonomy of the pastor and for voluntary cooperation between congregations and denominations on the basis of the dogmatic "fundamentals." They strictly rejected a functional expansion of the church and favored instead of a strategy of adapting to the needs of the clientele the traditional strategy of stimulating demand for "old-time religion" through a steady devotion to evangelism and revivalism. For them the purpose of a congregation was to pursue salvation and to provide a place for the religious community to join together in that pursuit. Functions that went beyond the worship service, Sunday school, and support for evangelists and missions did nothing but distract from these goals.

Neither, consequently, did fundamentalists seek any change in the role of the pastor. He was to remain a preacher rather than become a manager. As a result their financial needs were more modest, and they could concentrate their resources on fewer functions. At the same time, they chose not to focus on the new rising classes and thus the new market but attempted to transcend social distinctions and mobilize the entire traditionalist potential. Their emphasis in internal mission work thus lay on evangelizing the lower classes, not least the migrants to the city from rural areas.

Although liberal churches increasingly disappeared from the inner cities, moving with their more prosperous clientele to the suburbs, fundamentalist congregations tended much more to remain in city centers, near the quarters of the lower classes—the unemployed and hobos, foreign immigrants, urban migrants, and casual laborers—and in the residential districts contiguous to the city centers, home to tradespeople and white- and blue-collar workers.[165] Here the share of white Protestants in the population steadily declined with the arrivals of Catholics and blacks. And many of the Protestants that were located in these neighborhoods had become less open to the approach of the rational fundamentalist churches for these areas were also the strongholds of the charismatic fundamentalist sects. This crisis in the urban church was the subject of countless books, articles, and pamphlets, as well as the focus of considerable academic efforts to point a way to its resolution.[166]

The modernist program for overcoming the crisis of the urban churches promoted an adaptation to urban structures and functions, interpreted as functional expansion, bureaucratization, centralization, market agreements, an expanded role for pastors, and lending church organization a scientific basis. Fundamentalists, in contrast, supported voluntary cooperation, making traditional functions more effective, autonomy, and personalism. Both sides, therefore, were involved in an adaptation less to "the modern big city" than to their respective clienteles within the big cities.

A further important intrachurch conflict between modernists and fundamentalists concerned the nature of collaboration among the denominations. Given the crisis of the churches in both the city and the countryside, both parties were aware that collaboration among the denominations had to be improved in order, on the one hand, to avoid a ruinous competition and, on the other, to overcome the partial shortage of clerics.

Liberals pleaded for close collaboration among the denominations, a sentiment expressed in the foundation of the Federal Council of Christian Churches in America and in the Comity movement. The Comity movement represented an attempt to avoid competition between churches by regulating the market based on demand. Regulative measures included, for example, a limitation on the number of new congregations to be allowed and the supervision of the Comity committee over the establishment of any new congregations.[167]

Fundamentalists were not in principle opposed to interdenominational collaboration. Aside from cooperating in the World Christian Fundamentals Association, they participated in interdenominational conferences, in the exchange of preachers, speakers, and articles, and in the support of interdenominational congregations, Bible colleges, and periodicals. But as much as fundamentalists might have lamented

fragmentation into an excessive number of small, badly equipped congregations, they also rejected the conception and organizational structure of the liberal model of cooperation. For fundamentalists it was
unthinkable to agree to bureaucratic control over the founding of new
churches, in particular as the criteria for admitting new churches were
obviously shaped by the modern multifunctional conception of the
liberal church. Beyond this disagreement, and aside from the question
of the efficiency of congregations, the question in the foreground for
fundamentalists was the content of what was to be preached. In comparison, liberals were scarcely interested in substantive problems of
content in this context.

Another attempt at liberal interdenominationalism was represented
by the Interchurch World Movement of North America, which was
founded in 1918 to unite all social and missionary institutions within
American Protestantism. The goal of the new organization was to centralize and concentrate resources; thus fundamentalists were not altogether unjustified in seeing in it an attempt to spread liberal theology
with conservative money while, at the same time, bleeding them dry
financially.[168]

A summary of the intrachurch causes of fundamentalist mobilization
identifies, alongside the conflict over dogma and modern scientific knowledge, a series of institutional conflicts, all of which were connected to the
actual or intended creation of a bureaucratic apparatus by the liberals.
Now, it certainly would have been possible for fundamentalists to have
occupied positions in this apparatus and thus ensured their influence
among the denominations. It seems to me, however, that their principled
resistance to these institutions was founded not only on their rejection of
collaboration with liberal "heretics" but also on their opposition to principles of bureaucratic organization as such. The intrachurch mobilization
of fundamentalists was based substantially on a rejection of the structural
change of religious institutions from personalistic-patriarchal to bureaucratic organizational principles as they were pursued by liberals in regard
to congregations, confessions, and collaboration among denominations.
Not the least important characteristic was a defense of the individual
autonomy of clerics and believers against bureaucratic control.

SOCIOCULTURAL DIFFERENTIATION IN CITIES

The rise of fundamentalism as an urban protest movement occurred
during a phase of rapid urbanization in which the social structure of cities
was being revolutionized by the rise of new classes, migration from rural

areas, and heavy immigration. These also led to cultural pluralism, with both ethnic-religious and socioeconomic foundations.[169] The dominance of white Anglo-Saxon Protestant culture was in part relativized, in part broken, by the immigration of Catholic Irish, Italians, and Slavs; Eastern European Jews; and Central and Northern European Lutherans. To this was added the migration of blacks from the American South to the cities of the North.

But the Anglo-Saxon Protestant camp was also disintegrating—as evidenced by the denominational split between liberals and fundamentalists—into (at least) two sociomoral milieus, a "modernist" one, centered around the values of the rising middle classes, and a "traditionalist" one, centered around the established middle classes and migrants from small towns and the countryside.[170] Rapid urbanization, however, led not only to a pluralism of cultures but also to anomic phenomena. As we have seen above, a major part of the fundamentalist sociomoral critique was aimed at this transformative process. Which aspects of this development were responsible for mobilizing the fundamentalist camp?

I see the interests of fundamentalism affected primarily in two ways. First, it suffered an enormous loss in prestige. The exemplary status of its conduct of life, values, and norms, all essential aspects of its self-concept, were suddenly deprived of majority recognition and respect. Social control was no longer functioning; the previous proscriptions of things regarded as immoral were gone. Bars, gaming salons, dance halls, and bordellos had become normal features of the inner city, for which as a rule the immigrants were blamed.[171]

This development not only damaged the prestige of the traditionalist milieu but, above all, also considerably reduced and endangered its chances for sociocultural reproduction. Because of the plenitude of foreign cultural influences and anomic phenomena, the worth of traditional values and norms was no longer self-evident. To pass them on to the younger generation was becoming increasingly problematic in view of the expanding array of consumer and leisure-time activities being offered. Seen from this perspective, campaigns for Prohibition or for respecting the sabbath not only dramatized status claims but also served to enhance the appeal of the milieu by eliminating the profane competition to a religious use of free time.[172] Without strictly delimiting itself from new developments, the traditionalist milieu could not survive at all in the big city. Thus it was forced to become fundamentalist in order to be able to remain traditionalist.

The traditionalist camp was mobilized, however, not only by foreign cultural influences and anomie but equally by transformations within the family. Developments particularly in the big city led to an increase in the number of divorces, to changes in the received notions of sexuality and the role of women, and to a decline in parental authority and control over children. Women had an expanding role in national politics, above all in the Prohibition movement; in 1920 they received the right to vote on the federal level. More and more young women were attending institutions of higher education and universities; more and more women were pursuing professional employment.[173]

It was, however, precisely the maintenance of a patriarchal family structure, with marked sexual division of labor and paternal authority over the wife and children, that represented the core of the fundamentalist idea of a pious life pleasing to God's eye. Only the patriarchal family, from this perspective a positive commandment, fulfilled divine law. Because it symbolized the ideal of the established middle class, it could also be used as a means of demarcation from the modernist milieu. Here, again, two factors mentioned previously also had a mobilizing effect: the loss of prestige for a life conduct considered exemplary and pious; and the problem of preserving and transmitting this structure given a changed cultural context.

THE TRANSFORMATION OF POLITICS

A further process contributing to the mobilization of the fundamentalist camp was the transformation of political structures and values. This was manifest above all in the transformation of political parties, in a revision of the institutional division between the state and Protestantism, and in changes in the associated reinterpretation of the "national identity," or, in other words, the civic religion.

Political parties increasingly became mass parties, in which, on the one hand, the nouveau riche and "tycoons" and, on the other, non-Protestant immigrants as well as members of the new middle classes gained in power. The rise of "bossism" and urban machines transformed the character of the big-city parties. On the national level organized "pressure groups" of industrial associations, labor unions, and farmers were winning greater influence over Congress. Catholics and other immigrant groups were gaining political representation. The social reformist era of progressivism as well as the world war led, in addition, to an expansion of state bureaucracies.[174]

This growth in the political power of interest groups, non-Protestant immigrants, and state agencies meant a considerable loss of influence by the traditionalist camp and contributed accordingly to its mobilization. Fundamentalism as a political protest movement thus served to organize traditionalists, and it prompted a formulation of their claim to cultural leadership. In the process, because of fundamentalism's parochial, personalistic-patriarchal ideals, limits were set to its organizational boundaries. Since its values stood in direct opposition to the depersonalized bureaucratic structures then becoming dominant, all that remained was to develop a loose network among local and regional associations. Fundamentalism was capable of gaining influence on the national level solely by way of consensus and voluntary cooperation of various religious leaders and charismatic mass mobilization.

Aside from the loss of political power, the traditionalist milieu also suffered considerable losses in prestige. The nation was forced by growing cultural and religious pluralism to reinterpret the constitutionally prescribed separation of church and state under changed historical conditions. The broad evangelical consensus of the nineteenth century had required nothing beyond an institutional separation. With the growth of non-Protestant and non-Christian groups, the issue was posed anew in intensified form, now requiring the dissolution of the substantive blending of state institutions and traditional Protestantism.

This issue was symbolized by the conflict over curricula in the public schools. It concerned, first, the dissemination of evolutionary theory and, second, the prohibition of Bible readings.[175] With the prohibition of the teaching of Darwinian theory in a number of states, chiefly in the South, and the resulting Scopes trial in Dayton, Tennessee, fundamentalists won only a Pyrrhic victory, one which went a long way toward ruining their image. Parallel to this, however, was the conflict that finds scarcely any mention in the literature but which is, in my judgment, quite important for an understanding of precisely this debate over the spread of evolutionary theory: the conflict over Bible readings in public schools.

Up until the end of the 1920s, Bible readings in public schools were already prohibited in twelve of the forty-eight states.[176] More significant than this number, however, was the fact that in a country as strongly stamped by Protestantism as the United States there could be any debate at all as to whether the Bible was a "sectarian book." For Protestantism as a whole, and especially for the traditionalist camp, this debate represented a great deal more than a loss in prestige. It relativized or disputed the fundamental legitimation of the traditionalist-Protestant idea of the

proper conduct of life as well as the latter's exemplary status and universal validity. And, finally, the conviction held on the level of the civic
religion, that of the identity between the Bible and the Constitution,
between Protestantism and the nation, was subjected to doubt. All of
this represented to the fundamentalist camp a humiliation of epochal
proportions and posed a quite massive threat to its chances of cultural
survival.[177]

THE TRANSFORMATION OF ECONOMIC STRUCTURES
AND VALUES

The mobilization of the fundamentalist camp was, finally, the result of
the transformation of the economic structure. The established middle
class experienced the nationalization and internationalization of the
market and the rise of large industrial plants and interest organizations
as a threat to its monopoly of local and regional economies. The family
(or small) enterprise, managed under patriarchal direction and embody-
ing the ideal of economic independence, was seen as the vehicle of
upward mobility among working people, and it seemed threatened by
large operations with their bureaucratic, depersonalized organizational
structures.[178]

At the same time, labor unions were developing as a counterweight to
big business. But they appeared just as alien to the patriarchal ideal and
seemed to call the right of property into question. The traditionalist
camp thus saw itself being squeezed between, on the one hand, aggressive modern capitalism and, on the other, a yet more dangerous socialism, from which neither bolshevism nor anarchism were distinguished.
In addition, wage struggles began breaking out, transforming the image
of society from an organically integrated model, in which individuals
were "the architects of their own fortunes," into a conflict model, in
which organizations, not individuals, confronted each other with their
opposed interests. In the place of personalistic conflict regulation and
religious integration came class struggle, depersonalization, and legal
rationalization.

How, then, in view of the long-term process of transformation, is the
timing of fundamentalist politicization to be explained? The participation of the United States in the world war was an essential factor. It
enormously accelerated and intensified both the sociomoral dimension of
transformation and the entry of women into the professional world.[179]
But the war also had a strong impact on economic development. It stimu-

lated inflation and created an environment in which bankruptcies were juxtaposed with the enormous war profits of speculators. This transformation affected the traditionalist milieu in various ways. It stirred anxieties over social decline and the potential loss of one's livelihood, undermined hopes of social advance, destroyed ideals, robbed some of power, reduced prestige, undermined one's self-confidence as the representative of a pious way of life pleasing to the eye of God and thus as the legitimate representative of the national "identity," and made it more difficult for the cultural transmission of the milieu. All of these aspects of the transformation, which affected various groups and classes within the fundamentalist milieu differently, were melded by fundamentalist ideology into a synthesis that was both rational and emotional.

One important site of this development was the campaign against the theory of evolution, a controversy that had, accordingly, several dimensions. In the first instance it was a continuation of a conflict over worldviews that had been under way since the closing decades of the nineteenth century.[180] This is admittedly no explanation for why the topic received so much public attention precisely at the beginning of the 1920s, although there is no doubt that other topics discussed in fundamentalist periodicals were equally important.

The Scopes trial of 1925, however, was such a media event that, at least in hindsight, it overshadowed other events. Moreover, the powerful personal presence of William Jennings Bryan pushed the topic to the center of public attention. But Bryan, in particular, saw the conflict between Darwinism and the creation doctrine not as a natural scientific issue but as a political and moral problem. For him the fight against evolutionary theory was a fight against unbelief and immorality, which found expression in Social Darwinism and militarism. The creation doctrine, in contrast, symbolized to him social brotherhood and pacifism.[181]

Bryan, in holding this view, was not indeed typical of the whole fundamentalist protest movement. But through the popularity of his personality, his campaign became a symbolic crusade, one that fundamentalists of all shadings were pleased to join and that identified, whether explicitly or indirectly, all the other areas of contention between fundamentalists and modernists. Darwinism therefore provided a common cause to integrate the various wings of the fundamentalist camp and to symbolize the various experiences of deprivation.

The conflict between evolutionary theory and the creation doctrine was most importantly about whether human beings are a product of an anonymous natural process or the result of a personal act of creation.

This corresponded to the basic conflict between fundamentalists and modernists over the change from personalistic, patriarchal to depersonalized, bureaucratic structures in the churches and society. The theological conflict over Darwinism and creationism was particularly well suited to symbolize the broader social conflict as well.

Shi'ite Fundamentalism
in Iran, 1961–1979

Islam is not static, but as in other religions its dogma and practices have been subject to change in response to transformations in society, politics, and the economy. Islam appears differently in Indonesia than in Morocco, in Sunni countries differently than in Shi'ite, in the countryside differently than in the city. As in Christian countries differences in structural conditions either promote or hinder the rise of fundamentalist movements and influence the form fundamentalism takes.

Among such structural conditions are the autonomy of religion in relation to the state, the degree of religious legitimacy of the political regime, and the positions of both the clergy and believers in relation to the state. The rise of fundamentalist protest movements is particularly favored in Islam by a lack of religious legitimacy on the part of the state. In Sunni Islam, because of the limited significance of the clergy and the dependence of religious institutions on the state, lay persons usually appear as the movement's organizers and spokespersons. Shi'ite Islam, in contrast, is characterized by the institutional autonomy of religion from the state and by a powerful clergy closely connected to their clientele. For that reason the religious tradition is extraordinarily well suited to the formulation of social protest and the clergy to its organization.[1]

In order not to fall prey to the fundamentalist myth, it is wise to give a brief depiction of the development of these particular structural conditions in Iran since the establishment of Shi'ism. It is necessary to begin before the twentieth century, to ensure the least distorted perspective. For fundamentalism as a protest movement is produced by processes of social transformation only when the latter coincide with a tradition of religious and political thought and with a specific institutional structure and operations.

IRANIAN SHI'ISM AND POLITICS

Contemporary fundamentalism in Iran is not the reestablishment of the original Islamic order under Mohammed or Ali, but obviously one of many reactions to twentieth-century social change. In part it stands in the tradition of Shi'ite Islam, as it developed since the Safavids, and in part it breaks with this tradition. In any case, it represents a variation in a long-lasting conflict at the basis of Persian society, which is located in the altercation between political and religious rule, between monarchy and hierocracy.

Shi'ite fundamentalism in Iran is distinguished from comparable movements in Sunni Islam primarily by the prominence of the clergy and by its unique association with charismatic elements, which appear to be completely incompatible with its "basic Puritanical pattern."[2] These particularities are based on an institutional separation of political and hierocratic rule, as it has developed in Iran since the sixteenth century, solidly establishing itself in the nineteenth century, and on a monopolization of sacred knowledge through the hierocracy. Although in Shi'ite Iran as well a caesaropapist model of rule was first established, the clergy succeeded (in contrast, for example, to the Sunni Ottoman Empire) in gaining, on the one hand, a certain degree of autonomy for religious institutions in relation to the state and, on the other, in bringing popular (magical-ritualistic) religious currents under its control.

Although the Safavid and Qajar periods were significant, especially in the formation of the basic structures, the period of rule of the first Pahlavi shah is of primary interest for a specification of the causes of fundamentalist mobilization. Specific factors cited in the literature in the mobilization of fundamentalism in the 1960s and 1970s can be identified in the period 1925–1941, but with different consequences.

The Safavid Period (1501–1722)   In 1501 the Safavids, a militant order of mystics, proclaimed Twelver Shi'ism the religion of the Persian realm.[3] The Shi'ism of the Safavid dynasty was wholly characterized by charismatic-ecstatic features, expressed, for example, in the belief in the divine heritage of the leader, in ecstatic and egalitarian traits in the warrior orders, and anarchic elements among its tribal constituency. To consolidate their rule, however, the Safavids quickly dispensed with these features and established a caesaropapist system with a consistent religious policy. With great severity, they persecuted, on the one hand, the Sunnis, to prevent them from becoming adherents of the Ottoman Empire, and, on the other, the Sufi orders, whose chiliastic and anarchic features they feared.

To stabilize their rule, the Safavids sought support from the existing patrimonial administration, whose legal and religious offices were filled by notables who only over the course of time gave up their Sunni confession in favor of Shi'ism. These notables consisted of large property holders with strong local ties and were appointed by virtue of their descent from the Prophet.[4] Religious administration in Safavid Iran was therefore scarcely distinguished from Sunni practice as found in the Ottoman Empire. There was less a routinization of charismatic rule than a consciously introduced transformation into a caesaropapist system. In the latter there is no immediate impetus for an institutional separation of politics and religion and thus none for the development of a relatively autonomous and autocephalic hierocracy.

The seeds of such a development, however, were sown early on. For the Safavids brought Shi'ite theologians in from the Arabian regions of their empire to disseminate "orthodox" Shi'ism and to counterbalance the religious notables, who, though extensively converted, were still strongly stamped by their Sunni origins. At first, however, these imported theologians had no ties to the local population and were totally dependent financially on the rulers. Nevertheless, they succeeded over time in establishing themselves, ultimately gaining dominance over the religious notables. This development was completed in several stages and was obviously not as linear as might appear in this simplified depiction.

An important precondition to the establishment of the Shi'ite clergy was its assimilation into the local population. The Arabian scholars were increasingly replaced by their Persian students, who were frequently descendants of the religious notables, a circumstance that no doubt eased the acceptance of change. With this infiltration of the patrimonial religious administration, a tendential bifurcation between notables and Shi'ite scholars resulted. The notables continued to control the financial administration of religious institutions and justice, but the scholars increasingly took over such functions more narrowly described as religious, like the office of the imam, or prayer leader of the mosques, and of the *shaykh al-Islam,* the religious dignitary of a city. Beyond this, individual clerics were able to win great prestige outside of state functions as teachers and models of the pious life. Thus over time a consciousness of the difference between the political and religious spheres developed, which was intensified by the propagation of a particularly world-fleeing, nonpolitical variant of Shi'ism.

The competitive relationship between the religious notables and the clerics was reflected in opposing concepts of theology and the politics of religion, usually described as the controversy between traditionalists (Akhbaris) and legal scholars (Usulis). The Akhbaris emphasized the tradition of the imams and hermeneutics as an interpretive method in legal analysis. The Usulis, in contrast, represented a rational interpretation of the law and legalistic casuistry. They emphasized juridical knowledge, derived from the superiority of scholars, and demanded that believers adopt the legal opinion of the *mujtahids,* or legal scholars. The Akhbaris, for their part, held that the tradition of the imams was accessible to anyone capable of reading Arabic and familiar with a certain terminology.

Both positions imply power interests. The Usulis represented the interests of the scholarly class, whose chances to wield power rested on the monopolization of sacred knowledge. The Akhbaris, in contrast, formulated the interests of an educated class of notables whose legitimacy derived from their hereditary charisma, and whose chances for power rested on the preservation and fortification of the popular religious veneration of the imams and their descendents. Both positions, therefore, were equally elitist, if in different ways. Akhbari traditionalism divided believers into religious virtuosi, who achieved inner-worldly redemption through gnosis, and the rank and file, who were to exercise piety in the veneration of the imams and the ritualistic observance of their commandments. Usuli rationalism distinguished between scholars and uneducated people but bound the mass of believers to legal scholars in the form of a clientele.[5]

The two positions coexisted during many centuries, being able to usurp each other only temporarily. The victory of the Usulis during the reign of the Qajars was prepared to a great extent by their incorporation of critical elements of magical-ritualistic popular piety and thus their unification of the functions of scholar and saint in the clergy.[6] Texts were produced in which heaven and hell appeared in elaborate detail. Magical practices and prophecies were taken over by the clergy. Miracles, meetings with the Hidden Imam, and other supernatural abilities were attributed to the great theologians. All of this strengthened the ritualistic-magical aspect over the rational and created the precondition for the actual hierocratic monopolization of sacred knowledge. Twelver Shi'ism, moreover, was increasingly elaborated as a national religion. Anti-Sunni elements were emphasized, and universalist Islamic practices, like the pilgrimage to Mecca, were supplanted by those of national Shi'ism like the pilgrimage to the graves of the imams or their descendants.[7]

The hierocratic tendency, in addition, led to increasing emphasis on eschatological elements and the afterlife. Thus the chiliastic anticipation of the return of the Mahdi, the Twelfth Imam, was politically defused into a patient waiting for the Imam.[8] Imams increasingly took over the role of other-worldly mediators between God and people. At the same time, the theodicy of suffering, according to the paradigm of the martyr-dom of Imam Hussein at Kerbala, became a major focus of popular religious imagery and practices. The solution of the theodicy problem was thus transformed from a this-worldly "messianic eschatology" into the promise of a just reward in the other world.[9] This religious position contained two important implications. First, it prompted a dramatiza-tion of the separation between the "world" and the "beyond," of this-worldly and other-worldly interests and thus of politics and religion, that is, of the kingdom of the shah, on the one hand, and the kingdom of God, the Hidden Imam, and the hierocracy, on the other. Second, it implied a radical devaluation of the "world" and thus of politics, in the process promoting political apathy among the masses. At the same time, however, it occasioned the rise of a class of religious scholars, who, because of their support by the people, represented a potential counter-balance to the political rulers. By calling for the preservation of sacred interests, they could also mobilize their followers politically.

A permanent tension existed between this hierocratic view of politics and religion and the basis of the Safavids' legitimation, as they contin-ued to be represented by the religious notables. Although, as has already been pointed out, the messianic-charismatic rule of the early Safavids was quickly transformed into a caesaropapist one, its hereditary cha-risma remained the justification for its rule. The Safavid king continued to be a holy figure, the "shadow of God on earth," and failure to obey him meant disgrace in this world and hellfire in the next.[10]

The Qajar Period to the Tobacco Protest (1785–1890)   With the end of Safavid rule and a long interregnum in which Sufi currents experi-enced a renaissance, the tension between caesaropapist and hierocratic legitimation under the Qajars (1785–1890) was resolved through a division of power between the monarchy and the hierocracy.[11] An important reason for this development lay in the circumstance that the Qajars represented a tribal dynasty that could not trace its descent to the imams. Thus it had no hereditary charisma, like the Safavids (who had derived, among other things, their infallibility from that source), and required the clergy for its legitimation. In addition, the legal scholars succeeded in establishing a monopoly on religious rule over the population and in attaining autonomy and autocephaly. The theological elaboration and legitimation of this development were accomplished by the Usuli movement.

Prior to the beginning of Qajar rule the Shi'ite clergy found itself in the worst situation conceivable. During the interregnum (1722–1785) between the dynasties of the Safavids and the Qajars, in particular under the rule of Nadir Shah (1736–1747), it lost all of its income from religious offices and had its endowments confiscated. Thus it had to finance itself independently of the state, a circumstance that led to the closure of many *madrasas* (Muslim seminaries) and the deterioration of many mosques. And, at the cost of the scholars, the Akhbari position and mystical movements once again gained considerable ground.[12]

The shift in favor of the Usulis came with the rise of the Qajar dynasty, in particular under the second Qajar shah, Fath Ali (1797–1834). He strengthened the position of the legal scholars and provided them support while they attained autonomy and monopolized the means of salvation. This development had both economic and political-theological aspects. The financial foundation of hierocratic autonomy consisted, first, in the reinstatement and reinvigoration of endowments, and beyond that, in a monopoly on certain aspects of the administration of justice that were not controlled by the state and which represented a further source of income. Above all, however, the clergy was successful in securing institutionally its claim on levying religious taxes (*khums*). Half of these funds was to be devoted to social concerns. The other half was designated the "share of the Imam" (*sahm-i imam*) and was collected by the highest-ranking scholars, the *mujtahids*, in their capacity as representatives of the imam. This simultaneously entailed a further centralization of religious finances.[13]

In nineteenth-century Shi'ite political theory the shah was divested of his divine attributes. His office, however, was not delegitimized but only desacralized. Maintaining the worldly order and religious leadership, originally assumed by the imams, was now placed on two sets of shoulders, those of the king and those of the clergy. Both were taken to be representatives of the Hidden Imam, but in different functions. The shah represented the political function of the Hidden Imam; the clergy, the religious. The shah implemented the religiously commanded order and saw to the administration of justice; the scholars tended religious knowledge and thus exercised spiritual leadership.

This development and its theological justification demonstrated that the Usuli movement had succeeded in implementing a new interpretation of the *mujtahids* and their religious claim to rule. On the one hand it established a separation between political and hierocratic rule, which strengthened its power over the mass of the population and thereby limited the range of the patrimonial bureaucracy's arbitrariness. The Shi'ite hierocracy thus increasingly became the protector and advocate of the people, at least to the extent that role corresponded to its own interests.[14]

On the other hand, as the representative of the Hidden Imam on earth, it possessed a religious legitimation superior to that of the monarch in cases of conflict. It was incumbent upon the clergy to judge whether or not specific laws or political actions were compatible with the letter and the spirit of Koranic principles. Nevertheless, the rule of the shah was by no means illegitimate in principle, as many authors maintain. First of all, he was regarded as the "shadow of God on earth," and insofar as he stayed within the compass of Islamic ideas of justice, he was owed unconditional obedience.[15] In normal times the "political" role of the clergy consisted solely of praying for the shah. In cases of conflict, however, this theory gave the *mujtahids* considerable power, as the events of the tobacco protest and the Constitutional Revolution should demonstrate.

The power of the clergy was, nevertheless, relatively limited at the outset. Financial security did, indeed, mean a gain in autonomy, but, because of its weak institutionalization and meager organizational structure, the clergy did not possess any real autocephaly until probably the last third of the nineteenth century. For the internal structure of the clergy until that time was characterized only by the coexistence of the *mujtahids,* each with his own court, but not by procedures for mediating interests and resolving conflict. Thus sometimes mutual excommunications occurred, and a person seeking counsel who was not satisfied with the decision of one scholar could seek out another if necessary.

This situation changed only with the enormous increase in the number of *mujtahids,* which led to internal differentiation and the establishment of a hierarchy among them. Beginning in the late 1800s the scholarly estate underwent a process of differentiation of prestige and, accordingly, of authority and power, through which a single *mujtahid* frequently assumed the highest position as *marja' al-taqlid*.[16]

Alongside its financial autonomy as representative of the Imam, the practical realization and intensification of the duty of emulation (*taqlid*) contributed in particular to the hierocracy's increase in power. Building on the time-honored thesis that only high legal scholars, because of their knowledge, were competent to decide religious questions authoritatively, every believer was required to choose a *mujtahid,* whose interpretation of the law was unconditionally binding. With the decline of the Akhbaris and the enormous multiplication of *mujtahids,* this doctrine now acquired a wholly different practical significance.[17]

The power of the Shi'ite hierocracy, however, was and remained limited because it lacked a mechanism of enforcement. For the execution of the sentences of the religious court and for the struggle against "heretics," the clergy was thus ultimately dependent on the state, insofar as it did not have its own private armies or vigilantes (*lutis*).[18] Nevertheless, in the case of conflicts of interests with the state, through the *taqlid* on the one hand and through the simultaneous expansion of the communications media on the other, they did have thoroughly effective means of influence: the mass mobilization of their followers. This weapon of the hierocracy was particularly effective because the military power of the Qajar dynasty, like the entire apparatus of rule as such, was badly organized, limping far behind the standard of, for example, the Ottoman Empire.

The autonomous political role of the clergy thus depended upon the degree of its success in mobilizing followers, especially in the bazaar. It therefore had to pay particular attention to the desires and grievances represented there, but was then able to count on the bazaar's support. The reciprocity of interests between the clergy and the bazaar was considerable. They were bound to each other through common religious ideas, norms, rituals, traditional ways of life, and, not the least, by familial ties.[19]

The autonomous clergy supplied the bazaar with an intellectual stratum capable of formulating and religiously legitimating its interests before the state. For the clergy the bazaar provided a mass basis, which made considerable financial and political contributions to the preservation of its autonomy and the Shi'ite national culture it represented.[20] This alliance between a religious class and the bazaar was first tested, in the sense of modern mass politics, in the tobacco protest of 1891–1892 and then in the Constitutional Revolution of 1906–1909.

The Tobacco Protest and Constitutional Revolution   The first decades of Qajar rule led to the strengthening of the hierocracy described
above, but in the second half of the nineteenth century Western influences and efforts toward modernization made themselves felt at court.
Processes of sociomoral transformation as well as Western economic
interests, which found an eager response from a corrupt and notoriously
bankrupt court, were countered early on by a critique from the clergy
and its clientele, primarily in the bazaar. The conflict between worldly
and ecclesiastical power was considerably intensified, achieving dramatic expression in the tobacco protest of 1891–1892, which the clergy
brought to a successful end in alliance with the bazaar.[21]

Discontent grew with the increasing influence of alien powers because of the weakness and corruption of the court, erupting a second
time, in the Constitutional Revolution of 1906–1909. Although the
disturbance led to an alliance between enlightened political groups and
the religious camp, the "progressive" inclinations of the vast majority of
clergy and the bazaaris should not be overestimated. Many religious
adherents of the revolution had in mind only the immediate goal of
limiting the power of an incompetent, corrupt monarch and securing
their own economic and cultural-religious interests.[22]

As the revolution proceeded, a split developed between the proponents and opponents of a constitution and parliamentarianism. This
was, on the one hand, an expression of the divergence in the interests
and values of the respective followers.[23] On the other, however, it was
based on differing assessments of the results of constitutionalism. The
new Iranian constitution, which remained officially in force until 1979,
represented a compromise between Western-oriented liberal forces and
extensive segments of the religious camp. The model was the Belgian
constitution, in which a parliament limited the power of the king. Because of the protest of the conservative clergy, the constitution of December 30, 1906, was amended on October 7, 1907, with the changes
considerably strengthening the position of Islam and the hierocracy.
Both proponents and opponents of the constitution among the clergy
were more likely to have been shaped by traditional Islamic than by
Western liberal ideas. As revolutionary developments occurred, more
and more of the clergy withdrew support from secular forces, focusing
increasingly on the interests of their own estate.[24]

Western modernist elements in the constitutional struggle found their
most pronounced opponent in the conservative critic, the *mujtahid*
Shaykh Fazl Nuri. He took the view that the constitution was incompati-

ble with Islam for a number of reasons, no doubt referring to the version of Shi'ism established in the nineteenth century, which had institutionalized a strong position for the clergy. Nuri, in my opinion, was one of the few who recognized that the principles of the constitution critically undermined the hierocracy's claim to power.[25] The parliamentary system, equipped with legislative competence and majority rule, contradicted, according to Nuri, the status of the scholars as proxies for the Hidden Imam. In Shi'ite doctrine, decisions are to be made not by majorities but according to religious-legal educational qualifications. Equality before the law was counter to Islam, which provided for different rights for Muslims than for Parsees, Christians, and Jews; men and women also had different rights as did scholars and the uneducated.

Although an amendment to the constitution, included not least because of pressure from Nuri, provided for a panel of religious scholars to supervise the correspondence between laws concluded by parliament and the Shari'a, or religious law, Nuri was, in my opinion, correct in claiming that even the idea of a secular constitutional state was incompatible with Shi'ite political theory as established by the clergy in the nineteenth century. Despite its stipulation of a strong role for the clergy in the legal system, the constitution of 1906, with its amendments of 1907, signified a restriction of the clergy's previous role in Shi'ite political theory and practice.[26]

Above all, the role of the clergy as the protector of the Islamic character of legislation was being guaranteed by a constitution that simultaneously founded institutions and laws not subject to this clerical supervision. Henceforth, the function of religious legal scholars was no longer based on their proxy representation of the Hidden Imam but on a new political doctrine in which their rights were stipulated. The clergy thus became one institution among others within the political system and lost their traditional status of equality within, if not superiority over, a system founded on a distribution of the functions of the Hidden Imam both to the shah and legal scholars.

This process of integrating the clergy into the political system signified in a certain sense a reversal of the previous legitimation of rule, a process which became evident primarily in the procedure to elect the council of clergy. From a list of twenty candidates nominated by the legal scholars, parliament was supposed to select, either by acclamation or election, at least five, who, as a rule, were supposed to be *mujtahids* but did not have to be. Such a procedure flagrantly contradicted the elitist foundations of the hierocracy's legitimacy and undermined its autonomy. Legal scholars were no longer to be able to establish their own internal hierarchy through the informal recognition of leading *mujtahids* or a *marja' al-taqlid* based on extensive religious criteria; rather, religious or, as the case may be, fully uneducated parliamentarians were to select the persons who, in Shi'ite doctrine, were the representatives of the Hidden Imam on earth.[27]

However one might assess the position of the clergy in the new constitution, the clergy as a whole were deeply split, at least temporarily, by the Constitutional Revolution and thus weakened. The practical relation between the state and hierocracy after the period of disintegration (1909–1921) was determined above all by the formation of a modern bureaucratic nation-state by Reza Pahlavi, who possessed few scruples in regard to the functions and rights of the Shi'ite scholars as stipulated in the constitution. Over the long run the latter were unable to prevent the erosion of their power and the formation of a modern bureaucratic state.[28]

State and Religion under Reza Pahlavi (1921–1941)   Reza Khan's rise to power (1921–1925) was widely supported by the clergy and the bazaar. World War I, in particular, with the lengthy occupation of Iran by the English and Russians, with its disintegrating effect on state institutions, its revitalization of the power of tribal leaders and large landholders, and its political chaos and economic misery, had sharpened the sense of the necessity for a strong, independent state. Although Reza Khan was understood to be a supporter of republicanism, he managed, through skillful maneuvers, first to block his rivals' ascension to the prime ministership and ultimately to force the abdication of the last Qajar shah. He declared himself willing to relinquish his call for a republican constitution, which the religious camp, given the developments in Turkey under Mustafa Kemal, regarded as profoundly "anti-Islamic" and as the first step toward bolshevism.[29]

In Reza Khan the clergy and the bazaar saw a guarantee of settled domestic relations as well as an independent and Islamic Iran. In contrast to the weak Qajar shah he had strongly supported the Shi'ite clergy when they were having difficulties with the British occupation authorities and had contributed to reestablishing Qum as the center of Shi'ite scholarship. His support in the army in particular predestined him to introduce order into the chaos of domestic relations. At the same time, he skillfully courted the clergy, who lent his rule legitimacy, first as prime minister and then as shah, and branded his opponents as "polytheists."[30]

Reza also courted the clergy, whose cooperation he mentioned explicitly in his oath of office, at the beginning of his rule as shah. And among his first acts in office were symbolic bows in the direction of religious moralism, such as a prohibition on the sale of alcoholic beverages and the closing of all gambling halls. Yet these were essentially no more than strategies to secure his power. As soon as Reza felt himself securely in the saddle, it became apparent that his basic attitude was profoundly anticlerical.[31]

The conflict between Reza Shah and the clergy first emerged into the open in 1927. The occasion was a law that made the exemption of theology students and clergy from military service dependent on various conditions, including, in addition to proof of successful studies and full-time devotion to religious work, the passing of a state examination. The clergy undertook a protracted protest and the bazaars in Isfahan and Shiraz were closed in protest to this attack on religious autonomy. The government responded with threats to use force to open the bazaars and even to bombard Qum.[32] The conflict was resolved peacefully in the end, but it signified the last compromise Reza Shah was willing to make with the clergy.

From 1927 until the Allies forced him to abdicate in 1941, Reza pursued a strict course of antagonism toward the Shi'ite clergy. To this end he adopted the strategy of isolating the clergy from their clientele, of subjecting them to public ridicule, and of intimidating them through the application or threat of force. His success in this enabled him to put his policy of modernization into effect with no visible opposition.

The most important features of the shah's modernization policy were the rationalization and secularization of law, the centralization and bureaucratization of authority, state control over large parts of the modern economic sector, and the secularization of culture and the educational system. Thus, following a French model but including certain parts of Shari'a law, a new commercial code was introduced in 1925, a criminal code in 1926, and a civil code in 1928. The state expanded its sphere by establishing a monopoly on the legitimate use of force to the detriment of tribal leaders, taking over direction of economic policy, concluding trade and tariff agreements with Western nations, and transferring the traditional functions of the clergy in legal, economic, and educational affairs to civil servants.

Reza Shah thus considerably expanded the activities of the state and established a strict institutional separation between public and religious domains. And the state fought against the symbols of traditionalism on the cultural plane as well. Clothing laws were promulgated, for example, which prescribed a Western style of dress and headwear for men (1929) and prohibited women from wearing the veil (1936). Moreover, traditional religious festivals and gatherings were forbidden, especially the Ashura processions, which always offered the opportunity for political events to be interpreted religiously and gave the clergy and the bazaar a chance to express their political protest.[33]

This modernization policy signified far-reaching losses for the clergy, in functions, sources of income, power, and prestige; the bureaucracy, army, commercial middle classes, and large landholders derived, in part, great advantages from it.[34] In addition to the clergy, small merchants, artisans, and peasants were disadvantaged; their rights were abused to the benefit of large landholders, above all in land registration pursuant to civil law reforms.

The reformist policy of Reza Shah revolutionized the Iranian social structure. New middle strata arose, formed, for example, by state employees in the military, administration, and educational systems, by doctors, lawyers, and other professionals, and by people in technical professions and journalism. Tehran became a metropolis, expanding at the expense of provincial cities and the countryside. This was where economic growth took place, where the rural population was drawn in search of employment and inhabitants of small towns sought improved conditions and upward mobility, and where the sociocultural polarization of Iran began.[35]

Despite Reza Pahlavi's relentless policy of modernization, no fundamentalist protest movement took shape under his rule. The majority of the clergy were inclined to be passive. The reasons for this political reserve illuminate the later politicization of the clergy and bazaar. One frequent explanation is that the thoroughly brutal intimidation of the clergy left them no option but quietism: "Under these circumstances, survival and concern for the preservation of Islam became the major preoccupation of the clerical community."[36] Yet this explanation is not persuasive on its own; the political repression undertaken at the beginning of the 1960s was scarcely less perfect or brutal. Nor does the thesis that the shah's modernization policy caught the clergy unprepared and thus that the element of surprise was responsible for the absence of protest offer adequate explanation.[37] For the alliance between the clergy and the bazaar was still strong, both in its support for Reza Khan (1921–1925) and in its protest over the induction of theology students into the military.

In addition, a protest action was organized by the clergy in the summer of 1935 in Mashad. It was prompted by a law prohibiting the wearing of the veil and authorizing police to forcibly remove it from women. There were also reports of protests in other cities, so what was lacking, obviously, was support everywhere by the most important dignitaries.[38] "Sporadic protest and uprisings in Isfahan, Mashad, and Qum did not attract the support of the leading ayatollahs and hence did not turn into popular movements."[39]

Thus there is much to be said for the assumption that the primary reason no mass movement emerged was because the upper clergy did not consider such an escalation desirable. This could have been motivated by opinions that protest was pointless, there was no alternative to Reza Pahlavi, even more radical reformers would come to power after him, and he alone was able to secure national independence from foreign intervention.

Perhaps, however, no mass protests occurred because interests in the religious camp were not homogeneous. Even though the entire religious class had suffered a loss in prestige, segments of the clergy nevertheless profited to the extent that they were large landholders or merchants. The bazaar, too, was divided among small merchants and artisans, on the one hand, and large merchants, on the other. Large landholders, as supporters of the regime, might well have encouraged the ayatollahs allied with them to adopt a quietistic position. And, finally, the regime skillfully coopted the rising generation of clergy, a key reservoir of fundamentalist activists in the 1970s, by offering them employment opportunities in the state bureaucracy and thus chances for upward mobility: "Many students of religious schools were recruited by the government, and after proper training, found employment in government offices."[40]

From World War II to the "White Revolution" (1941–1961)   The end of the rule of Reza Pahlavi offered the clergy a chance to regenerate itself and recapture lost influence. Their initial demands included repealing the prohibition on passion plays and religious readings, the lifting of restrictions imposed on Ramadan and pilgrimages to Mecca, and the reestablishment of traditional public morality. Prescriptions on Western dress and the prohibition of the veil, in particular, were no longer respected.

At the same time, the Allied occupation of Iran in the Second World War intensified Western influence, threatening traditional Islamic culture. In addition, the war had created economic and social problems. On the one hand, increased demand as a result of the presence of Allied troops stimulated an economic boom; on the other, it led to supply bottlenecks, inflation, and hoarding. In December 1942 bread riots broke out in Tehran. Opposition formed in the press, unions, and political parties, above all in the communist Tudeh party.[41]

Shah Mohammed Reza Pahlavi, whose position had been weakened by British and Soviet policy, patronized both the tribal leaders in the south and the opposition in the north. He brought American advisers into the country, who were active primarily in economic and military affairs, thus marking the beginning of American influence in Iran.

The end of the war brought economic crisis, especially for the bazaar. Demand declined, with imports of foreign goods increasing at the same time. Other social groups, like the industrial work force and white-collar employees, were growing in number and influence. Dependence on foreign countries, in particular the United States, became increasingly palpable. Urbanization and the accompanying processes of social structural transformation were quickly accelerated. At this time a small fundamentalist group, the Fedayan-i Islam, formed, garnering attention through terrorist attacks.[42] Influenced by Ayatollah Borujerdi, however, who had meanwhile risen to become the highest-ranking Shi'ite scholar, the clergy generally refrained from political involvement.

The wide-ranging Western influence on Iran at the beginning of the 1950s centered on and was symbolized by the question of nationalizing the petroleum industry. The National Front, a coalition of religious and secularly oriented parties under the leadership of Mosaddeq, won the elections on this issue. The resulting boycott of Iranian oil organized by the Americans and British worsened the economic situation of the country. Mosaddeq was toppled in 1953 by a joint action of the CIA and the army, but meanwhile the religious camp had also turned away from him. As popular as Mosaddeq's policy of national independence may have been, his adherents proved themselves just as divided over issues of domestic reform, such as the introduction of female suffrage or his decree on agrarian reform.[43] The splitting of right and left, as well as of the religious and secular wings of the National Front, thus led ultimately to its failure.

The religious camp was split among various factions, of which three were of particular significance: the higher clergy, the terrorist Fedayan-i Islam, and the lower clergy allied with the bazaar and the lower strata. The conservative higher clergy pronounced a prohibition on political activity for all clergy at the Qum Conference in 1949, threatening ex-communication for violations.[44] They feared the influence of the left and, in particular, rejected their social reformist tendencies. The fundamentalist Fedayan-i Islam argued for a theocracy, criticized the political abstinence of the higher clergy, and carried out assassinations not only against opponents of the policy of national independence but also against nonreligious and leftist members of the National Front. The lower clergy and the bazaar, led by Ayatollah Kashani, who had proved his mettle in the struggle against the British, suffered from the economic crisis of the postwar period and withdrew support from Mosaddeq, actively contributing to his fall.[45]

The relationship between the clergy and politics was stamped, until his death in 1961, by the conservative quietism of Ayatollah Borujerdi. His position in no way implied a renunciation of the exercise of political influence but only a reserved strategy, confined as a rule to the communication channels within the elite. The regime cooperated with the clergy in several areas, such as the intensification of Islamic instruction in public schools and in opposing the Baha'is, who were considered heterodox. Borujerdi's great achievement in the 1950s was above all the securing and fortifying of religious autonomy and the rationalization and modernization of religious institutions. Under his leadership, the number of mosques, *madrasas,* and theology students once again increased.

Disagreements between the clergy and government began in 1959, when the question of the legal status of women, especially their right to vote, was discussed in parliament and the government considered holding a "Women's Day" parade in Tehran. The conflict grew sharper at the end of 1959, when the first draft of a law on land reform was circulated. The disagreement thus was sparked by the same questions that had already led to alienation between the National Front and its religious adherents.[46] As yet, however, the protest remained confined to the usual legal reports (*fatwas*) or letters of grievance from high-ranking clerics. When Borujerdi, for example, declared the land reform law of May 16, 1960, to be incompatible with Shari'a law, it was withdrawn by the government.[47] As long as Borujerdi lived, there was no mass mobilization and thus no escalation of the conflict. This changed, however, shortly after his death in March 1961.

From the "White" to the "Islamic" Revolution (1961–1979)   I now turn to the period in which modern Shi'ite fundamentalism took shape under the leadership of Ayatollah Khomeini. This period began with a "revolution from above," the "White Revolution of the Shah and the People," and ended with a revolution from below, carried by a broad alliance of groups and classes, that resulted in the victory of the fundamentalist wing of the clergy and its extensive assumption of political rule.

The traditionalist camp was shaken out of its quietism and became politically mobilized by the proclamation of the "White Revolution" by the shah. This modernization program began in 1962 with six projects, which were later supplemented by others: land reform, the nationalization of the forests, the privatization of state enterprises, profit sharing for the work force, electoral reform, and the organization of a literacy corps.[48]

Land reform and the introduction of women's suffrage in particular were met by significant portions of the clergy with decided opposition, which was intensified even further by the provocative manner in which the shah and the government demonstrated their power in an attempt to intimidate their religious opposition.[49] First, pursuant to the implementation of reforms, parliament was dissolved (from May 1961 to October 1963) and a referendum on the six points held on January 26, 1963. Moreover, three days before the referendum took place, the shah traveled to Qum and there made a great show of distributing land in a peasants' assembly. In a speech given in a courtyard adjacent to a holy shrine, he characterized the clergy as "parasites" and "black reactionaries" and compared them to unclean animals: "We are done with social and political parasites; I abhor the 'black reaction' even more than the 'red destruction.' "[50]

Not the least target of this attack was Ayatollah Khomeini. The latter had already given fiery speeches as early as 1962, in opposition to the planned extension of suffrage to women on a local level, and had been arrested for them. In January 1963 he was taken into custody once again, for allegedly characterizing the planned land reform as incompatible with Islam.[51] In March 1963 the regime brutally put down student protests in Qum. With that, Khomeini began his rise to national prominence as the leader of opposition against the policies of the shah.

The extent to which land reform helped mobilize the clergy, and, in particular, Khomeini, against the "White Revolution" is disputed in the literature. On the one hand, there is much to indicate that a major segment of the clergy was not opposed in principle to land reform, which would benefit the class of small peasants from which they themselves had come. On the other hand, however, they must have felt themselves threatened as an estate, because the reform did not exempt the clergy's own endowments of land, on which the material existence of many clerics depended. Nevertheless, the majority of the clergy was united in its protest against the provocative manner in which land reform had been put through.

Although the significance of the land reform for the mobilization of the clergy is disputed, that of the woman's question is not in doubt.[52] In June 1961, on Ashura (a holy day of atonement), Khomeini delivered a public address in Qum in which he sharply attacked the shah in personal terms. After his arrest on the following day, there were mass protests before the bazaar in Tehran, which also spread to other cities, such as Mashad, Qum, Isfahan, and Shiraz. Unrest continued for several days and was bloodily repressed. This was the first nationwide mobilization of the religious camp to have taken place for a long time, and the last until the end of the 1970s. For the next fifteen years, resistance was pushed underground or played itself out in smaller groups.[53] In 1964 Khomeini was forced into exile, first going to Turkey and from there to Iraq. The occasion was his strong critique of laws guaranteeing diplomatic immunity to all American advisers, as well as Iran's enormous indebtedness to the United States for arms purchases.

In the beginning of the 1960s lively discussions inside the religious camp led to new definitions of the political role of Islam, which I will treat in more detail in the next section. Relations between the clergy and the government worsened in subsequent years, however, for many reasons, touching ultimately on the purported certainty of the regime, which no longer felt obliged to extend special consideration toward the traditionalist-religious camp. The occasions and symbols of this progressive alienation were contained above all in the new "Family Protection Law" of 1967, which considerably improved the position of women and rendered the old prescriptions of Shari'a law invalid. The Islamic identity of the Iranian monarchy was also annulled by way of the 2,500th anniversary of the monarchy in Persepolis (1971), and the Islamic calendar was replaced by an Achaemenidian one in 1976.

Because of severe state repression and the continuing reorientation of the religious camp, but quite likely as well because of economic prosperity that also benefited the bazaar, the opposition hardly appeared in public but organized itself in small discussion circles and, in part, in militant movements. Thus there are estimated to have been approximately 12,300 religious associations in Tehran alone by 1974, and the number of persons making a pilgrimage to Mashad, the most significant holy shrine in Iran, rose from 332,000 in 1966–1967 to 3.5 million in 1976–1977.[54] In this period the conservative quietistic camp clearly lost influence to both the fundamentalist and the social revolutionary camps. As long as the economic boom of the 1960s and early 1970s continued, no confrontations resulted. This changed with unsuspected speed, however, with the beginning of the economic crisis and the provocative responses of the government, which affected small merchants and thus the bazaar in particular.

From 1977 to 1979 the latent confrontation between the regime and the clergy became more intense. As late as 1975, the rather moderate, conservative Ayatollah Shari'atmadari, the leading cleric in Qum, kept silent as the shah's troops beat down a demonstration of theology students in Qum, arresting four hundred because their slogans praised Khomeini and cursed the shah.[55] Yet, following the clashes of November 1977 to January 1978, he broke his silence and declared the regime un-Islamic. What was it that moved him to give up his otherwise quietistic attitude?

On November 3, 1977, a son of Khomeini died in mysterious circumstances; many immediately suspected the shah's secret police of having killed him. Mourning services took place throughout Iran. In the Tehran bazaar there were clashes between mourners and police.[56] This took place shortly before the beginning of the month of Muharram, in which the most important Shi'ite holidays dedicated to the martyrdom of Hussein occur. To inhibit further demonstrations, the government prohibited observance of the traditional memorial on the fortieth day after the death of Khomeini's son.

The conflict finally came to a dramatic head in January 1978, when the final Muharram holidays coincided with the regime's newly introduced holidays, including the anniversary of women's emancipation (January 7) and that of land reform (January 9). At the same time, in a newspaper closely associated with the government, an article appeared sharply attacking the clergy in general and Khomeini in particular. The clergy was charged with being composed of "black reactionaries" working together with the communists to undermine the "White Revolution." Of Khomeini it was claimed, among other things, that he was in reality Indian, had worked as a British spy, led a dissolute life, and written erotic Sufi poetry.[57]

In Qum a wave of protests erupted in response. The seminary and bazaar were closed, and about four thousand theology students demonstrated against the regime, demanding the return of Khomeini and the application of the constitution of 1906–1909. There was no mention of an "Islamic republic."[58] Police shot into the crowd, killing ten in the official version, seventy according to the opposition, and wounding many more. These deaths and the memorial services following them resulted in more deaths, a *perpetuum mobile* leading ultimately to the Islamic revolution.

The protest was not at all limited to religious forces, but over the course of the 1970s the religious camp clearly took over the lead of the opposition. The masses followed it. Within the religious camp were three major factions, which, to be sure, worked together in the protests: first, the conservatives, led by Shari'atmadari, who desired the retention and enforcement of the constitution, which also recognized the monarchy as the established form of government; second, the social revolutionaries driven primarily by the theories of Ali Shariati, a lay preacher and graduate of the Sorbonne, who wanted a Islamic-modernist reformation of society but who were decidedly anticlerical in their attitudes; and, finally, the fundamentalists under the leadership of Khomeini, who sought a consistent "return" to the principles of an Islamic way of life under the leadership of the clergy. The rank and file of the protest movement did not always recognize these divergent goals, in particular as those involved, in view of their common opposition to the regime, were not especially concerned to express them.[59]

The history of subsequent developments in Iran is known and is not pursued further here.[60] The object of this investigation is an interpretation not of the Iranian revolution but of fundamentalism as an urban protest movement. I therefore turn to the various religious positions that took shape in Iran between 1961 and 1979 in reaction to rapid social change.

PROFILE AND BOUNDARIES OF THE FUNDAMENTALIST MOVEMENT

William McLoughlin, in his analysis of the movements of awakening in the United States, argued that such phenomena are universal. They are popular movements by means of which an adaptation to changed social conditions is accomplished: "Revivals and awakenings occur in all cultures. They are essentially folk movements, the means by which a people or a nation reshapes its identity, transforms its patterns of thought and action, and sustains a healthy relationship with environmental and social change."[61]

An application of this generalization to Iran of the 1960s and 1970s proves problematic in several respects. Under Iranian political conditions neither the structural functionalist theory of adaptation nor the rosy belief in progress is very persuasive. It is true that in Shi'ite Iran one can find a number of approaches to a reinterpretation of the religious tradition, with which various social groups attempted to respond to processes of social, cultural, and political transformation. Yet Shi'ite fundamentalism was not just a "folk movement." It was also a gathering of religious intellectuals—clerics and educated lay persons—who were seeking an answer to the problems of the time, while the faithful masses remained substantially traditionalist.

And McLoughlin's thesis that essentially two parties confront each other within such revitalization movements—the conservative to reactionary "old lights" and the innovative, social reformist "new lights"—fails to apply precisely to the Iranian case. For here the "old lights" and "new lights" allied with each other against the "Aryan sun."

The "White Revolution" and the measures adopted toward its implementation provided the point of departure for the various approaches to a reinterpretation of the religious tradition. In opposition to the "Western" modernization model of the shah and, especially, as a reaction to the traumatic experience of the massacre of thousands of demonstrators in June 1963, a younger generation of clerics and students, many of whom came from a traditionalist milieu, was increasingly radicalized.[62] In distinction to the opposition of the 1950s they attempted to reinterpret and politicize the religious tradition. In a common front against the quietistic understanding of Islam by the leading legal scholars, two positions in particular took shape: a social revolutionary and a fundamentalist reinterpretation of Islam. Parallel to this, a reform faction among the younger clergy, supported by lay persons, argued for a reorganization of religious institutions. Many of them later represented the tie between the social revolutionary and the fundamentalist wings of the revolution.

Reformers of Religious Institutions   The first religious reform movement began in the beginning of the 1960s. It had about twenty members, mostly clerics but some lay intellectuals. The new ideas they advanced found scant reception among the population at large because of their predominantly intellectual style, but they clearly enjoyed considerable resonance among theology students, preachers, and younger clerics. The movement is noteworthy in that several of its participants in

later years exercised great influence over Iranian youth and had important roles in the Islamic revolution and republic. Among these were the
clerics Mutahhari, Beheshti, and Taleghani; Mehdi Bazargan, the first
prime minister after the overthrow; and the "vanished Imam," Musa
Sadr.[63]

The goals of this reform movement were concentrated primarily in
four areas. First, it was directed against the political quietism of the
leading *mujtahids*. It sought a repoliticization of Islam and its establishment in the consciousness of the masses as an ideology encompassing all
areas of life and summoning believers to action. Second, the reformers
wanted to reorganize the hierocratic leadership through the institutionalization of a council of several top-level clerics, each with specific areas
of competence. A chance for such a reorganization existed particularly
after the death of the *marja' al-taqlid* Borujerdi in March 1961. A third
goal of the group was to rationalize and centralize the financial foundation of the clergy, in order to gain greater independence from the
traditionalist- and quietistic-minded masses. Finally, they were concerned about raising the intellectual niveau of religious education, in
order to attract intellectually promising youth.[64]

These goals are remarkable in that they were essentially limited to a
reorganization of religious institutions and did not promote social reforms. Nor did religious reformers offer any critique of the shah's modernization policy, thus distinguishing themselves sharply from Khomeini, who in these years had begun to see his main task as formulating
just such a critique. This reform movement can probably best be interpreted as a critique of the conservative religious establishment. Beyond
this, its great importance is its historical role as predecessor to the
second, social revolutionary movement.

Religious Social Revolutionaries   The development of a Shi'ite social
revolutionary ideology is inextricably bound to the name Ali Shariati.
As Ervand Abrahamian has pointed out, however, Shariati himself ac-
knowledged that his social revolutionary Shi'ism was to a large extent
anticipated by the guerrilla group Mojahedin. Shariati took up the critique of the quietism of the religious leaders and laid a claim to leadership by modern, educated Shi'ite lay intellectuals, who, in contrast to
the clergy, did not represent a corrupt "Safavid" Islam but an authentic
"Alid" one. "Safavid" Shi'ism, in his view, was shaped, on the one
hand, by the ossified power structure of the monarchy and hierocracy
and, on the other, by unquestioned adherence, superstitious practices,

and the passivity of the traditional masses. "Safavid" and "Pahlavid" Shi'ism were thus identical. He identified "Alid" Islam, in contrast, as the original, pure Islam of the prophet and imam Ali. This Shi'ism was revolutionary and just, opposed to tyranny and exploitation. It called for an active emulation of Ali, not just blind veneration.[65]

According to Shariati, the carriers of this Alid Shi'ism were not the clergy but the "enlightened," whom he compared to prophets and religious founders. The "enlightened" obviously represented an avant-garde of religious lay persons, whose task was "assisting the popular masses toward self-consciousness." Shariati thus not only distinguished himself from the traditionalist camp but also stood counter to Khomeini's fundamentalist-hierocratic claim to power. Opposing both the traditionalist Shi'ite and Western cultures, but simultaneously using the Shi'ite religion for the "re-creation of tradition" and the formation of a national cultural identity, Shariati was similar to the writer Jalal Al-e Ahmad, who coined the expression *gharbzadegi*, a "plague from the West."[66]

Shariati's revolutionary ideas were of less import as political or economic conceptions than as visions of a cultural identity and future for Iran that lay neither in "Safavid" traditionalism nor in an imitation of the West. One vision was of a new role for women, derived, in distinction to the Western ("barmaid") and the traditional ("religious cry-baby"), from a reinterpretation of Fatima, the daughter of the prophet, wife of Ali, and mother of Hassan and Hussein. She provided a role model not only as daughter, wife, and mother but also "as a stalwart and responsible woman in view of the needs of her time and society." "She is herself an 'imam,' an ideal type, and model for all women concerned with the development of their personalities." In his image of women Shariati openly reveals his antitraditionalism and also distinguishes himself clearly from Khomeini's politicized, radicalized traditionalism.[67]

The Pahlavi regime initially tolerated Shariati's statements because it welcomed his critique of the clergy and probably hoped to see it eventuate in a split in the religious camp. Only later did the regime recognize the explosive nature of his social revolutionary ideas and try to stop them. But by then Shariati had already won such great popularity among the youth that repression and imprisonment served only to increase his appeal.

What was Shariati's appeal? Aside from the fact that he was apparently a gifted speaker, he represented the ideal of a modern Iranian-Islamic intellectual who had preserved his cultural identity despite his Western education. His theories justified the claim to power of an avant-garde of Islamic intellectuals, rejected the political and cultural hegemony of the West, and fulfilled the desire for a "special path" to modernity growing in many on account of foreign cultural dominance. Neither East nor West, neither socialism nor capitalism, but an authentic Islamic path to modernity was the promise of the vision. In his utopia this special path was formulated as "Alid Shi'ism," a classic case of the "re-creation of tradition."

The alliance between social revolutionary and fundamentalist Shi'ism came about in the late 1970s. It was based on a common opposition to the conservative-quietistic clergy and their apolitical interpretation of Islam. It was further shaped by the common experience of political persecution at the hands of the Pahlavi regime. These two factors in particular obscured the differences in basic positions for many adherents and allowed them to appear meaningless, at least temporarily, for most representatives of both movements. Nevertheless, it is important to distinguish social revolutionary from fundamentalist Shi'ism.

Religious Fundamentalism   The differences in ideology and carriers between the various groups will be treated in the following chapter. My initial concern here is to chart the organizational lines of demarcation, which is difficult if not basically impossible. First, political repression in Iran meant that there were no associations or parties in which the fundamentalist opposition would have been able to organize itself. Second, religious leaders traditionally recruited their followers through clientelist relationships and personal loyalties. Thus there are no institutions but only clientelist ties and "networks" that can be drawn upon to identify the fundamentalist movement. In despotic societies, however, data on such networks are simply not readily available.

Thus, the fundamentalist movement in Iran can only be inadequately defined as the sum of such clientelist relationships, tied ultimately through hierarchical networks to the person of Khomeini. In a more narrow sense this characterizes the circle of clergy and lay persons who recognized Khomeini as the authoritative legal scholar, who oriented themselves according to his interpretation of Shari'a law, and who paid their religious taxes into his network. Beyond this, the network encompassed people who supported him as the political leader of the struggle against the shah's regime and who, above all, affirmed his claim to leadership on behalf of the legal scholars and supported his ideas of a just, legitimate order and his ideals of the proper conduct of life.

Because of the relatively low degree of institutionalization, it is clearly not possible to be certain that the social revolutionary and the fundamentalist wings of the opposition did not overlap; the same circle of people may have shared texts or audio cassettes by both Shariati and Khomeini. This was probably the case in particular among the students of Qum.[68] Because of the opposition's common political front in the 1970s, these contradictions between the two groupings first emerged in practical terms after the revolution.

THE IDEOLOGY OF SHI'ITE FUNDAMENTALISM

As has already been indicated above, the ideology of fundamentalism can be viewed from three perspectives: that of the social critique, the salvation history, and the mentality expressed by the first two. An investigation of the salvation history is concerned with one's ideas of the theological meaning of the social crisis of the present within the tension between, on the one hand, revelation and the original Islamic congregation as a "Golden Age" and, on the other, the expectation of future salvation brought by the return of the Twelfth Imam from his concealment and the realization of a divine order. Seen in these terms, fundamentalism appears chiefly as mythical regress and nativism, as millenarianism and messianism, as a charismatic movement with the claim of being the instrument of divine action on earth.

A social-critical dimension can be distinguished from this theological-historical dimension. In its social critique fundamentalism identifies those phenomena, social groups, and powers that, in its view, contribute to or are responsible for the decadence of present society. Here we discover information about the possible economic, political, legal, or cultural grievances of the traditional camp, about the causes of its mobilization, about the justifications for the actions it undertakes, and about its reproval of other social groups, classes, strata, or milieus. In fundamentalism these two dimensions, the theological-historical and the social-critical, are inseparably united but can, of course, be distinguished analytically, in particular because the fundamentalist social critique is also capable of mobilizing people who do not necessarily share its historical theology.

THE FUNDAMENTALIST SOCIAL CRITIQUE

The primary sources for investigating the social critique are writings of the leading personalities of the fundamentalist movement that found a broader dissemination in brochures, fliers, or tracts. Alongside these, however, certain recorded events also yield information about the specific occasions that led to the mobilization of the fundamentalist camp, for example, in protest demonstrations or closings of the bazaar. And, finally, in the case of Iran, postrevolutionary political measures implemented by the fundamentalist camp supply important information and insights.

As has already been mentioned, a major problem in the treatment of the fundamentalist movement in Iran is to isolate it from other aspects of the protest. Because of the prevailing political conditions, institutional boundaries, such as those marked by periodicals, associations, and parties, cannot be drawn. Accordingly, there is the danger either of arbitrarily compiling compatible claims from writings by various authors or of claiming that the whole of the opposition movement was involved in protest and revolution for the fundamentalist camp. The revolutionary movement, however, represented a coalition of, in part, quite heterogeneous groups, classes, milieus, and interests, which were subject to integration only under the specific political conditions prevailing in Iran at a certain time. Fundamentalism was only one element of the revolution, even though it was a central one.

As is appropriate given my provisional limitation of the fundamentalist movement to those hierarchically structured clientelist networks centered on the person of Khomeini, his writings and speeches provide the midpoint for the analysis of fundamentalist thought. And, indeed, he is regarded throughout the literature as the undisputed representative of Shi'ite fundamentalist thinking par excellence.

Nevertheless, such a concentration on the person of Khomeini harbors the possibility of misinterpretation because it does not allow for a distinction between typical cognitive figurations and atypical, accidental, or individual ones. At the same time, there is the danger of emphasizing all the characteristics that fit well for a comparison with Protestant fundamentalism and overlooking other characteristics of Shi'ite fundamentalism that do not conform.

For these reasons, I have also used the program published in 1950 by the Fedayan-i Islam ("devotees of Islam"), a small group of militant fundamentalists. This violation of my self-imposed temporal limitations appears to me sensible for a number of additional reasons. First, comparable writings from the years that are treated here, 1961–1979, are lacking. Second, the Fedayan-i Islam embody a continuity—one to be found all the way up to the revolution—of a fundamentalism shaped by petit bourgeois and proletarian lay persons and uneducated clerics. Although their methods might not have been shared, their goals certainly did find support in the bazaar milieu and among younger legal scholars. Thus, two of Khomeini's later comrades-in-arms, Ayatollah Murtaza Mutahhari and Ayatollah Mahmud Taleghani, who had outstanding roles in the formulation of a fundamentalist ideology and the organization of the Islamic Republic, maintained very close contacts with the Fedayan-i Islam in the early 1950s in Qum (Mutahhari) and Tehran (Taleghani).[69] The program of the Fedayan-i Islam was reprinted in 1979 and their representative, Ayatollah Khalkali, was a major figure as the supreme revolutionary judge. And, finally, they were the first to raise the call for an Islamic republic. The Fedayan-i Islam leaders can thus be regarded as the relatively uneducated precursors to Khomeini.

The multitude of individual themes addressed in the fundamentalist social critique can be summarized in their essentials by four categories: first, the moral decay of the Iranian people, focused above all on sexual morality, the role of women, and leisure-time and consumer behavior; second, the government's policy of secularization, encompassing primarily the forced institutional differentiation of religion on the one hand from politics, law, the economy, and education on the other; third, the loss of national independence and the influence of foreign powers; and, fourth, social and economic injustice, referring chiefly to the contrast between the public extravagance and ostentation of the rich and the poverty of the masses.

Moral Decay   The central significance of questions of sexual morality and the social role of women, alongside changes in consumer and leisure-time behavior, was expressed repeatedly in fundamentalist writings, protest actions, and measures implemented after the revolution. Moral decay was interpreted in this context as a decline in the validity of Islamic norms and their repression by a foreign culture. Complaints about the moral decay of society referred above all to the loosening, which is to say, general decline, of sexual morality: lewd behavior, vices, and depravity were seen as having gained the upper hand everywhere.[70]

At the top of the list of crisis symptoms was the public display of female sexuality. Above all, women were wearing indecent dress, some of them strolling through the public streets unveiled or worse. "Flames of passion rise from the naked bodies of immoral women and burn humanity into ashes," according to one dramatic statement by the

Fedayan-i Islam,[71] and "the unveiling of women has caused the increasing number of broken families and divorces. . . . women also become less attentive toward their families and husbands and its result are divorce and prostitution." It was also argued that youth were seduced by women's behavior and kept from their work.[72]

The decay of sexual morality was promoted above all by the cinema and periodicals. Pornography was propagated in films and magazines. But the schools, too, were agents of corruption; coeducation was threatening the innocence of young girls.[73] Opportunities for men and women to meet without supervision stimulated the passions in general: "Day and night, men and women face each other in the streets, offices, schools, plants and in other public places and this sense is stimulated at all times without control. This continuous stimulation of the sexual sense gradually paralyzes the nervous system and weakens the other senses of the people."[74] A further result of moral decay was seen in prostitution and the spread of venereal diseases.[75]

Next to female sexuality, the change in the legal status of women ignited a major part of the resistance to the Pahlavi regime. The early protest against the "White Revolution" of 1963 had been directed in particular against the extension of voting rights to women. In any case, that had been a more important issue than, for example, land reform. It was, however, the passage of the "Family Protection Law" in 1967, as well as its heightened enforcement in 1975, that prompted bitter criticism from the fundamentalist clergy.[76] This law, which superseded the provisions of Shari'a law that had been valid previously, reordered family, marriage, and divorce laws and considerably elevated the legal status of women. Further government measures on women's issues that inspired protest from the fundamentalist camp were the admission of women to judgeships, their enlistment in the armed forces, and the prohibition of the veil for women and girls attending school.[77]

In the fundamentalist critique of the change in leisure-time and consumer behavior, the consumption of alcohol was a major target. The sale of alcoholic beverages in stores and bars was tolerated and even encouraged by the government, which allowed sales in state hotels.[78] Leisure activities had meanwhile expanded to include such widespread excesses as gambling—likewise supported by the state—dancing, playing and listening to music in public, and attending films.[79]

The central significance of the issues of sexual morality, the position of women in society, and consumer and leisure-time behavior for the mobilization of the fundamentalist camp was unambiguously mani-

fest in prerevolutionary demonstrations and postrevolutionary practices of the new regime. Protest demonstrations often targeted for
violence and arson, in addition to police stations and banks, cinemas
that presented sexually uninhibited films as well as cafes, bars, night-
clubs, gambling casinos, and bordellos. Prostitutes were beaten, frequently severely injured, and the bordello district of Tehran was partially burned down.[80]

Among the first to suffer retaliation following the mullahs' seizure of
power, besides political enemies and religious minorities, were prostitutes, adulterers, and homosexuals. Many of them were brought to trial,
and not a few executed. The Family Protection Law was replaced by
Islamic law, and women were ordered to put their veils back on. A law
promulgated in 1981 to codify the provisions of the Koran in regard to
infringements of rights, sexual behavior, and alcohol consumption consisted of 195 articles; of these, 107 referred to the punishment of sexual
activities, from adultery, male and female homosexuality, incest, and
prostitution to two unrelated persons of the same sex lying naked under
a blanket.[81]

The delight taken in details alone indicates that the issue of sexual
morality was not an artificial one covering their "real motivations" but
a quite central commitment on the part of the fundamentalists. Their
protest actually was ignited by concerns revolving about the family,
gender roles, the legal position of women, and female sexuality. Alongside these, other vices, such as alcohol consumption and gambling, were
also critical issues, but these were of concern primarily for their destructive effects upon the family.

Loss of Religious-Cultural Identity   A further complex of issues in the
fundamentalists' social critique referred to the loss of Iran's Islamic
identity. This was manifested, in their eyes, in several areas: in the
nationalization of social spheres previously subject to religious control;
in the replacement of an Islamic foundation of state legitimacy by a pre-
Islamic, Achaemenidian one; in the emphasis on Iranian national culture at the expense of the universalist religious tradition; and in the
public devaluation of the clergy and pious living in the traditional sense.
The secularization policy was begun, for the most part, under Reza
Khan and was merely being continued by his son. Nevertheless, the
latter undertook a few spectacular steps in the sphere of religious-
political differentiation, outstanding examples of which were the (self-)
coronation ceremony in 1967, the 2,500th anniversary celebration of

the Iranian monarchy in 1971, and, finally, the abolition of the Islamic calendar in 1976.

In contrast to previous practice, which varied between limited compromise with the clergy and disrespect for their constitutional rights of supervision, the Islamic foundations of legitimacy for the political system were now done away with. The last two measures, in particular, represented a violation of the constitution and a deliberate provocation of the whole religious camp. With the celebration of the 2,500th anniversary of the Iranian monarchy the foundation of legitimacy was pushed back into the pre-Islamic, Zoroastrian period. This was probably what finally pushed Khomeini to declare the monarchy incompatible with Islam.[82] And the abolition of the Islamic calendar appeared to him, understandably, as the high point of the shah's anti-Islamic policy: "He is against the Islamic calendar. To be against the Islamic calendar is to be against Islam itself; in fact the worst thing that this man has done during his reign is to change the calendar. Changing the calendar is even worse than the massacres; it is an affront to the Most Noble Messenger himself (peace and blessings be upon him)."[83]

Further governmental measures aiming at the separation of politics and religion included the suffrage, eligibility for political office, and appointment of non-Muslims to judgeships and the associated substitution of the Koran with "a holy book" to swear in representatives, which put Muslims, Christians, Jews, and Zoroastrians all on an equal level. The conscription of theology students into military service and the organization of literacy corps, health workers, and religious educational corps, with the task of providing for and indoctrinating the rural population, also implied an erosion of the special status of Islam and thus an automatic reduction in the influence of the clergy, especially in the countryside, where they had preserved their dominance despite decades of reform.[84]

The regime's campaign against the oppositional Islamic clergy was also expressed, finally, in deliberate attempts to lower their public prestige and even in brutal attacks on them. Thus the protest gatherings of clerics and theology students against the "White Revolution" in 1963 in Qum and the student protest there in 1978 were put down with extreme severity, and some protesters were even killed.[85] The protests of the fundamentalist camp were inspired not only by political measures but also often precisely by such brutal treatment by the regime and its direct attacks and slander campaigns against leading clerics. Thus the protest demonstration of 1963 had been preceded by a provocative appearance of the shah in Qum.[86] And the religious protests in January 1978 were spurred by an article in a newspaper with close ties to the regime, in which Khomeini was depicted as an unreligious reactionary, an author of erotic poetry, a spy in the service of Britain, and, on top of that, of Indian descent.[87]

All of these measures were intended to keep the clergy out of politics and thus to separate politics and religion by force. In fact, however, the slander campaigns and the brutal treatment of the religious camp initiated politicization, thus making fundamentalists out of traditionalists. The deaths of demonstrators, according to Islamic custom, called for memorial gatherings for the victims, which regularly turned into political protests, which—once again brutally put down—created more victims and thus called for more memorial services.

Foreign Political Influence   A third complex of issues around which the fundamentalist critique crystalized concerned Iranian national independence, which was seen as closely related to its identity as an Islamic state. Iran's government was perceived as having fallen under the influence of foreign powers, in particular the United States and Israel, who were using the government as the agent of their own anti-Islamic policies. Although the reform policy of the "White Revolution" was begun largely under the pressure of the Kennedy administration, Israel was regarded initially as the major guilty party. After the army's massacre of theology students and clerics for the antimodernization protests in Qum in March 1963, Khomeini charged the government with being subservient to Israel: "It was Israel that assaulted Fayziya Madrasa by means of its sinister agents. It is still assaulting us, and assaulting you, the nation; it wishes to seize your economy, to destroy your trade and agriculture, to appropriate your wealth."[88]

The Pahlavi regime was criticized primarily for its cooperation with Israel, which critics saw proceeding in politics, the economy, and the military. As his central reproach in 1963, Khomeini cited a treaty being planned for conclusion with Israel. Moreover, the opposition claimed that Israel exercised considerable economic influence over Iran and maintained close contacts with the army and secret police. In exchange, Iran was supposed to have supported Israel with oil deliveries during its wars with Arab states.[89]

The charge that Iran was subservient to the United States was reinforced in 1964, when parliament passed a law providing diplomatic immunity to all American military and civilian advisers in Iran. More-

over, Iran was to receive a $20 million loan from the United States for
the purpose of purchasing American armaments. Khomeini issued a
forceful attack, for which he was exiled from Iran.

> They have reduced the Iranian people to a level lower than that of an Ameri-
> can dog. If someone runs over a dog belonging to an American, he will be
> prosecuted. Even if the Shah himself were to run over a dog belonging to an
> American, he would be prosecuted. But if an American cook runs over the
> Shah, the head of the state, no one will have the right to interfere with him.
> Why? Because they wanted a loan and America demanded this in return. . . .
> The government has sold our independence, reduced us to the level of a
> colony.[90]

Criticism of the United States picked up enormously with the revolutionary movement at the end of the 1970s. And the protest actions during
the Iranian revolution, culminating in the seizure of the American embassy and the taking of its personnel as hostages, as well as the slogans
against the United States, the Soviet Union, and Israel that were used at
mass demonstrations, show clearly the great significance the fundamentalists attributed to national independence and Islamic identity.

Public Extravagance and Mass Poverty   Another important target of
the fundamentalist social critique was mass poverty, especially that
found in the large cities. The Fedayan-i Islam had already complained
about mass misery in Tehran: "half of the nation is poor, starving, and
prostituting itself because of the crimes and frauds of the traitors to the
country and the rich, whose cars send dust and dirt to the chests of the
poor."[91] The poor were without work, the critique continued, suffered
from the cold in winter and heat in summer, were unable to feed their
families, and starved on street corners, while the wealthy and corrupt
elite and the government paid no attention. But, one day, the poor
would rise in revolution: "the pressures of poverty and misery will
overcome the resistance and patience of the poor and a sudden natural
explosion will happen when the bones and the flesh of the rulers and the
rich will be eaten in revenge."[92]

Khomeini likewise denounced government extravagance and the ostentation of the rich, contrasting them with the poverty of the masses,
especially in the large cities such as Tehran: "Go take a look at the south
of the city—go look at those pits, those holes in the ground where
people live, dwellings you reach by going down about a hundred steps
into the ground."[93] In contrast, the Iranian upper classes and foreigners
lived in gigantic palaces and extreme luxury. As the culmination of such

extravagance, Khomeini criticized the coronation ceremonies of 1967 and the 2,500th anniversary celebration of the Persian monarchy in 1971.[94]

Complaints about the poverty of the masses, up until the beginning of the 1970s, referred primarily to the urban lower classes, whose number had grown enormously because of the migration of impoverished peasants and nomads into the cities. At the beginning of the 1970s the charges were expanded: "You witness complacently the hunger and poverty of our people, the bankruptcy of the bazaar, the unemployment of our educated youth, the sorry state of our agriculture and industry."[95]

The rich and the institutions of state had failed and betrayed the country—in economic and social policy, in educational policy and the administration of justice. Responsible for this in the critics' eyes, aside from the turn away from Islam, was the bureaucratic organization of the state apparatus.

> When the juridical methods of Islam were applied, the shari'a judge in each town, assisted only by two bailiffs and with only a pen and an inkpot at his disposal, would swiftly resolve disputes among people and send them about their business. But now the bureaucratic organization of the Ministry of Justice has attained unimaginable proportions, and is, in addition, quite incapable of producing results.[96]

THE SALVATIONAL DIMENSION

The fundamentalist critique of existing society, however, was by no means confined to a summary listing of actual or suspected wrongs. Expressions of discontent over the changes in values, over immorality or the younger generation do not, taken in themselves, identify fundamentalism but represent a general phenomenon of traditionalist dissatisfaction or conservative social criticism. Traditionalism is transformed into fundamentalism when the individual elements of the critique are unified by religious intellectuals into a systematic whole with the salvation history, which compels individuals to take a position and become active politically. Such a transformation also implies the fundamentalist revision and reinterpretation of critical points in the theology of traditionalism. It is precisely this process of innovative reinterpretation of the religious tradition that deserves our particular attention.[97]

The structural problems of society, understood by the critics as a crisis of epochal dimensions, appeared henceforth to be the result of the fall away from the divine law of the Koran. The contemporary conflict among various social groups over power, income, privilege, and prestige was interpreted as a struggle between good and evil, between God and Satan. The position of fundamentalists in these conflicts was seen as parallel to Hussein's in his battle against Yazid at Kerbala and his heroic death, thus glorifying a believer's readiness for martyrdom and the charisma of suffering. The action of the individual therefore acquired significance in the context both of the salvation history and world history. It became a part of the divine drama. This consciousness was apparent in particular in the mass demonstrations and street battles of the revolution.[98]

The complex ideology of fundamentalism in which the social critique is embedded can be viewed according to three temporal perspectives: first, as a mythical regression to an idealized past ("Golden Age"); second, as a struggle between good and evil in the present; and, finally, as the anticipation of a future millennium, prepared by the holy warriors of fundamentalism and inaugurated by the imam returning from his concealment.

The Religious Tradition   The basis of the split between Sunni and Shi'ite Islam was the question of Mohammed's successor as leader of the Islamic community.[99] A majority faction assumed that Mohammed had declined to stipulate his successor and that, therefore, he would have to be chosen by election. A minority faction, in contrast, claimed that Mohammed had named his stepson, Ali, as his successor. From this divergence grew the split between Sunnis and Shi'ites, the party of Ali. Ali was, indeed, elected as the fourth caliph, but the election was challenged by Muawiya, and Ali lost most of his influence to the former, the founder of the Umayyad dynasty. Ali was murdered in 661 in Kufa (near present-day Najaf). His sons, Hassan and Hussein, withdrew to Medina, and Hassan (d. 669) renounced all claim to rule.

With the death of Muawiya in 680, Hussein—encouraged by his followers in Kufa, who regarded him as the legitimate caliph—refused allegiance to Yazid, Muawiya's son. Hussein withdrew with his small following, first to Kufa, then to Kerbala. There the group was surrounded by a superior Umayyad force, cut off from supplies, and then brutally massacred. With that, from a Shi'ite perspective, Imam Hussein, the third legitimate successor to Mohammed, after Ali and Hassan, was subjected to a martyr's death.

Further splits ensued within Shi'ism, resulting from disagreements over which genealogical line was legitimate and which imam was the last bearer of the original charisma. Of interest here is Twelver Shi'ism, which had been the state religion in Iran since the Safavid seizure of power in 1501. It recognizes a genealogical succession of twelve imams, the last of which, Mohammed al-Mahdi, is supposed to have vanished in 873–874, to live on in concealment until his return. His return is to initiate the reestablishment of a just order, the end of oppression and tyranny. The idea of a "Golden Age" in which the Islamic principles of a just society were realized thus refers in Shi'ite Islam to the few years in which Mohammed was leading the congregation from Medina and Ali that from Kufa.[100]

Bound up with Shi'ite imamology are questions of the legitimacy of rule for the phase prior to the return of the Hidden Imam. These questions, as we have seen above, have been given different answers at different times and have been the subject of continual conflict and power struggles between political and clerical rule. Khomeini's fundamentalism devoted extensive attention to the problem of legitimate rule and the role of the clergy, adding a surprising variation to the controversy in the beginning of the 1970s: the illegitimacy in principle of the monarchy as an institution and the postulate of an Islamic republic under the control of the clergy.

The "Shadow of God" and the Hidden Imam   Reacting to Mohammed Reza Pahlavi's efforts since the mid-1960s to replace the Islamic legitimation of rule with a pre-Islamic, Achaemenidian one, Khomeini radicalized his critique of the shah into a general critique of the monarchy, thus depriving the shah of any possibility to recapture legitimacy for his rule. He now declared the constitution of 1906–1907 an act of fraud against the Iranian people orchestrated by British agents and equated the monarchy with the Fall. Mohammed, he continued, had established his holy Islamic order in opposition to the monarchies of the time, and Ali had been toppled by the successor monarchy of the Umayyads.[101] The sole legitimate order was one led by the imams. Since the concealment of the Twelfth Imam, this function had been transferred to the clergy. Therefore, the only legitimate Islamic order was one led, or, as the case may be, supervised, by Islamic legal scholars.

In view of this argument many orientalists have also made a point of the limited and precarious nature of legitimation for all monarchies in Twelver Shi'ism. It is one of the accomplishments of Said Arjomand to have thoroughly criticized this unrealistic perspective. In *The Shadow of God and the Hidden Imam*, he showed that the shah of Persia—like monarchs in all patrimonial systems—was regarded as having been divinely ordained. Under the caesaropapist regime of the Safavids even a hereditary charismatic legitimation of rule prevailed. And under the Qajars the clergy supported the king because of his stabilizing function, even when his behavior was scarcely "Islamic." Their fear of chaos was greater than their religious objection.

The foundation of the legitimacy of a ruler was his "justness." As long as he governed society "justly," he was regarded as having been ordained by God and was due obedience. During the period in which the imam was concealed, nothing in this foundation of legitimacy changed. Only the parousia of the imam would create a new order, one in which the shah would have to join the ranks of the imam's followers. Just as the assumption that Christ was the only true sovereign of the eastern Roman empire did not diminish the legitimacy of the Byzantine rulers, so the true sovereignty of the Hidden Imam never signified the illegitimacy of a just king.[102]

This interpretation can also be found in Khomeini's own writings. In the 1960s he had called for the reinstatement of the constitution of 1906–1907, which foresaw a commission of the top-ranking legal scholars to examine new laws for their agreement with Shari'a law but did not contain any further political responsibilities for the clergy and, above all, firmly established the monarchy. Conservative clerics continued to represent this position into the 1970s. No challenge to the legitimacy of rule by the shah ever referred to the institution but only to a particular shah's conduct in office. This was also for a long time Khomeini's view, as he stated in 1941: "When a government does not perform its duty, it becomes oppressive. If it does perform its duty, not only is it not oppressive, it is cherished and honored by God."[103]

According to traditional Shi'ite doctrine, it was thus quite possible to confirm the illegitimacy of the rule of Shah Mohammed Reza Pahlavi, because he pursued policies directed against Islam. Khomeini's position after 1971, however, that the monarchy as an institution was illegitimate in principle, represented a clear break with tradition. Many of his adherents failed to notice this break or, if they did, to take it as seriously as it was meant. For in demonstrations and protest gatherings prior to the revolution the call for the reinstatement of the 1906–1907 constitution continued to be raised.[104]

The Rule of Law under the Legal Scholars   If, however, the monarchy now fundamentally typified illegitimate rule, who should be in power? Khomeini's answer—Islamic legal scholars—was unambiguous in theory but not so in its practical effects.[105] He spoke in one instance of the rule of the legal scholars, in another of their guardianship. This apparent contradiction is resolved, however, if the justification of the claim to rule (or to guardianship) is considered. What was supposed to rule was, namely, the law. Because, however, the victory of the Usulis had established in Shi'ism that only the *mujtahids* were competent to issue valid interpretations of the Shari'a and further its creative development, Khomeini's formula implied that only legal scholars could guarantee the rule of law. In doing so, it was a matter of relatively little importance whether they wore the robes of government officials or not. Of sole importance was that they have control: "Since Islamic government is a government of law, those acquainted with the law, or more precisely, with religion—i.e., the fuqaha—must supervise its functioning. It is they who supervise all executive and administrative affairs of the country, together with all planning."[106]

Because of the legalistic character of Islam, however, it is true at the same time that the legal scholars were not free in the exercise of their supervisory function. They drew from their office the legitimacy solely to fulfill the law in a literal sense.

> The fuqaha are the trustees who implement divine ordinances. . . . They must not allow the laws of Islam to remain in abeyance, or their operation to be affected by either defect or excess. If a faqih wishes to punish an adulterer, he must give him one hundred lashes in the presence of the people, in the exact manner that has been specified. He does not have the right to inflict one additional lash, to curse the offender, to slap him, or to imprison him for a single day.[107]

This statement clearly illustrates yet again the distinction I emphasized at the outset between the social revolutionary Shi'ism based on an ethic of conviction, found, for example, in a Shariati, and the statutory ethical, fundamentalist Shi'ism of a Khomeini.

Fundamentalist Millenarianism   Shi'ite traditionalism is at bottom quietistic. This quietism is essentially based on its premillenarian doctrine of the imam, that is, that the millennium, the realm of peace and justice, is not the work of man but will be established by the Imam Mahdi. The imperfection of the world is, therefore, a fact to be accepted, which, to be sure, does not forbid one from rebelling against an unjust ruler once his tyranny has become intolerable.

Like its social revolutionary counterpart, Khomeini's fundamentalism not only transformed political quietism into activism but also modified the premillenarian doctrine.[108] Khomeini distinguishes between the religious status and function of the imams, and thus between their charismatic quality and the objective-technical tasks with which they are charged.[109] In regard to their status, they are far superior to all normal mortals: "In fact, . . . the Most Noble Messenger and the Imams existed before the creation of the world in the form of lights situated beneath the divine throne; they were superior to other men even in the sperm from which they grew and in their physical composition."[110]

Their extraordinary qualities, however, by no means extend to their political capabilities, according to Khomeini. For the exercise of governmental functions, all who have the requisite religious knowledge and are personally moral and just are equally qualified. The task of government is the faithful implementation of the letter of Islamic law. The necessary legal knowledge and personal integrity were to be found in numerous contemporary legal scholars.

> The two qualities of knowledge of the law and justice are present in countless fuqaha of the present age. If they would come together, they could establish a government of universal justice in the world. . . . The idea that the governmental powers of the Most Noble Messenger [i.e., Mohammed] were greater than those of the Commander of the Faithful [i.e., Ali], or that those of the Commander of the Faithful were greater than those of the faqih, is false and erroneous.[111]

The establishment of a just order, however, does not require the return of the Hidden Imam. And the attempt to encourage his return, for example, by encouraging sin and decline, is to be avoided absolutely.[112] Thus the political quietism and historical pessimism of premillenarianism become illegitimate attitudes and ways of behaving in Khomeini's fundamentalism.

Kerbala as a Model for Action   As indicated above, the massacre at Kerbala and the martyrdom of Hussein have been of central importance in the self-concept of Shi'ite Islam. The first ten days of the month of Muharram are devoted to the memory of Hussein, with readings of the story of his passion, passion plays (*ta'zieh*), and processions. Those days, and especially Ashura, the tenth day of Muharram, are the yearly climax of popular Shi'ite piety.[113]

In Khomeini's interpretation of these holidays his transformation of a quietistic traditionalism into an activist fundamentalism is also evident. In traditional Shi'ism both the passion plays and the religious readings are designed to bring the events at Kerbala to life for believers. Imam Hussein, as the legitimate ruler of the Muslim community, along with his family, friends, and companions, is cruelly killed by the usurper and tyrant Yazid. The drama embodies the struggle of good against evil, the just against tyranny. The grief over Hussein's death, however, is tied to a belief in his apocalyptic triumph.[114]

In popular Shi'ism the imams have a role similar to that of saints in the Catholic church. They are regarded as mediators between God and the people. The shedding of tears for Hussein's sake earns the mourner an intercession. At the same time, the mourning of Hussein's martyrdom signifies a lamentation of the injustice and wickedness of the world.[115] In the popular religious tradition this implies that believers are not to accept injustice, which, however, will be abolished only with the return of the Twelfth Imam. Khomeini took up this religious practice but reinterpreted it as a guide to political action.

> Make Islam known to the people, then, and in so doing, create something akin to 'Ashura. Just as we have steadfastly preserved the awareness of 'Ashura ... and not let [it] be lost, so that people still gather during Muharram and beat their breasts, we should now take measures to create a wave of protest against the state of the government; let the people gather, and the preachers and rauzankhwans [reciters of the lives of the imams, in particular the passion narrative of Imam Hussein] firmly fix the issue of government in their minds.[116]

Thus the lamentation of Hussein became the emulation of Hussein, the active struggle against tyranny, oppression, and injustice. And, in the course of the revolutionary conflicts, the apocalyptic victory of Imam Hussein over Yazid became the imminent victory of the faithful, under the leadership of Imam Khomeini, over the present-day Yazid, Shah Mohammed Reza Pahlavi. This dramatization of the political struggle of the 1970s in terms of the salvation history is no scientific construct presented solely for its aesthetic appeal, but, as Hans Kippenberg has impressively shown, it can be identified in the symbols and rituals of the street battles.[117]

BASIC PATTERNS OF SHI'ITE FUNDAMENTALIST THOUGHT

In its social critique and its interpretation of the present crisis in terms of the salvation history, features of a mentality become apparent that are of significance for the characterization of Shi'ite fundamentalism and its comparison with Protestant fundamentalism. The basic pattern of fundamentalist thought reveals fundamentalism's images of the world, society, and self and thus the psychological disposition of the fundamentalist camp. Five features in particular stand out: Manichaeism, xenophobia, religious nativism, a paranoid certainty of conspiracy, and gender dualism.

Fundamentalist thinking is Manichaean, marked by an extreme moral dualism. The social crisis in Iran was interpreted not as the result of structural problems but as a struggle between Islam and Satan, between good and evil. That was manifest simply in the juxtaposition of Hussein and Yazid and its transfer onto the believers and the shah. Nor is there any middle ground between good and evil, but solely those two poles. Those who did not take the side of Islam were regarded as enemies, branded as traitors. Imperialism stood opposed to Islam, oppressors against the oppressed, satanic powers against the true Islam.

Fundamentalism is xenophobic. Evil, the satanic, is, first of all, "foreign." It does not stem from one's own religion, culture, or people but is imported from without. The corrupt and repressive regime of the shah, the decadent elite stratum, the sociomoral decay of society, the economic and social misery of the poor—all of this was traceable to foreign influences and intrigues, which, in part, made use of local accomplices. Foreign influences were not understood, for example, as the interest-oriented politics of West and East or of the domestic elite and rising middle class, but as a demonic assault on Islam with the goal of destroying it. The United States and Israel, above all, but also the Soviet Union were the embodiment of evil in the thinking of Shi'ite fundamentalism.

Fundamentalism is nativist. Because society's crisis is regarded as having been initiated from without, only two measures offer the possibility of salvation: first, the repression and annihilation of the foreign; second, a recollection of and return to indigenous religious and cultural roots. These latter represent the divine principle versus the foreign and satanic one. Fundamentalist nativism, however, is based solely upon religious criteria. It is in no way limited by categories such as class, nationality, ethnic-cultural identity, or race, thus distinguishing it from radical right-wing secular ideologies. The historical ideal of Shi'ite fundamentalist nativism is represented by the original congregations of Mohammed and Imam Ali, in which divine law is supposed to have been realized. Yet the legal scholars, with their knowledge of the proper interpretation and application of divine law, are the carriers in the present of the religious legacy promising salvation.

From the fundamentalist point of view it is part of the character of evil that it is cunning. The enemy does not fight fairly but resorts to conspiratorial means. The conspiracy is structured hierarchically. At the top is the worldwide Jewish conspiracy, which is in the main supported and promoted by the major powers. To implement their goals, they use local agents, who thus become traitors to their own people: "We must protest and make the people aware that the Jews and their foreign backers are opposed to the very foundations of Islam and wish to establish Jewish domination throughout the world."[118]

Variations of this conspiracy theory arose in prerevolutionary Iran. In these the main conspirators were the imperialists—the British, Americans, and Russians. "The British imperialists penetrated the countries of the East more than three hundred years ago. Being knowledgeable about all aspects of these countries, they drew up elaborate plans for assuming control of them. Then came the new imperialists, the Americans and others. They allied themselves with the British and took part in the execution of their plans."[119] In this variation, Jews appeared solely as "agents" of imperialism.[120]

The writings of Khomeini are filled with "agents," "traitors," and "conspiracies." These account for all turmoil, from the beginning of imperialism through the Constitutional Revolution to threats against the Islamic Revolution. Despite the xenophobia expressed in the use of such terms, they serve to isolate domestic opponents as persons on the outside of the Islamic (or national) community, whose "just punishment" is already implied in their characterization as the hacks of foreign powers.

Khomeini's conspiracy theory was closely bound to a pronounced anti-Semitism. He did not rest with a critique of the state of Israel or of Zionism, which would be thoroughly understandable from an Islamic point of view, given the wars between Israel and its neighbors. He went on to represent Jews as the enemies of Islam and the divine order from the very beginning. Even the prophet himself had been "forced" to oppose them: "Since the Jews of Bani Qurayza were a troublesome group, causing corruption in Muslim society and damaging Islam and the Islamic state, the Most Noble Messenger . . . eliminated them."[121] In another place Khomeini stated: "From the very beginning, the historical movement of Islam has had to contend with the Jews, for it was they who first established anti-Islamic propaganda and engaged in various stratagems, and as you can see, this activity continues down to the present."[122]

Another feature of the Shi'ite fundamentalist mentality is reflected in its dualistic view of gender. Men and women, because of their biological differences, represent two opposed but mutually complementary principles, which imply a natural division of functions and a separation of their respective spheres. The functions allotted to women are those of wife, housekeeper, and mother. Their most important task is to bear and raise children. Women unable to fulfill this task were permitted to work in offices, factories, or schools, but they had to be segregated from their male colleagues.[123]

The necessity of segregation is justified by the belief that female sexuality poses a threat to men and can be appropriately domesticated only in marriage. Female sexuality confuses the senses of men, stimulates their passion, and holds them back from the performance of their religious duties. This thesis, already presented by Ghazali, is to be found in essentially identical form in the writings of the Fedayan-i Islam, who state that "all parts of a woman's body are stimulus for [the sexual] sense in men."[124]

In distinction to Fatima Mernissi, I regard this not as a question of a more active or passive view of female sexuality in various cultures but as the typical "Eve myth" of patriarchally stamped societies, in which woman, accorded nearly magical powers, is the potential seductress of man into sin.[125] As I demonstrated above, this image of woman as femme fatale is found in comparable form in Puritan-Protestant fundamentalism in America.

THE IDEAL ORDER

Theocracy, the rule of divine law on earth, the "Islamic government," is the ideal order of Shi'ite fundamentalism. The rule of God on earth can be accomplished, in this view, through the consistent enforcement of the laws revealed by God to Mohammed and set down in the Koran.[126]

Divine revelation and the legal prescriptions based upon it provide the foundation for a universal ethical monism. The law is valid for all people of all times and for all social spheres. A cultural or structural ethical pluralism is thus excluded. At the same time, the claim is made that, in principle, the Koran provides the basis for the regulation of all interpersonal relations. Yet how does one implement the law, who are its legitimate interpreters, and who oversees its application?

The "Islamic Republic" represents for fundamentalism the ideal form of the state. Such a republic rests on the severe subordination of individuals and society to divine law.[127] In practice this means that all social spheres have to be structured to correspond to these Islamic principles.

Who exercises power in such a republic? Democratic elements are, indeed, present, such as the election of the president of the republic and the representatives to the national council or the holding of popular referenda, but these elements are structurally subordinate to the rule of the legal scholars, whose legitimation as Khomeini argued it has already been analyzed above.[128] Because they alone are the legitimate representations of the Hidden Imam and only they hold the knowledge requisite to an interpretation of divine law, only they can decide which secular legislative initiatives are compatible with divine law and which candidates are fit to hold political office. One cannot speak here, then, as one can in relation to Protestant fundamentalism, of a tension between republicanism and democracy but only of a hierocratically controlled republicanism with elements of rule by plebiscite.

The ideal community for Shi'ite fundamentalism is not the nation but the Islamic world community, the *umma*. This is clearly reflected in the preamble to the Iranian constitution, in which the "advent of a unified world community" or the "struggle for the spreading of the sovereignty of the rule of God on earth" is repeatedly affirmed. Khomeini declared that the formation of nations was the work of imperialists intent on artificially fragmenting the *umma*, which must be reestablished.[129]

Iranian fundamentalism regards itself as an Islamic avant-garde, a model for the world, which is to be disseminated throughout the world. This ambition has two contrary implications. First, for its own legitimation it has to play down the differences between Shi'ite and Sunni Islam in favor of a "true" Islam.[130] Second, its ideological-political expansionism leads unavoidably to an intensified emphasis on the split between Shi'ites and Sunnis by those governments that feel themselves threatened by it, particularly in countries where Shi'ite minorities, or even majorities, are living, such as Iraq, Lebanon, or Kuwait.[131] For Iran is the only state in which Twelver Shi'ism is the state religion, and it is, additionally, separated from the other Arab states in culture and language. Its missionary ambition, moreover, puts Shi'ite groups in other countries in a difficult position, in that it attempts to force them to choose between religious and national loyalty.

All of these factors together necessarily lend the universalistic Islamic claims of Shi'ite fundamentalism in Iran the flavor, if not actually the character, of an Iranian Shi'ite nationalism. It is subject to the same structural conditions as the "proletarian internationalism" of the Soviet

Union under Stalin. What is good for the Islamic Republic of Iran is also good for the Islamic *umma*. This tension between Islamic universalism and Iranian Shi'ite nationalism is irreducible. But political development favors an intensification of religious nationalism. Like Protestant fundamentalism in the United States, it is therefore possible to characterize Shi'ite fundamentalism in Iran as an exemplary, expansive religious nationalism with a claim to universal validity.

What, then, does the ideal economic order of Shi'ite fundamentalism look like and what is its attitude toward modern industrial capitalism, toward organized labor, and toward the concept of social class? In view of the "mythical" orientation of fundamentalism, it is not surprising that few concrete descriptions of this ideal economic order of the future are found. Even in the constitution of the Islamic Republic of Iran, to the formulation of which social-revolutionary forces also contributed, there is little that is explicit.

The fundamentalist ideal is most readily understandable as a traditional economy subject to intensified religious regulation. This is manifest directly in the abolition of all economic forms regarded as incompatible with Islam. This applies, to name one example, to the implementation of a prohibition on earning interest and the corresponding reorganization of the banking system. Another is the elimination of all immoral sources of income, such as prostitution, the sale of alcoholic beverages, and gambling casinos. Finally, it is necessary to protect the Islamic population from the competition of nonbelievers, an imperative that applies in particular, but not exclusively, to artisans and merchants, as the economic ideal as such is borrowed from the bazaar.[132] Thus, for the Fedayan-i Islam the ideal finance minister is a shopkeeper, and the economic interests that must be attended to first of all are those of the bazaaris.[133]

The economic function of the state is primarily to organize patrimonial-state relief for the poor and to supervise general adherence to Islamic law. The concept of class interests is repudiated for a religious model of integration, understood by the Fedayan-i Islam as follows: "The minister, the deputy, the poor, and the shopkeeper all gather together 3 or 5 times a day for prayer and this results in a bond of friendship among the people and creates a kind of mutual respect and affection among all classes of the community."[134] It is formulated more abstractly, but in the same sense, in the constitution: "Government, from the point of view of Islam, is not a product of any class position or the supremacy of an individual or group. Rather, it is the crystallization of political ideals of a people of the same religion and thought." And Taleghani adds: "The appearance of classes is the result of individual and social deviations from the principle of truth and justice, and the strengthening of attitudes corresponding to transgression, exploitation, and imperialism."[135]

The economic model of fundamentalism thus combines a patrimonial welfare state with a petit bourgeois, capitalist, private industry. The ideals are the paternalistic state and the small enterprise under patriarchal management. Bureaucratic organizational structures are generally rejected as contrary to Islam. This applies as well to the modern mode of industrial production, which is regarded as enslaving the individual and being solely profit oriented. In the West this is done by the capitalists; in the East, by the state: "While these powers do oil the factory machinery and ready it to run, they also seize on various deceitful pretexts to restrict individuals' means of livelihood and rob them of their freedom, independence, and very identity, things more precious than all else."[136]

Also predominant is a general compassion for the "little people," not only the poor in the slums, petty merchants, and artisans in the bazaar but also the lower ranks of white-collar employees, who are often paid starvation wages and left unable to feed their families adequately. At the same time, a remedy is offered in the form of the patrimonial state, which, in Islamic modesty, limits its financial outlays to be able to alleviate the problem of mass poverty solely by means of the religious taxes at its disposal. Postrevolutionary politics also clearly renounced the modern bureaucratic welfare state and state guarantees of the rights of workers.[137]

The ideal work relationships of the "little people" are also strongly marked by a patriarchal traditionalism, as is evidenced both in postrevolutionary practice in Iran and in studies of other Islamic countries. Thus Pierre Bourdieu reports on the responses of Algerian workers to different work environments: "Algerian workers . . . tend to react with pain to . . . cold or brutal impersonal work relations . . . [but] most workers and clerks in small businesses where patriarchal- or paternalist-style working relations still survive say they like their jobs even when they are dissatisfied with their wages."[138]

Peter von Sivers, also using the example of Algeria, referred to the unity of work and leisure time as well as the differences in the working hours between traditional and modern economic sectors, which manifest many structural differences. He named this different attitude toward work and leisure as one of the essential factors in the rise of fundamentalist movements.[139]

The same holds true for Shi'ite fundamentalism in Iran. Its ideal economic order is stamped by traditionalist values, which are expressed above all in the ethics of work and consumption. The work ethic of the bazaar is characterized by long working hours, by an integration of work and leisure time, and by a high degree of autonomy. The high value placed on this personal autonomy within the bounds of religious legality is also clearly expressed in the writings of Taleghani.[140] The value of work lies not so much in its provision of a livelihood nor in its support of expensive leisure-time activities. Work is much more an integral component of a way of life. The consumer ethic of the traditionalist camp is also sharply distinct from modern Western ideas and behaviors. If only for reasons of political caution, wealth is not traditionally put on open display. Nor does consumption have here the function of differentiating levels of prestige, which is accomplished by other means.[141]

The family ideal of Shi'ite fundamentalism is naturally the "holy family," consisting of Imam Ali; his wife Fatima, the daughter of Mohammed; and their children Hassan, Hussein, and Zainab. Ali, Hussein, and Fatima are particularly important symbolically. Ali is the just ruler, who combines esoteric knowledge with religious legality. Fatima, like Mary in Catholicism, combines the roles of virgin and mother. And Hussein, through his heroism and martyrdom, is the redeemer.[142]

Khomeini also drew on this model to exemplify his ideals of the family and relations between the sexes. Women are to take guidance from Fatima, whose status as a model derives above all from her surrender to her father, Mohammed, and to her husband, Ali. A woman's lot is to be mother and housewife and to raise the children; she is of a different nature than man, a fact that must be respected. This, however, does not signify inequality between men and women but an equality appropriate to their respective destinies.

Only in the context of the patriarchal family does woman achieve her true dignity, thus escaping the misuse to which she is put in the capitalist system of the West and in the collectivism of the East. "The family is the fundamental unit of society and the main center of growth and transcendence for humanity.... a woman, as a unit of society, will no longer be regarded as a 'thing' or a tool serving consumerism and exploitation."[143]

This dramatization of gender-specific differences underlies additional features of the fundamentalist ideal of women and the family, such as the strict separation between male and female spheres and between public and domestic spheres. The postulate of such a separation leads to conflicts over women's rights, reflected in the wearing of the veil, segregation in schools and leisure-time establishments, education, and, at least for a certain time, the right to vote.

In earlier times the veiling of women was a status symbol of the elite that indicated the women's freedom from household work. As the elite increasingly conformed to Western models of gender integration, the lower classes adopted the former behavior of the elite. Contributing above all to this development were rapid urbanization, increasing population density, and modern urban architecture.[144]

Bound up with the idea of gender separation is the extensive repudiation of women's employment. This can be well documented in Tehran, given the contrast between the modern, Western-influenced northern part of the city and the traditionalist southern part, including the old city. In the bazaar, for example, the entirety of commercial and crafts activities are undertaken by men, and women appear there only as customers.

The dominance of traditionalist values is evident in a comparison of working women in the modern and older sections of Tehran. The employment of women in the modern center of Tehran was 23 percent of the work force in 1966, but in those areas inhabited by traditionalist strata their share was 3.8 percent to 9.9 percent.[145] In addition to the influence of values these numbers were certainly determined as well by the large number of men in these areas who were available for work, and whose chances for employment would have been considerably diminished by female competition.

Moreover, the small number of employed women within the traditionalist milieu was also based on their relatively low level of education, which, in turn, represented an index of the significance of the traditionalist separation of roles. Although the literacy rate among women also rose rapidly with decreasing age in the traditionalist camp, their participation in higher levels of the educational system remained low. Although the shah's regime attempted to provide equal access to higher education, the fundamentalist regime partly reversed this trend. With gender segregation in the schools the number of teaching personnel available for girls was also reduced. For the latter were to be taught only by female teachers, of whom there were many fewer than male teachers. A further influence in this direction came from the lowering of the marriageable age for girls to thirteen.[146]

As, finally, for the right of women to vote, it was one of the central points of the "White Revolution," prompting dramatic protests by the clergy and bazaar in 1963. Although fundamentalism tended, therefore, to oppose suffrage for women, it has not abolished it, because of the conservative role of many women in and after the revolution. Lower-class women in particular offered support for the regime and were courted as producers of cannon fodder for the war with Iraq. Other measures aimed at the improvement of women's legal status, on the other hand, were immediately repealed after the Islamic revolution, including the appointment of women to judgeships and other high governmental posts as well as the "Family Protection Law" of 1967.[147]

Shi'ite fundamentalism's concept of order was thus generally based on a personalistic-patriarchal model, which underlay both the paternalistic state, small family enterprises, and the family itself.

THE CARRIERS OF SHI'ITE FUNDAMENTALISM

For an interpretation of Shi'ite fundamentalism as an urban protest movement, a survey of its social critique, salvation history, mentality, and conception of an ideal order, naturally, does not suffice. The significance of the ideology becomes apparent only when it is referred, on the one hand, to the carriers of fundamentalism and, on the other, to their specific experiences in the process of rapid urbanization and economic, political, and cultural "modernization."

The carriers of Shi'ite fundamentalism cannot just be equated with the followers of Khomeini during the Iranian revolution of the late 1970s. From the fall of 1978 to February 1979 many groups joined with Khomeini in the common goal of toppling the shah that in other respects had completely different ideas about the future order of society. For that reason I take a more generous historical view and include protest actions beginning in 1962–1963 in the analysis of the carriers of fundamentalism.

CONSTITUENT GROUPS OF THE FUNDAMENTALIST MILIEU

The incisive events marking the birth of a Khomeini-led fundamentalism might well be the protest actions, above all those of 1963, against the "White Revolution." Instances of comparable drama began occurring again only immediately prior to and during the revolution of 1978–1979. Based on analyses of these events, the literature has identified three social groupings in particular as the carriers of fundamentalism: the clergy, the bazaar, and the subproletariat. In this chapter I examine the internal differentiation of these groups according to their positions in the production process, income level, education, and political influence. In my opinion, developments since the mid-1970s in particular make it necessary to add a fourth group, which I designate as "border crossers" between the milieus. This category mainly includes lower-level white-collar employees in the modern sector and youth from the traditional milieu with a modern education.

The Clergy   As I have already demonstrated, the Shi'ite clergy by no means represented a homogeneous class or stratum. Their social origins ranged from large landholder to rural worker, from big merchant to porter in the bazaar. Most of them came from rural or, at least, small-town provincial circumstances and were of (lower) middle-class backgrounds. Nevertheless, many of the leading *mujtahids* came from families of big merchants and large landholders.

The clergy's income also varied considerably, depending on origin, hierocratic status, and clientele. The income of an ayatollah, from religious endowments, voluntary contributions from followers, juridical functions, and religious instruction, far exceeded that of a village mullah, who frequently was unable to live solely from his professional religious activity. The standard of living and cultural niveau of a cleric from a big merchant or large landholding family cannot be compared with that of a mullah from a petty rural or provincial circumstance.[148]

There was vast variation especially in education. As described above, the degree of religious education served as the preeminent criterion for internal status differentiation within the Shi'ite clergy. Not every theology student received at the conclusion of his studies the *ijtihad*, the certification of competence to determine the meaning of religious law independently by means of reason and apply it to new problems. Not every cleric, in other words, was a *mujtahid*; most in fact were uneducated or semieducated mullahs.

The group of *mujtahids*, scholars with the *ijtihad*, can be broken down roughly into three categories: the majority of *mujtahids*; the outstanding *mujtahids*, or ayatollahs; and the *marja' al-taqlid*, the "source of emulation." This latter, the supreme authority, consisted of one or sometimes several of the most prestigious and educated Shi'ite legal scholars, who also carried the title "grand ayatollah" (*ayatollah ozma*).[149]

How strongly were these various groups represented within the clergy? Hooglund estimates that the clergy in Iran in the 1960s and 1970s totaled approximately 150,000 to 180,000.[150] About 100,000 of them were men (with a few women) who had received little or no theological education and exercised their religious activities to a considerable extent as a second profession. They fulfilled a variety of religious functions, above all in the poorest rural regions and urban districts, and represented a kind of "deputy mullah." Not the least of their activities involved engaging in the kind of folk religious practices no longer deemed acceptable by the educated clergy.

Alongside these were the mullahs; Hooglund estimates their number roughly at 14,000 to 44,000. They lived primarily from their religious activities, but enjoyed neither official recognition nor long-standing ties to institutions. In the main they were probably active as preachers. Hooglund describes the remaining 36,000 clerics as students in the institutions of higher religious education and professional mullahs and legal scholars. Students in the *madrasas* were required to complete a minimum of five years of education, characterized by various levels of academic achievement. Hooglund estimates their number at more than 21,000. They represented a significant share of the occasional preachers who were important in the dissemination of Khomeini's ideas. The remaining 15,000 clerics were professional mullahs accounted for in the statistics; of these about one hundred bore the title of ayatollah in the 1970s and six of grand ayatollah.

Given this heterogeneous composition, the chances of any particular cleric exercising political influence varied widely. With the exception of popular preachers only the narrow stratum of *mujtahids,* the legal scholars, had any real opportunity to influence a large number of people for any length of time. For every Shi'ite was obligated to select a *mujtahid,* whose decisions he or she was obligated to follow in religious-legal matters. As a rule the dominant criterion in such a selection was religious education and the legal scholar's conduct of life. There exists in Shi'ism no charisma of office. The power of an individual cleric is inextricably bound up with his personal prestige, which is equally based on legal expertise and model piety and righteousness. Prestige in this sense leads to the development of clientelist relationships and thus to the allocation of resources, which, in turn, form the basis for political power. Only the upper reaches of the clergy, in the traditional Iranian system, are part of the political elite. And up to the death of Borujerdi in 1961, their objections to legislation were respected, even by the last shah. Since 1961, however, the clergy's power has been primarily in their capacity to organize mass protest, such as demonstrations and closings of the bazaar.

In view of the clergy's internal differentiation, we must now examine its political consequences, if indeed there were any. More concretely, we need to delineate the political factions existing within the clergy and identify those belonging to the fundamentalist camp. Ashraf distinguished within the upper Shi'ite clergy two factions, one that was more likely to be allied with large landholders and another that tended more to speak for the bazaar middle class. Akhavi, in contrast, identifies four groups: first, the radicals surrounding Khomeini (fundamentalists), whose goal was the establishment of a hierocratically dominated order; second, social reformers, among whom Akhavi counts both reformers of religious institutions (Mutahhari) and sympathizers among the clergy of lay social revolutionaries (Shariati); third, conservatives in the tradition of Borujerdi (Shariatmadari, Milani, and others), who were more concerned with tending religious institutions and only rarely made political declarations (even then, they did not mobilize the masses but sought to influence the shah or his elite representatives directly); and fourth, those clerics who were well disposed toward the regime. This breakdown clearly demonstrates that the clergy in these years was scarcely less split than Iranian society as a whole. At the same time, it shows how closely the selection of a *mujtahid* or *marja' al-taqlid* was connected to one's own political stance.[151]

The dominant faction consisted of conservatives who were either officially neutral toward the shah's modernization policy in the period since 1962, but rejected it in private, or who distanced themselves cautiously from the policy in public. Only a minority freely criticized the regime or even took part in demonstrations.

An attempt to interpret the various political positions according to class or stratum has been made, thus far, only by Hooglund. He expresses the suspicion, based, to be sure, only on incomplete data, that it was primarily the lower-level clergy, that is, the preachers and the students of the *madrasas,* who lent the most unqualified support to Khomeini. Theology students obviously were prominent in the protests of both 1963 and 1978–1979, and the preachers contributed considerably to the dissemination of fundamentalist thought. Within the stratum of ayatollahs, however, fundamentalism found little resonance, and among the six grand ayatollahs the five who equaled Khomeini's legal scholarship rejected his political interpretation of Islam.[152]

Of greatest interest in the present context are investigations of the social origins of the lower clergy. Hooglund's comparison of two samples of theology students in Shiraz and Tehran indicates that approximately

50 percent of them came from the countryside and 24–30 percent from modest social conditions (peasants, workers, petite bourgeoisie). For them a religious career was bound up with hopes of upward social mobility, which, however, were destined for disappointment because of both the widespread disdain for uneducated clerics in the cities and the anticlerical policy of the shah. The dominance of both the middle and lower clergy as well as students in theological seminaries has also been confirmed by Shaul Bakhash's study of the spread of Khomeini's ideas through pamphlets and audio cassettes.[153]

Undoubtedly, the clergy was the driving force in the fundamentalist movement in Iran, but it is equally clear that they would not have been successful without the support of the bazaar. What, then, were the causes of the politicization and organization of parts of the clergy in opposition to the policy of the shah's regime? Hamid Algar has advanced the thesis that their oppositional attitude was inherent in the self-concept and tradition of the Shi'ite clergy. The clergy, in this argument, existed in constant tension with the limited legitimacy of the monarchy because of its supervisory role during the absence of the Imam Mahdi. This contention, however, is not supported empirically as Floor has shown, but even if it were true, it would be of little help in explaining the fundamentalist movement since 1961.[154]

In the relationship between the clergy and the monarchy it is, in fact, possible to identify phases of opposition and support, as well as quietistic retreat from politics. All three positions can be easily justified theologically. The first dramatizes the necessity of defending the just order against injustice and tyranny; the second affirms the divinely ordained monarchy as the "shadow of God"; and the third emphasizes the futility of human deeds and insists on awaiting the return of the imam. To derive the clergy's fundamentalism from the logic of a religious idea would be in this case a hopeless endeavor.[155]

The clergy in Iran did indeed oppose the Qajar monarchy in both the tobacco protest of 1891–1892 and the Constitutional Revolution of 1906. At the same time, however, they contributed substantially to the preservation of the institution when they pressured Reza Khan to continue the monarchy in 1926, rather than establish a republic according to the Turkish model. Under Mosaddeq the upper clergy remained largely quietistic, although a few younger clerics supported him. Out of fear of the left, however, they then encouraged the fall of Mosaddeq and the return of the last shah from exile.

Aside from external events, the internal organizational structure of

the clergy itself greatly influenced its mobilization. Because of the hierarchy of the Shi'ite clergy, its role in politics depended strongly on its
highest representative or, as the case may be, representatives. If the
leadership tended toward quietism, then the bulk of the middle and
lower clergy would be more likely to stay out of politics. Moreover, the
political engagement of the *ulama* depended heavily on encouragement
from the classes of landholders and bazaaris on whom they primarily
relied for their support. And, finally, the various degrees to which those
in power exercised a policy of intimidation had an important role.

As described above, the clergy suffered a considerable loss in prestige
as early as the rule of Reza Shah (1925–1941): religious institutions
were subjected to state regulation and control; Islamic law was replaced
by a new civil law; the juridical functions of the clergy were taken over
by state civil servants; and the system of religious education was increasingly supplanted by secular schooling. Nevertheless, a significant opposition involving the participation of the clergy did not arise during those
years.[156]

In the period from the "White Revolution" to the Islamic Revolution
as well the highest-ranking clergy refrained from political involvement
and from actively supporting Khomeini's radical opposition. That
might have had to do with their reluctance to push the conflict with the
regime to the point of endangering religious institutions in general. Or,
perhaps, their privileged position encouraged them to maintain a distance from daily politics.

The primary carriers of fundamentalism among the clergy were clerics of middle and lower status with ties to the bazaar and students of the
madrasas. As to the clergy, the severe effects they suffered because of the
cultural and economic marginalization of the bazaar probably explains
their particular susceptibility to politicization, a circumstance we will
return to later. Among theology students, a high percentage of whom
came from a rural milieu, the disappointment of their chances for upward mobility, alongside a conflict of values, certainly contributed to
their radicalization. With the decline in the significance of religious
education in comparison with modern secular knowledge and the general loss in prestige on the part of the clergy, a religious career was no
longer a vehicle for talented young people from modest circumstances
to better themselves socially.

The Bazaar   The literature is unanimous in naming the bazaar, also
termed the traditional middle class or the petite bourgeoisie, as the

second major group of carriers of fundamentalism.[157] The extent to which this is accurate will be discussed below. The bazaar as the traditional economic center differed from the modern economic sector in that it continued, and continues even today, to deal predominantly in domestic goods. In the bazaar the agricultural and industrial products from the urban environs were sold or further processed or both. In terms of class, that is, according to its relationship to the production process, the bazaar can be regarded as a relatively homogeneous unit of independent merchants and artisans. These in turn provided work for a small number of employees, who were often family members or other relatives.[158] Further constituents of the bazaar complex included moneylenders (who can also be assigned to the middle class) and also workers, porters, and employed artisans and sales personnel.

An income analysis of the various groups making up the bazaar yields a much more heterogeneous picture. They ranged from wealthy merchants to porters, from dealers in expensive cloths to tanners, from goldsmiths and moneylenders to butchers; thus, according to sociological criteria, from the upper-middle down to the lower class. More interesting than these imposed categories is the status differentiation within the bazaar itself. For this differentiation expresses the ideals and values of the bazaar and structures its social interaction, like commercial relationships, membership in associations, shared leisure activities, intermarriages, and so forth.

Status differentiation among the various occupational groups is marked first of all by religious criteria. In the narrow sense only adherents of Islam are part of the bazaar milieu. Jews and Christians are present in the bazaars, of course, to carry out the activities prohibited or frowned upon by Islam. Thus in the Tehran bazaar, for example, Armenian Christians were specialized in the manufacture and sale of musical instruments; the moneylenders and gold- and silversmiths were Jews. Christians as well as Jews dominated the production and sale of alcoholic beverages.[159] Yet both groups were excluded on religious grounds from the social clubs, from marriage, and from the (nearly exclusively religious) elaboration and practice of leisure-time activities. They were tolerated outsiders, with whom believers interacted in the economic but not, as a rule, the social sphere.

Among the occupations legitimized by Islam, status differentiation was based on the degree of or proximity to manual labor, income, and the value and purity of the materials involved. There was a fundamental separation between manual and nonmanual activities. A wealthy merchant, because of his relative proximity to manual work, lagged behind the large landholder in prestige, even if the former disposed over greater wealth than the latter. Within the bazaar the same criterion created a principled distinction between merchants and artisans. Big merchants, particularly those in import-export trade, enjoyed the greatest prestige. Other retailers and shopkeepers were ranged below them, after which came the artisans, graduated by income and the prestige of the goods they dealt in and the materials they processed.[160]

The bazaar was also heterogeneous in the educational levels of its constituents. Moreover, it had gone through generational change. Traditionally, the bazaar had been unanimous in the view that education and culture were in the hands of the clergy, and the substance of what the latter conveyed, alongside the skills of reading, arithmetic, and so forth, was primarily Islamic ethics. From the village schools to the city schools in the bazaar up to the *madrasas*, the educational status varied according to the relative levels of depth and intensity of knowledge. This relative homogeneity had been increasingly modified in recent decades by the introduction and expansion of secular educational institutions.

The older generation of bazaaris had grown up nearly exclusively inside the religious educational system, but considerable numbers of their children and grandchildren learned mathematics and natural science, history and foreign languages, and some even studied at universities in Iran, France, Germany, or the United States. Although the bazaar and the clergy had been involved much less than other social groups in the modern, secular educational system, there nevertheless arose a split within the bazaar milieu. The older generation of bazaaris had been formed to a substantial degree by traditional education, which closely conformed to its conduct of life.

The younger generation, in contrast, possessed an at least rudimentary secular education. This, in interaction with the experience of cultural change in the city, left its mark. The sociocultural differentiation of Iranian society into modern and traditional sectors split not only the clergy into numerous factions but also the bazaar. Some of the younger generation sought careers outside the bazaar, and many of them broke with its traditional values. A central experience of the retailers and artisans was thus generational conflict.[161]

The bazaar's opportunities to wield political influence have also been subject to historical processes of transformation. Traditionally, access to positions of political power depended directly on wealth, which was based nearly exclusively on the ownership of land. Those who possessed landed property and, therefore, money were able to purchase offices, which, in turn, secured and increased revenues. And those who successfully rose into the political elite acquired land to stabilize their income. Thus has the political elite in Iran, well into the twentieth century, been composed predominantly of large landholders.

In the course of the twentieth century, but especially after the "White Revolution" of the early 1960s, this recruiting mechanism underwent change. With land reform and the policies of industrialization and urbanization, for one thing, there came a diversification of the preconditions for and acquisition of wealth. Large landholders, who had been partially dispossessed of their property, and the nouveau riche invested in state enterprises, urban real estate, buildings and apartment houses, and foreign securities. Second, with the intensification of the modernization policy, Westernized education increasingly became the decisive criterion for access to positions of political power and thus upward social mobility in general. For, in comparison with the private economic sector, which the government held in check, the state employed 80.7 percent of the most highly educated Iranians.[162] At the same time, the government controlled access to the modern educational system by fixing educational fees, curriculum, and textbooks; by controlling the education of teachers; and by establishing state schools or certifying private ones. Simultaneously, the religious educational system was fully marginalized.

The ruling elite went about structuring access to the modern educational system, and thus to political power, so that their children had the best chances of advancing into favorable positions. Thus people in rural areas were all but excluded de facto from higher education, in that scarcely any institutions of secondary education were established there. In the cities the poorer classes were excluded from higher education by the burdens of tuition and the costs of textbooks, uniforms, and so forth. Moreover, entrance into institutions of higher education was channeled through a system of state-controlled examinations, with the result that the existing elite was able to maintain its privileged position.

This limited access meant that the children of only the most affluent merchants of the bazaar had a chance to improve their social status and rise to positions of power through modern education. The participation of the children of merchants and artisans has been correspondingly small compared with that of children from families of large landholders, upper civil servants, and big merchants.

As suggested at the outset, the literature identifies the bazaar as the most important component of fundamentalist protest, at the same time characterizing it as a traditionalist middle class or petite bourgeoisie. As we have seen, its social composition was substantially more complex, although merchants and artisans did form the core of the Islamic-traditionalist bazaar milieu. However, despite the bazaar's middle to lower social ranking in terms of income, access to power, and occupational prestige, it enjoyed, at least in its own self-conception, the distinction of being the model for the pious life. In this, shared values and norms enabled the bazaar to act as a collective, despite its internal economic and social differentiation. And its close reciprocal connections with the clergy contributed to the acceptance of religious regulation, as well as to a legitimation of its way of life.

This specifically "pious" way of life was reflected primarily in four areas: first, the fulfillment of the general Islamic codex of obligations (prayers, fasts, alms, pilgrimages); second, the regulation of occupational life according to the dictates of the Koran (economic morality) and the subordination of the former to general religious prescriptions concerning the conduct of life; third, the religious regulation of leisure-time activities (religious associations, pilgrimages, commemorations of the death of Imam Hussein); and finally, close social and economic interrelations with the clergy (kinship, friendship, clientelist relationships, donations).

Moreover, these close ties between the bazaar and a "pious" way of life were manifest architecturally in the central location of mosques and *madrasas* within the bazaar complex. I will treat these mechanisms of integration on the part of the traditional milieu in more detail below.

Urban Migrants and the Lower Urban Strata   In the literature the urban lower strata, also designated the subproletariat, are often counted as significant carriers of fundamentalism. Moreover, there frequently arises the impression that the subproletariat and the class of urban migrants were essentially identical. This view requires correction. Thus Kazemi, referring to Tehran, distinguishes three groups of urban migrants. The first group consisted of members of the upper-middle class who had moved to Tehran from other Iranian cities to enhance their participation in economic development and improve future opportunities for their children. The second group consisted of members of the lower-middle class with artisan skills, which allowed them to gain a footing in Tehran and establish for themselves a modest but secure livelihood. They, like the first group, were subject to the "pull effect" of Tehran. The third group, finally, was subject to the "push effect," that is, because of poor conditions in the countryside, they were driven by need, in the truest sense of the word, to migrate.[163]

This third group of urban migrants formed the lowest class, though it is possible to identify two major settlement patterns, which obviously depended in part on preexisting economic and educational attributes and in part on the presence of social relationships. One group settled in the slums of the city, the second in provisional shantytowns.

Inhabitants of the shantytowns, usually erected illegally on the edge of the city, were primarily those who had just migrated from the countryside, a group recruited from small peasants, tenants, rural workers, and nomads. They lacked regular employment as a rule and lived from occasional jobs, street dealing, and so forth. A move to the slums for them was already an indicator of social betterment. The slum dwellers were typically urban migrants successful in finding work from which they derived a small but regular income. For newcomers this was usually possible only with the help of relatives or friends who had already gained a footing in the city.

The inclusion of the urban lower classes among the carriers of the fundamentalist movement in Iran is recent. In any case, they took no notable part in the demonstrations of the early 1960s. As was seen in the analysis of fundamentalist ideology, the urban poor nevertheless were important in the writings and speeches of Khomeini. With repeated reference to miserable living conditions especially in the southern part of Tehran, which he contrasted with the extravagance of the rich and the courtly celebrations of the coronation ceremony (1967) and the 2,500th anniversary festival, Khomeini disputed the legitimacy of the monarchy.

The participation of the urban poor in the fundamentalist movement was largely a product of the late 1970s and, in intensified form, a postrevolutionary development. There is even some evidence that the postrevolutionary support of Khomeini by the urban poor led to an overestimation of their role in the prerevolutionary period. Kazemi does report a series of demonstrations and disturbances in the poorer residential districts but shows that only a small part of the urban poor was subject to any significant political mobilization. The inhabitants of the shanties were scarcely involved at all in political activities. Among the slum dwellers the factory workers were most readily politicized because of their relatively high degree of organization at the workplace. Insofar, therefore, as it is possible to speak of the urban poor's participation in the revolution, it was clearly less an original contribution than a quite late involvement in a process that had already been under way for some time.[164]

To what extent, then, can these urban poor be characterized as adhering to fundamentalism? They were not involved in the protests of the fundamentalist camp against the "White Revolution" and appeared only to a modest degree and in a subordinate role in the demonstrations and disturbances of the late 1970s. Since the revolution, however, they have represented one of the supports of the fundamentalist wing of the Iranian revolution. How is this apparent contradiction to be explained?

My thesis is that the fundamentalism of the lower classes, in particular of the urban migrants, was of a different sort than the fundamentalism of the traditional middle class. The fundamentalism of the lower classes was, in nearly all cases, strongly charismatic. It was centered around magical notions, holy persons, and individual crises. This is related to a series of factors, such as the migrants' peasant background, the lack of religious regulation of peasant, proletarian, and subproletarian employment, and the actual situation of the lower classes in an alien social environment, which they can neither understand nor control. In their case an active rationalization of their way of life based on values had a smaller chance of being realized than a flexible strategy of survival adapted to actual conditions. It was, therefore, less rural religious notions that encouraged the charismatism of the lower classes than the continuity of the experience of living in an incomprehensible and uncontrollable world.

The fundamentalism of the bazaar milieu and the middle classes that lent it form was, in contrast, primarily rational. Admittedly, it also had charismatic and magical elements. Thus the memorialization and reexperience of Hussein's suffering in the religious readings or self-flagellation in the Ashura processions represented popular charismatic religious traditions. And in daily life in the bazaar a multitude of superstitious and magical practices had been retained. Nevertheless, Islamic traditionalism represented in the first instance an ethical regulation of the entire conduct of life. The clergy—above all, of course, the *mujtahids*—emphasized this rational side exclusively and even attempted to use "acceptable" charismatic elements to motivate and provide a model for ethical, value-rational action.

The way in which the lower classes participated in pre- and postrevolutionary processes and their veneration of Khomeini as a saint, or even as Imam Mahdi returned from his concealment, clearly demonstrated the charismatic-magical character of their fundamentalism. This assessment was also confirmed by the dramatic scenes of mourning following the death of Khomeini. In my opinion Khomeini recognized the particularity of the fundamentalism of the lower classes and formed his strategy accordingly. He not only referred occasionally to the miserable living conditions of the lower classes but also took a stand in favor of using the popular religious, charismatic elements present in the veneration of Hussein to politicize the masses. At the same time, however, as Hans Kippenberg has suggested, he also attempted to reinterpret the symbolism of Ashura and Kerbala in terms of its ethical-rational content.[165]

"Border Crossers" between the Milieus   In addition to the main carriers of fundamentalism—the clergy, the bazaar, and the subproletariat—Khomeini's teachings and charisma also attracted other people. These people can be designated "border crossers" between the traditional and the modern milieus. Two groups especially are relevant: youths and white-collar employees.

Many of Khomeini's young followers came from the traditionalist milieu (bazaar, small town, rural areas) but had received a modern secular education. Their education alienated them from the milieu of their origins, but their predominantly traditional values distinguishes them from the modern, Western milieu.[166] The same applies to a segment of state white-collar employees, in particular those in the lower service grades. Because of their education and as a part of the modern bureaucracy, they were alienated from the traditional religious milieu and the target of its disdain. They may have profited from corruption because of their occupations, but only to a limited degree; moreover, they were exposed to unfamiliar organizational patterns and arrogant superiors, seeing perhaps for the first time the whole extent of bureaucratic corruption and disorganization, cliquey set ups, and foreign intervention.

Along with their professional ambivalence they often had other negative experiences. Thus, for example, they could not as a rule afford the rents in the modern part of Tehran, which had risen astronomically primarily because of the presence of a multitude of foreign experts and businesspeople, and lived as before close to the traditional old city. In their private lives they frequently had difficulty coming to terms with the extremely rapid changes in the role of women and sexual morality. As "modern" as they may have been in many respects, they were still traditional when it came to their image of women.

Positioned thus in a kind of limbo, both groups sought to interpret their situation and reconcile traditional and modern values and ideals.

To people in this predicament the traditionalist mullahs were of no help, but the politically activist reinterpretation of traditionalism by Khomeini or the re-creation of tradition by Shariati undoubtedly offered an anchor. Both models overcame the conflict between modern education and traditional values, proffered both an individual and a collective cultural and national identity, and recaptured pride, self-confidence, and a sense of honor. Shariati's vision of a social revolutionary Islam appealed more strongly to the college-educated youth; Khomeini's politicized traditionalism was more likely to reach the "little people," such as those employed in the modern sector or youth in the bazaar.

MECHANISMS OF INTEGRATION IN THE TRADITIONALIST MILIEU

Social movements do not involve isolated individuals but people with previously existing associations.[167] This generalization applies as well to Shi'ite fundamentalism. The bazaar, with its religious associations, economic relationships, kinship and friendship ties, and its homogeneous values and ideals of life conduct, supplied the basis for fundamentalism in Iran. This milieu integrated merchants, artisans and urban migrants and preachers, scholars, and students in the *madrasas* in a complex network of social relations.

The integration of the milieu was the result not only of shared ideas of order but also of an agreement on the practices of daily life, such as conventions or habitual consumer or leisure-time behavior. In what follows I address briefly the mechanisms of integration in the traditionalist Shi'ite milieu, on the basis of which Khomeini's fundamentalism was able to arise: religious gatherings and celebrations, and economic and kinship relationships, which were often intensified by ties of neighborhood, place of origin, or friendship.

Among the numerous religious gatherings, two types were dominant in particular. One was based on membership in a professional group ("guild") in the bazaar, the other on membership in a residential community. Among the urban lower strata, there was yet another type of religious gathering, based on common ethnic or geographical heritage.[168]

Religious gatherings were not entertained by organizations, such as the guilds, but exclusively by pious individuals who made their houses or apartments available for such purposes. The gatherings took place weekly on a set day, usually alternating among places supplied by the various participants. They began at sundown and lasted several hours.

The readings, delivered by a low-ranking cleric, revolved around the lives and suffering of the imams, above all, the massacre at Kerbala and the martyrdom of Imam Hussein. Once the readings were concluded, personal, business, or social affairs were discussed.

As a rule among the bazaar merchants and artisans, everyone belonged to at least two religious associations, one professional and one residential. Beyond this, the gatherings were also interconnected with one another, so that the system of religious associations formed a loose network beyond neighborhood and class boundaries.[169]

These two elements, the professional and the residential (apparently identical with mosque membership), in addition to those of religious adherence to a particular *mujtahid* and nonreligious clientelist relationships, formed the foundations for the organization and supervision of the parades on the occasion of the most important religious events in Shi'ism, the Ashura processions. Processions as well as the passion plays were financed in the main by bazaar merchants and artisans and also frequently took place in the bazaar.[170]

Ashura processions centered on the theme of Hussein and were full of symbols referring to the massacre at Kerbala. They were accompanied by self-flagellation with swords, knives, or chains. Religious celebrations, therefore, dramatized essentially the same social relationships as the religious associations. And, here as well, mourning for Hussein and the demonstration of individual readiness for self-sacrifice formed the paradigm.

Religious associations and processions integrated the bazaar and the lower strata outside the bazaar not only with one another but also with the lower clergy, the prayer leaders in the mosques, and the preachers and reciters in the gatherings. The higher clergy made up of legal scholars, the *mujtahids,* rejected pictorial representations for the Ashura processions and the passion plays (*ta'zieh*) as well as self-flagellation.[171] In addition to these associations and celebrations other religious relationships, such as attendance at the same mosque, daily public prayers, pilgrimages, funerals, and redemptions of votive offerings, served to integrate the traditional bazaar milieu. In many cases the bazaar was also the site of those religious activities.[172]

The integration of the bazaar was further based on economic relationships. The first of these, as has already been mentioned, were the guilds or professional associations. Although originally created by the state to facilitate taxation through collective liability, they nevertheless had forged close ties among the members of an occupation. Collective liability for taxes intensified the association between members and led to the institutionalization of mutual emergency assistance in matters extending beyond taxation, as Thaiss reports in reference to the religious associations based on guild membership.[173]

Additional economic networks existed among wholesalers and retailers. The shortage of capital meant that individual merchants could afford scarcely any surplus inventory. They were therefore required to replenish supplies from the wholesaler regularly, in some cases several times a day. This led to the creation of "location-specific associative ties" within the bazaar, such as also existed in handicrafts between production and sale.[174] In addition, clientelist relationships arose as well between wholesalers and retailers based on credit purchases.

As retailers were associated with wholesalers, on the one hand, and with producing artisans, on the other, so were their customers bound associatively with them. Although in earlier times the bazaar had offered a comprehensive supply of goods for all social classes, it had developed into an economic center primarily for middle- and lower-class shoppers; the upper-middle and upper classes increasingly took their business to the newly established modern shopping districts.[175] This intensified the separation between the modern, Western and the traditionalist-Islamic milieu and thus reinforced milieu consciousness.

Most significant for the integration of the milieu, however, were the economic relationships between the bazaar and the clergy. Thus merchants and artisans were essentially responsible for the livelihood of the clergy to which they were associated, and they paid them for their religious services. In addition, they financed religious institutions; made donations, for example, for the construction of a new mosque or *madrasa;* paid their religious taxes; and, occasionally, even made additional money donations to their *mujtahid.*[176]

Yet these economic relationships were by no means one-sided. Thus were the bazaaris partly dependent on religious institutions. Many bazaar buildings belonged to religious endowments, to which rent had to be paid.[177] And the clergy aided bazaaris who got into trouble by putting at their disposal part of the religious taxes of another bazaari upon the latter's request.[178]

Kinship relationships represented a third source of integration in the traditionalist milieu. A notable share of the Shi'ite clergy in Iran was characterized, on the one hand, by internal kinship relationships and, on the other, by kinship relationships with the bazaar. Big merchants, following other clerics, constituted the group with the strongest kinship ties to the highest clergy.[179] A large share of theology students in the *madrasas,* as well as the middle and lower ranks of the clergy, came from rural areas or small towns, often belonging to families of the lower-middle stratum, that is, small merchant and artisan families.[180]

The bazaar, too, was made up of an extensive network of kinship relationships. There persists to the present day a marked preference for marriages within the bazaar, one strictly observed among the small merchants in particular.[181] In addition to kinship ties, relationships based on friendship and neighborhood, in part encouraged by common socialization, represented a further aspect of integration.

In earlier times the only source of education for bazaar members and the lower clergy were religious schools under the clergy's direction. Yet Marvin Zonis has demonstrated that even in more recent times "both groups have consistently failed to participate in the formal, Western, modern educational system in anywhere near the proportions of other groups in society."[182] The dominance of religious education applied especially to the mass of urban migrants from rural areas, in which the mullahs continued to head the village schools. Their integration in the traditionalist urban milieu was considerably facilitated by this common education and by shared values and ideals regarding the conduct of life. A further characteristic of this education was its ignorance of foreign languages and cultures, which made it particularly susceptible to xenophobia. As Zonis has shown, knowledge of foreign languages and travel in non-Islamic countries were experiences of the elite, not of the bazaar, particularly in the older generation.[183]

Khomeini was able to use these mechanisms of integration in the traditional milieu to mobilize the masses with his fundamentalist version of Shi'ite Islam. Of course, he was not followed by the entire bazaar, and even those who supported him for a time were not all fundamentalists or even "temporary fundamentalists." Many remained traditionalistic, guided by a basic model of social protest that they neither expected nor hoped to see transformed into hierocratic rule. For, despite their piety, bazaaris remained businesspeople, with no interest in subordinating the economy to ideological concerns, in the tutelage of the clergy, or in the ruination of the economy by a missionary foreign policy. But it is probably a characteristic of successful social movements that, in the end, parts of the carriers will not have "wanted" the results, leaving some groups to speak of a "betrayal" of the revolution after it is over.[184]

THE CAUSES OF SHI'ITE FUNDAMENTALIST MOBILIZATION

The analysis of the carriers of Shi'ite fundamentalism has shown that at its core was the mobilized traditionalist milieu, which was characterized in essence by an alliance between the clergy and the bazaar. This is not particularly surprising, but corresponds to a basic pattern of mass political protest in Iran for more than a century now.[185] Yet, as we have seen, fundamentalism did not represent all the partial groupings within the milieu to the same degree, and it cannot be reduced to this milieu. For it also appealed to parts of the new middle class and to lower-class urban migrants. On the basis of the preceding analyses of the carriers and the ideology, I will now turn in conclusion to the question of which processes of social change were primarily responsible for prompting the transformation of traditionalism into fundamentalism.

An investigation of the structural change occurring in Iran in the 1960s and 1970s makes it possible to identify changes in all social spheres that affected the carriers of fundamentalism in a specific way and that were thematized, either explicitly or implicitly, in the fundamentalist critique of society. Sociocultural differentiation in the cities, cultural transformations within the bazaar milieu, and general political structural and value transformations all contributed to the overall process of change. Because each of these developments was concentrated with particular intensity, speed, and drama in the capital city of Tehran, I investigate the causes of mobilization there, offering first of all a brief overview of developments up to the beginning of the 1960s.[186]

The formation of a modern Western countermilieu to the traditionalist milieu was indeed already under way at the time of the Qajar dynasty in the nineteenth century but was considerably intensified with the rule of Shah Reza Pahlavi and the introduction of his modernization policy. Under his rule the Western orientation of the upper class was completed. Through his creation of a modern military and administrative apparatus a new middle class arose. The upper and new middle classes moved in increasing numbers away from the old city to the north, where new residential districts and lavish suburbs were being built. The first business streets on a Western model outside the bazaar likewise appeared there. This marked the beginning of the development of Tehran as a "dual" city.

The dualism concept is not meant to imply that relations between the traditionalist and the modern sectors were always hostile, that there were no relationships of a social, political, cultural, or economic nature, or that there were no paths of transition between the two sectors. The concept refers more to the rise of two urban areas that were distinct in principle concerning their ideal social relations within the family, politics and economics, and their general conduct.

The Western center was rebuilt in the postwar period, forming a modern counterbalance to the bazaar. Westernization then continued at a rapid pace in particular beginning in the 1950s, with the construction of a new Western center with modern major business streets. The first Western center gradually deteriorated, but the new business district expanded vigorously beginning in the early 1960s.[187] This development in Iran represented fertile soil for the rise of a fundamentalist mass movement in the 1960s and 1970s and was, in a certain way, the extreme version of a trend that can be found in all the cities of Iran and the Middle East in varying degrees and tempos.[188] The transformation of the cities had cultural, political, and economic implications for the traditional milieu, to which I now will turn.

The Cultural Polarization of Tehran   In terms of culture the development of Tehran as a dual city signified a spatial separation between social classes and milieus with different values and ideals of life conduct. The upper and modern middle classes, in particular, left the old city and moved to residential districts and suburbs farther north. The traditionalist middle and lower classes continued to live in the old city and the adjacent southern part of Tehran. This process was certainly determined in part by economic factors, for the rents in the new Western residential districts were beyond the reach of the lower-middle and lower strata. In addition, however, the cultural-religious dimension was important. Central values, such as the separation of men's and women's spheres, the isolation of women from strangers, and the integration of religion and the economy, of bazaar and mosque, were hardly practicable under Western architectural conditions. Only an orientation to new ideals of life conduct led to the acceptance of Western architecture, which, indeed, structured and symbolized modern social relationships.

The division of Tehran into two sociocultural milieus was quite clearly manifest in educational levels, the participation of women in employment, and the consumer and leisure-time behavior of the populations in the respective residential districts. Table 4 gives a comparison of residents' education in the old city and the Westernized part. These ratios are founded partially in the structure of the economy. The chil-

TABLE 4.
EDUCATIONAL LEVEL IN TEHRAN

	Old City	Western City
Literacy		
Age 6 and above	57.0%	80.0%
School attendance		
Age 10	86.0%	94.0%
Age 14	68.0%	83.0%
Age 20	16.0%	43.0%
University qualified	3.8%	13.3%
University attendance	0.9%	6.3%

SOURCE: Seger 1978, 56–65; percentages, 60.

dren of small merchants, artisans, and petty entrepreneurs often had to help out in the family business and thus were unable to attend school regularly, to say nothing of ascending to higher educational levels.

Regarding professional activity on the part of women, there was also a clear decline in the figures from the modern north to the traditionalist south of Tehran.[189] Only 10.1 percent of all women were employed in the period under investigation, with the majority in the service sector (72 percent) primarily as domestic workers and sales personnel in the modern stores, where the employment of women at all stands in sharp contrast to the bazaar. Thirty-two percent of working women were employed in state services. Women from the traditionalist milieu were less likely to be working, partly because of their lack of education and partly because of the religious-cultural prejudices against female employment in the public sphere. Moreover, there was a surplus of male labor power precisely in the poorer districts.

Finally, the sharp polarization of the city was expressed with particular clarity in the significance of religion as a factor determining the shape of daily life, leisure time, and consumer habits. The strong influence of Islam on the traditional middle and lower classes was manifest in the distribution of religious structures, such as mosques, graves of the successors of the imams, and religious libraries. Sacred structures were largely absent in the Westernized districts, but they were found in the old city, in the southern districts, and also in the northeastern suburbs, which were relatively recently settled by members of the poorer classes.

The difference between the modern and traditional Tehran was also evident in the distribution of traditional snack shops, bathhouses, and athletic facilities (*zurkhaneh*) and that of modern fast-food restaurants, swimming pools, and tennis courts.[190] Comparisons of this sort can be multiplied at will. All of them document the impact of cultural orientation in the division of Tehran into a city stamped by two milieus, a traditionalist milieu and a modern, Western countermilieu.

What, then, were the effects of this sociocultural differentiation on the traditionalist milieu? One was an enormous loss in prestige. The model conduct of life of the bazaar, which had been traditionally regarded as the refuge of piety, was no longer recognized and was demonstratively disdained or even made to appear ridiculous by a part of the population that had adopted more Western ways. The consumption of alcohol, gambling, theater and cinema, a changed sexual morality, and a profound break with traditional ideas concerning the social position of women all demonstrated to the bazaar milieu that it had lost its previous function as a cultural model. The rise of the modernized milieu in itself confronted the traditionalist milieu with a heightened sense of its otherness. And to that was added the role of the state, which unambiguously encouraged the modernized sector and presented it as a new model. In the competition for prestige between the two milieus the state was not neutral. Thus both sociocultural differentiation and state institutions created the basis for the delegitimization of the modern middle and upper strata from the traditionalist perspective.

Cultural Differentiation within the Bazaar   The values and life conduct ideals, the leisure-time and consumer habits, of the modernized milieu were not confined in their impact to the modern sector of Tehran but penetrated the traditionalist milieu in various ways. Gustav Thaiss has illustrated this effect in an example of a marriage between the son and daughter of two bazaar merchants. The religious-cultural divergence among the members of the two families made it necessary to hold two receptions. At one, alcoholic drinks were served and music was played. Men and women danced with each other, and women wore miniskirts. At the other, men and women sat in different rooms, the women wore veils, and verses from the Koran were recited.[191] The fundamentalist critique of moral decline in society was thus not limited to the modern middle and upper classes but also referred to the cultural polarization taking place within the traditionalist milieu and frequently appearing in the form of a generational conflict.

We can identify four basic reactions by the bazaar milieu to the penetration of modern sociomorality and values: traditionalist isolation; modernist conformity; and both fundamentalist and social revolutionary reinterpretations of the Islamic tradition. For youth with modern schooling the traditionalist variant was largely ruled out because it was closely bound up with the knowledge acquired in religious schools and thus largely an affair of the older generation. Modernist conformity was certainly the rule in many cases, as was the fundamentalist countermovement in others. The social revolutionary variant, in contrast, was not as widespread in the bazaar milieu as it was in the universities.

Traditionalist withdrawal as well as modernist conformity both meant giving up long-term preservation of tradition. Fundamentalism, in contrast, actively defended traditionalist values and thus attempted to secure their reproduction. It was therefore an attempt at self-preservation by the traditionalist milieu against progressive extinction or gradual conformity; it was a protest against cultural alienation between the generations and between members of the same families. From this perspective fundamentalism represented a countermovement against the transformation of sociomoral ideas, not only in the part of the city oriented toward the West but also and precisely within the bazaar itself.

Transformations in Economic Structures and Values   The development of the second modern business district in particular had far-reaching effects on the structure of the bazaar. As long as the bazaar was still the economic center for all social classes, Tehran had been a city differentiated socially by neighborhood but not yet a polarized one. With the rise of the Western business district, high-priced consumption goods were no longer for sale in the bazaar. The wholesale trade in all upmarket domestic and foreign goods except rugs shifted to the northern part of the city. The bazaar experienced thereby a considerable loss in prestige, but the process of economic differentiation thus by no means led to bankruptcy or even to a clear decline of the retail trade and handicrafts. On the contrary, the steady increase in the population of poorer classes brought on by rapid urbanization increased the demand for goods offered at the bazaar, and it was able to consolidate and stabilize itself on a lower level.

Moreover, the modern and traditionalist economic sectors also became differentiated organizationally and ethically. Although personalistic-patriarchal organizational principles and the embeddedness of economic ethics in religion continued to dominate in the bazaar, depersonalized organizational structures and the removal of religious regulation of life conduct in general characterized the modern sector. This affected work schedules, the perception of work and leisure time, and the employment of women.[192] Thus the supermarket operated by hired employees appeared alongside the small, family-run shop in the bazaar, the large-scale bank alongside the moneylender, industrial manufacture alongside artisanal shops. This development may not, indeed, have led to the immediate economic ruin of the small operations, but it incited anxiety as to the viability of such livelihoods over the long term. At the same time, it contributed to alienation between the bazaar and the state and encouraged both xenophobia and nativism. For a major part of the modern economic sector was dominated by the state itself and by Iranian and foreign entrepreneurs enjoying privileges dispensed by the state.

Not only was there an open competition between the modern and traditional sectors, however, but the state itself increasingly joined in a direct struggle with the bazaar. This took the form of assaults on the bazaar's physical existence, such as the bulldozing of facilities, planned though only partially carried out; the architectural redesign and separation of the bazaar and mosques in Mashhad and Tehran; and the support and encouragement lent intentionally to the competition in the government's economic policy. As the shah wrote following his overthrow: "The bazaaris are a fanatic lot, highly resistant to change because their locations afford a lucrative monopoly. I could not stop building supermarkets. I wanted a modern country. Moving against the bazaar was typical of the political and social risks I had to take in my drive for modernization."[193]

In its most direct attack the newly founded state-run Resurrection party (Iran's only political party after the others were abolished) decreed a vexatious system of price controls in 1975, intended to dampen the high rate of inflation caused by unrestrained state expenditures and imports and bound up with further threats to the traditionalist milieu. The state initially targeted the wholesalers but then primarily individual merchants. Numerous minor merchants were executed, and countless numbers were ruined economically and deported. These steps did not, in fact, lead directly to an uprising by the bazaar, but they did do irreparable damage to the legitimacy of the regime.[194]

The bazaar was confronted not only with competition from modern economic organization and ethics but inside the bazaar from a new generation. For many younger bazaaris with a modern education were themselves carriers of the new ideas. Two typical sorts of conflict resulted, as Gustav Thaiss has reported. Some of the younger bazaaris forsook the traditional economic sector altogether to pursue professional opportunities in the modern sector or in state administration; "one of the numerous social consequences of this widening of opportunities [was] the increasing economic independence of sons which . . . had the corollary effect of reducing the power and authority of the father in the home."[195] Other younger bazaaris, in contrast, attempted to take over businesses from their fathers and reorganize them according to a modern economic point of view. This, in turn, frequently led to differences between fathers and sons over who had the power to make decisions concerning the business: "The father/son conflict which appears so evident in the bazaar in relation to commercial practices and decision-making is evidence of the growing gap between the older generation and the newer generation."[196]

The structural and value transformations in the economy were thus not confined to the modern sector of the city; rather, they penetrated the bazaar itself, often in the form of a generational conflict. Against these transformations fundamentalism represented an active defense of traditionalist economic organization and ethics, not only against external competition but also against its own internal disintegration. At the same time, it signified a strengthening of the patriarchal family structure and thus of paternal authority.

Transformation of Political Structures and Values   Recent Iranian history has witnessed two phases in which the formation of a modern bureaucratic national state was promoted. The first was begun by Reza Shah, who laid the foundations for a modern administrative apparatus in the period from 1925 to 1941. His son, Mohammed Reza Pahlavi, continued the process, especially in the 1960s and 1970s, by shifting the basis of his power from the large landholders to the bureaucratic apparatus and to the military and secret police.[197] That was where the bulk of educated youth went to pursue professional opportunities, not into the private sector. The structural and value transformations in politics had three effects that touched primarily on the traditionalist milieu of the bazaar and the clergy: a secularization of state institutions; a bureaucratization of the whole of economic life; and a diminution of the political influence of the bazaar and clergy.

With the death of Borujerdi in 1961 and the onset of the "White Revolution," the leaders of the Shi'ite clergy were essentially excluded from the Iranian elite. The members of the clergy that were identified with the regime enjoyed little respect and scarce support among the masses. With the polarization of Tehran, the rise of the new middle class in the government apparatus, and, finally, the founding of the state Resurrection party, the traditional channels of interest mediation and conflict regulation ceased to function between the bazaar and the clergy on the one hand and the court on the other.

The bazaar, with the exception perhaps of a few large wholesalers, had never had direct access to power. Nevertheless, channels of communication did exist through which it had been able to articulate its interests and grievances: the "guilds" and the clergy. The guilds clearly did not operate to represent the economic or political interests of the artisans and merchants organized in them but were obligatory corporations subject to collective liability, created by the state to facilitate the collection of taxes. Thus they had no political significance that would be even approximately comparable to that of their European counterparts. Nonetheless, the religious associations organized by the guilds constituted a forum in which their interests could be articulated and passed on to government officials, who would also be present at meetings. With the incorporation of the guilds into the state party, these rudimentary opportunities for exercising political influence were eliminated.[198]

A complex clientelist network existed between the bazaar and the clergy, however, which reached all the way up to the peaks of the hierocracy.[199] As long as the latter remained part of the elite and had influence over the court, the bazaar used it as a channel to have its interests heard. With the exclusion of the religious leaders from the elite, this possibility was no longer available. Thus the structural impoverishment, bound up with the polarization between state institutions and the traditionalist milieu of values and ideals of conduct, necessarily led to changes in the formation, articulation, and mediation of interests. It was all but unavoidable that public protest replace clientelist mediation.

The withdrawal of the highest-ranking clergy from the elite and the rise of the new middle class were part of a secularization process that, in its furthest extension, represented the de-Islamicization of Iranian national identity. Reza Pahlavi had already emphasized the pre-Islamic tradition in Iran. His son focused even more on the Achaemenidian foundation of his legitimacy, with his self-coronation, the celebration in Persepolis, and the replacement of the Islamic by an Achaemenidian calendar.[200] This de-Islamicization of national identity represented a symbolic exclusion of the traditionalist milieu from the collective bond of the "modern nation." At the same time, the bureaucracy forced the guilds to contribute "voluntarily" to this change by lending their financial support to the spectacles of 1967 and 1971.[201]

A further effect of the structural and value transformations of politics was the extension of the power and regulatory competence of the state bureaucracy. The traditional patrimonial bureaucracy had also possessed power and been corrupt. But both aspects were intensified in the semimodern, neopatrimonial bureaucracy. In addition, it combined in a particularly unfortunate way the disadvantages of both modern and patrimonial administration, for it was largely "modern" and depersonalized in its organizational structure but patrimonial in the "spirit" of those working within it. That meant, as a result, that its procedures become yet more unpredictable, but the level of corruption did not decline. It was more likely increased by the elevated consumer demands of the new middle class. To this was added the arrogance toward the traditionalist camp on the part of civil servants and employees with a modern education.

The State as Provocateur and the Timing of Mobilization   All of these processes of change contributed to the transformation of traditionalists into a fundamentalist opposition. Nevertheless, it is possible to identify as the decisive factor in the permanent alienation of broad classes from the shah's regime the establishment of a one-party system by the founding of the Resurrection party (Rastakhiz) in 1975. This step represented an attempt to transform the neopatrimonial dictatorship into a totalitarian system. Its two most important measures were an aggressive policy toward the traditionalist camp, above all, the bazaar and clergy, and an attempt at political mass mobilization of the population through forced membership in the party.[202]

The price controls mentioned above were part of the hostile policy toward the bazaar, as were the threat to tear down the bazaar and replace it with modern supermarkets, the support of the bazaar's economic competitors, and the dissolution of the guilds and their reformation as party suborganizations. The party was also blamed for the repeal of the Islamic calendar and an intensified enforcement of the Family Protection Law. The clergy was also threatened with the nationalization of their endowments and press. Clerics were supposed to have been recruited into SAVAK (the secret police), with those who cooperated generously provided for.

The clergy protested vigorously against the Resurrection party. Two opposition clerics were conspicuously murdered. Khomeini warned all

believers to beware of the party, which, he said, was bent on the destruction of Islam and the ruination of the country. The government responded by arresting large numbers of Khomeini's followers. The attempt to politicize the masses in the interests of the regime backfired as
well. Its practice of forcing people to take sides politically, to append their
signatures to proclamations, and to join the party provoked its own
opposition.[203]

The expansion of the fundamentalist base and the mass support lent
Khomeini by forces not categorizable as fundamentalist become understandable only against this background of political developments, the
goal of which, among others, was the liquidation of the traditionalist
milieu of the clergy and the bazaar. It is reasonable to surmise that the
policy of the Resurrection party toward the bazaar contributed to the
shift of power among the clergy toward the radical wing surrounding
Khomeini and its support by religious taxes.

Alongside the long-term structural change and the immediate threat
to the traditionalist milieu it is possible to see in the government's symbolic degradation and intentional provocation further factors of mobilization. As early as 1961, Mohammed Reza Pahlavi had altogether given
up attempts to pacify the religious camp, and had begun simply to
humiliate it whenever he could. It was precisely these symbolic acts,
however, that led to an eruption of all the stored-up frustrations resulting from the processes described above. Thus a provocative appearance
of the shah, in which he was contemptuous of the clergy as a whole,
preceded the protest demonstration of 1963. And the Islamic revolution
got under way in response to a slanderous article about Khomeini in an
official newspaper, which, as previously mentioned, accused him of being Indian by birth, of having worked for the British secret service, and
of having composed erotic Sufi poetry.[204] In response to the assaults by
police and military units, resulting in deaths among the demonstrators,
more memorial services for the dead were held—resulting in new demonstrations and new victims—which proceeded ever more strictly in accord with the religious rituals and symbols of Ashura processions.[205]

A summary of the various factors contributing to the mobilization of
Shi'ite fundamentalism reveals their roots in cultural, political, and economic change. Taking into account the fundamentalist critique of society, the most important factors were sociocultural polarization and the
penetration of Western ideas of the family, of relationships between the
sexes, and of sexual morality into Iranian society in general, but above
all into the traditionalist camp. This point makes it particularly clear

that fundamentalism primarily represented a defense of a patriarchal order and social morality.

This interpretation finds confirmation in a consideration of postrevolutionary policy in the "Islamic Republic." Despite all manner of dramatic reference to the misery of the masses in Tehran, the oppression of the bazaar, and the plight of the small peasantry, the regime has not yet made much use of its power to solve structural economic problems. Much more energy and "imagination" has been invested, in addition to strategies purely for staying in power, in the control of sexual morality and the female body. Ervand Abrahamian has spoken accurately of a dual policy of cultural-political radicalism and socioeconomic conservatism, which he regards as typical of the traditional middle class.[206]

Processes of political and economic transformation, such as policies working systematically to its detriment and the cutting of its vertical channels of interest mediation, which left the traditionalist camp no alternative between quietism and revolt, had a clearly subordinate but still important role in the mobilization of the traditionalist camp up until 1975. Yet the bazaar even then continued to conform relatively flexibly to given political circumstances and available market opportunities and niches. Only the Resurrection party's clear policy of annihilation toward the bazaar and the clergy caused political and economic problems to move into the foreground as matters of immediate concern. For this policy offered no opportunity whatever for them to conform to "modern" conditions, but drove those affected into an irredeemable situation and thus into Khomeini's arms.

The experience of the traditionalist camp was expressed in a general critique of change in the principles of social organization and the ethics associated with it. The depersonalized bureaucratic organizational principles represented, by virtue of their antagonism to traditionalism, a negation of the whole traditionalist ethos; traditionalists therefore regarded them as "un-Islamic" and saw them as having been introduced by foreign powers and their Iranian agents for the purpose of destroying the Islamic order. Considering the interplay between the state bureaucracy, the military, the police and secret police, the state party, and the modern economic sector, all of which rested on bureaucratic organizational principles and presented an actual threat to much of the bazaar and the clergy, this interpretation is understandable.

Manifest here is a clear correspondence between fundamentalism's social critique, its ideas concerning a just social order, and the processes of transformation that led to the mobilization of the fundamentalist camp. In politics and the economy as well, fundamentalism thus opposed an unjust order of depersonalized bureaucratic structural principles with an Islamic order of personalistic-patriarchal principles. Therefore, as we have seen of Protestant fundamentalism, Shi'ite fundamentalism was also at its core a movement of radical patriarchal moralism.

CHAPTER 4

Fundamentalism as
Radical Patriarchalism

The goal of this work has been to investigate fundamentalism as an urban protest movement in the United States (1910–1928) and Iran (1961–1979). This was intended to test whether such a cross-cultural comparison makes sense and is useful for other societies and cultures. We have investigated the ideology, carriers, and causes of mobilization of two fundamentalist movements. The overall design makes it obvious that the generalizations herein apply to the two cases under investigation with no further claim to validity. The term fundamentalism as used here, therefore, refers to the characteristics of a "rational fundamentalism of world mastery" as they have emerged from the comparison of Protestant and Shi'ite fundamentalism as protest movements in the given time periods.

This comparison, of course, has also identified significant differences, which are by no means to be denied. Shi'ite fundamentalism was organized in hierocratic and clientelistic structures and became revolutionary; Protestant fundamentalism was democratic, individualistic, voluntarist, and reformist. The respective political structures of the United States and Iran, within which fundamentalism developed, are also essentially dissimilar. And Protestant fundamentalism evidenced no parallel to the Shi'ite charisma of suffering.

Despite these and other differences, structural characteristics of fundamentalist protest movements can be identified, which make it appear worthwhile to continue serious attempts to take fundamentalism as the research subject of a cross-cultural comparative sociology.

What features, then, do Protestant and Shi'ite fundamentalism have in common?

FUNDAMENTALISM AS RADICAL TRADITIONALISM

Fundamentalism can be characterized generally as a radical or radicalized traditionalism. For fundamentalism represents not a continuous constituent of ascetic Protestantism or Shi'ite Islam but a position that recurs periodically over time. It may be that there is at its core a continuity of ideological content. Yet it is also true that each instance of fundamentalism bears innovative elements issuing from the specific conditions of its constitution, which any interpretation must take into account.

The point of departure is a traditionalism that is called into question by manifold processes of transformation. Traditionalism becomes subject to new pressures for legitimation, a circumstance that leads to a reformulation of the tradition that necessarily includes the introduction of novel aspects, whether in the form of accentuations, the shifting of emphases, or true innovations. Both Protestant and Shi'ite fundamentalism are instances of a traditionalism that has become reflexive and radicalized.[1]

In both cases, however, fundamentalism exceeds the compass of an intellectual disposition or ideological position and is transformed into a movement, initially into a religious movement and then into a protest movement, which in Iran became revolutionary and in the United States remained reformist. Fundamentalists revitalize existing institutions and create new ones, found publications and associations, and organize regular gatherings of the like-minded. They mobilize their sociomoral milieu and recruit new adherents. Fundamentalism is thus a mobilized traditionalism, a social phenomenon in the sense that it effects new associations; it reanimates both existing institutions and noninstitutional relationships and it prompts the creation of new ones.

A "rational fundamentalism of world mastery," as we have seen in both the United States and Iran, is primarily an urban movement. In both countries all of the significant fundamentalist institutions, the leadership associated with them, and the mass of followers are found in the city. It may be true that many of them spent their childhood in villages or provincial towns or even that they are new arrivals in the cities, yet their political-religious mobilization occurs only under an urban influence. The countryside or provinces have, if any, a marginal role in fundamentalism.

This confirms the old sociological observation that the city, rather than, for example, peasant or nomadic societies, is always the site of a statutory ethical regulation of life conduct, represented by orthodox text-based faiths and rationalist exegesis.[2] Accordingly, fundamentalism is typically not a rural type of religiosity that is imported by migrants into the city, but one that is urban in origin. It is the means by which the traditional middle class conveys to a part of the population of urban migrants the principles of its statutory ethical, rationalized life conduct. Fundamentalism is thus a radical-traditionalist protest movement within the rapidly growing cities by means of which rural migrants are socialized into their new social environment. At the same time, it sponsors the integration of the city-dwelling traditional middle class and the new urban migrants.

I will return to the concept of radical traditionalism in conclusion, for I believe that it is necessary to introduce greater precision into the term "tradition." Tradition in this sense does not refer exclusively to the preservation of arbitrary, received conventions, ethical precepts, or customs but implies quite specifically structured social relationships and an ethical regulation of life conduct the transformation of which is protested. As I will discuss in more detail, these are derived primarily from patriarchal structural principles and culturally specific patriarchal structural forms, which fundamentalism attempts to preserve and recreate. Radical traditionalism under the influence of rapid urbanization and modernization is thus in essence a radical patriarchalism. In practice, fundamentalism adapts to some of the societal changes but creates new forms of personalistic-patriarchal relationships. In terms of this capacity for innovation it is always a neopatriarchalism.[3]

BASIC PATTERNS OF FUNDAMENTALIST IDEOLOGY

The analysis here of two fundamentalist ideologies has identified basic similarities with regard to not only the social critique but even the salvation history, the conceptual model, and the ideal notions of order. Fundamentalist thought can be characterized primarily according to six structural criteria: its primary as well as secondary patriarchal moralism; its organic social ethic; its statutory ethical monism; its religious republicanism; its religious nativism with a claim to universal validity; and its messianism and millenarianism.

Fundamentalism as Patriarchal Moralism   At the center of the fundamentalist critique of society is the moral decay of society, which is regarded as the result of a turn away from divine law. Social decadence is overwhelmingly identified in phenomena displaying a lack of self-discipline and self-control. Passions, compelling dependencies, and materialist greed are revealed in prostitution and pornography, adultery and divorce, music and dancing, the consumption of alcohol and gambling, and crime and class hatred.

A large share of these phenomena refer to the role of women in society or, more precisely, to the sexual aspect of the female body. Fundamentalism is particularly occupied with the public display of the female body. In both the United States and Iran its themes are the immoral dress of women in public, the creation of a uniform type of "decent" women's clothing (veiling, national costume), the stimulation of male sexuality by women (dress, films, theater, swimming pools), and unsupervised contact between the sexes and opportunities for meeting (dance halls, swimming pools, coeducation).

Behind this critique, as I documented above, is the idea of woman as the potential seducer of man into sin. Female sexuality is an instrument of Satan, which is to be rendered harmless and subdued within a patriarchal family structure. Outside of this institution, however, it poses a danger to the stability of the worldly order and to religious salvation.

This point of view necessarily creates a division of roles between men and women, in which men find their gender-specific ("natural") tasks primarily in the public sphere and women find theirs in the home. From sexual difference is derived, however, not only a division of roles but also—admittedly much more markedly in Iran than in the United States—a distinct legal status for men and women. This, in turn, is interpreted not as discrimination but as an expression of the proper consideration of gender-specific attributes.

The fundamentalist critique of changed consumer and leisure-time behavior likewise emphasizes above all their destructive effects on the family and morality. In Shi'ite Iran as well as in Protestant America, alcohol consumption, gambling, public dancing, musical events, and attendance at the cinema and theater were regarded as the most damaging symptoms. Such activities, in their various ways, were seen as stimulating the passions, which hindered men, in particular, from adopting a moral way of life and thereby destroyed families and plunged them into poverty and misfortune. Against these modern leisure-time practices conducted under the influence of Satan, fundamentalism juxtaposes religious activities. In Protestant fundamentalism this meant, above all, respecting the sabbath and going to church and Bible readings; in Shi'ite fundamentalism it meant attending Friday prayers, religious gatherings, and pilgrimages to holy sites.[4]

Although fundamentalism thematizes the dissolution of patriarchal structures and morality above all in reference to primary social relationships, the same basic pattern can also be found in its critique of politics and the economy. Depersonalized (and therefore morally vacuous) bureaucratic structures appeared to both Protestant and Shi'ite fundamentalists as tyrannical institutions exercising illegitimate power over the individual. Modern large-scale industrial enterprises and unions—"big business" and "big labor"—as well as the modern state bureaucracy were regarded as reprehensible from a religious-moral point of view. Fundamentalism's economic ideal is the small enterprise organized along personalistic-patriarchal lines as the cornerstone of an economy regulated by religious moralism.[5]

Fundamentalism emphasizes the individual freedom of economic activity and the individual right to property insofar as they remain within divine commandments. It regards property gained from religiously proscribed activities, such as gambling or prostitution, as illegitimate and immoral. It rejects all forms of "conspicuous consumption" and has a clear "ascetic-puritan" idea of what a person really needs and what goods are superfluous luxuries.[6]

Fundamentalism recognizes the obligation of the rich to provide for the poor. However, it rejects bureaucratically organized welfare, which construes support as a right and is not combined with any kind of social control. As a rule, charity is to be practiced either by individuals or the church, whereby religious-moral supervision is guaranteed as to whether the welfare recipient deserves it or is truly needy. For poverty is worthy of assistance only when it has been caused by a blow of fate and not when it comes from immorality, such as laziness, alcoholism, or a passion for gambling. Thus, in reference to the organization of the economy, property rights, and welfare, fundamentalism is based on a personalistic-patriarchal model with religious-moral social control.

Despite these basic correspondences between Shi'ite and Protestant fundamentalism, Shi'ism tends to put greater emphasis on the obligation of providing assistance to the poor. One reason for this concerns the traces of the Calvinist tradition still palpable in American Protestantism, which tends to identify misfortune with sin. Moreover, the lower classes in the United States often belonged to non-Protestant confessions, but in Iran they were, as a rule, adherents of the same creed.

Fundamentalism as an Organic Social Ethic   In line with its patriarchal moral ideas, fundamentalism also rejects modern conceptions of class and class struggle, opposing them with a religious model of integration. Fundamentalism does not perceive any conflict of interest between industrialists and workers or between the poor and the rich because these relationships are regulated religiously through the protection of property, one's duty toward one's fellows, and patriarchal or patrimonial charity.

In modern industrial society, therefore, it is not social classes that stand opposed, but believers and unbelievers, people who obey the religious commandments and those who disdain them. From this there frequently derives a critical position toward both industrialists and unions; toward the rich when they live in luxury, neglect their charitable obligations, or fail to support the church or mosque adequately; and toward the poor when they raise unjustified demands.

This organic religious social ethic represents the fundamentalist countermodel to modern formulations of class and class conflict. It is the basis of the ideology of the "special path," in which only the terminology varies. In Shi'ite fundamentalism the special path is Islam as such and is distinct from both capitalism and socialism. In Protestant fundamentalism it is (religiously regulated) capitalism, which is distinguished on the one hand from socialism, anarchism, communism, and bolshevism and from bureaucratic, "social Darwinist" industrial capitalism on the other. What is meant in both cases is the defense of a petit bourgeois capitalism subject to religious-moral regulation as opposed to large-scale depersonalized enterprises, whether state run or privately operated. Nevertheless, the organic social ethic is not merely "ideology" but also corresponds to the practice of fundamentalist associations. For these associations actually transcend class boundaries and thus symbolize the possibility of integration on the basis of religious-moral values, rather than conflict on the basis of material interests.

Fundamentalism as Statutory Ethical Monism   Both the patriarchal moralism and the organic social model of fundamentalism are based on its statutory ethical monism. There is only one morality, namely, the one revealed by God and contained in the holy texts of divine law. This morality is regarded as universal in a twofold sense. On the one hand it is valid for all people of all times and cultures, and on the other it regulates all situations and spheres of life.

Fundamentalism thus represents a total religious statutory ethic. It rejects all forms of cultural or structural pluralism, whether it be the ethics of other social groups or foreign cultures, or the particular ethics of specific social subspheres and the groups of individuals within them. Its rejection of cultural pluralism means that, though it accepts other cultures as given, it regards its own as superior and expects, over the long run at least, that missionary work will convert others to the "true religion."

The denial of structural pluralism signifies the unified whole fundamentalism sees formed by private life, the family, politics, the economy, justice, and culture through the subordination of all of them to religious law. Society is not differentiated into particular spheres with particular ethics. All people are equally subject to the law in all spheres of life and society, meaning that fundamentalism rejects any privileging of particular persons or groups through a limited exemption from particular ethical obligations.[7]

Fundamentalism as Religious Republicanism   Fundamentalism derives its political ideals from its statutory ethical monism. Its ideal of government is republicanism, as the embodiment of and attempt to realize divine law. This republicanism, depending on the respective constitution of religious institutions, bears either hierocratic or democratic features.

In Iran the hierocratic moment dominates because of the legal scholars' monopoly on interpretation; in the United States the democratic moment prevails because of the belief in individual religious autonomy. Accordingly, Shi'ite fundamentalism bears features that are structurally antagonistic to democracy, which are legitimized rhetorically by reference to its origin in foreign cultures. But Protestant fundamentalism is also subject to a certain tension in relation to democracy, and even becomes antidemocratic when majority decisions fail to harmonize with what it regards as a divine commandment. In Protestant fundamentalism as well, the republican ideal is clearly superior to the democratic.[8]

Fundamentalism as Religious Nativism with a Claim to Universal Validity   A further characteristic of fundamentalist thought is its nativism, which has two aspects, one regressive and one expansive. The basis for both is Manichaeism, a division of the world into two opposing forces, good and evil, light and darkness, God and Satan.

Regressively, nativism signifies the turn to one's own religious roots and the rejection of all influence defined as foreign. Both in Shi'ite and in Protestant fundamentalism the changes perceived in worldview, culture, society, and politics are interpreted as foreign imports. In Iran the source is the United States, Israel, the Soviet Union, or Western imperialism in general; in the United States it is German "Kultur," Rome, or bolshevism. Native religious roots are interpreted as "pure," "good," and received of God; the foreign as "impure," "evil," and stemming from Satan. This correspondence is remarkable insofar as many have interpreted Islamic fundamentalism primarily as a reaction to neocolonialism of the superpowers, referring to the dominating influence of Western politics and culture and the low status of Islamic countries in international comparison.[9] This does indeed appear plausible at first glance, but, given the example of Protestant fundamentalism, it can be seen that internal processes of social transformation, such as, for example, a heavy influx of poor immigrants, suffice to summon up anxieties and bring the nativist-xenophobic pattern of thought into play.[10]

Nativist-xenophobic characteristics combine with a conspiracy theory. The foreigner comes into the society in question not by accident but intentionally, in accord with the secret plans and designs of satanic powers. In pursuit of his plans the foreigner makes use of domestic agents who contribute, either out of naïveté or malevolence, to the corruption of society.

In a fundamentalism of world mastery these regressive elements of nativism do not lead to withdrawal and renunciation of the world, although this development is also possible, but to an offensive position. The revitalization of the domestic religious-cultural roots serves as a model for the world. Fundamentalists regard themselves as the avantgarde of a radical movement that gains legitimacy through their religious-nativist model's claim to universal validity. They are expansive, building their organization worldwide through missionary activities. Thus Shi'ite fundamentalism attempted to spread the revolution to other countries, such as Lebanon and Iraq, and Protestant fundamentalism vigorously pursued its worldwide mission, especially in Latin America and Asia.

Fundamentalism as Messianism and Millenarianism   Fundamentalism regards itself, however, not only as the carrier of divine law on earth but also as the herald of the approaching millennium and vanguard of the coming messiah or, in the Shi'ite case, Imam Mahdi. One essential peculiarity of Shi'ite as well as parts of Baptist fundamentalism is its mobilization of people accustomed to thinking primarily in quietistic-messianic, profoundly apolitical categories. The premillenarians' focus on catastrophe and their millenarian-messianic anticipation of salvation, however, infuse their political action with a high degree of willingness to suffer. The politicization of premillenarianism necessitates a reinterpretation of millenarian expectations, at least in the sense that the believers have to give up their passive anticipation in order to contribute personally to the return of the messiah or imam and the dawning of the millennium. Neither in Baptist nor in Shi'ite fundamentalism did this reinterpretation proceed altogether consciously or even coherently.[11]

Summarizing fundamentalist ideology once again, we find relationships between the central characteristics of the social critique, the ideas of religious salvation, and the intellectual projections of the social order. The core of the social critique is the decay of morality in the family and society, in the economy and politics, in leisure-time and consumer behavior. The salvational ideas polarize the world into two antagonistic camps, excluding the carriers of social and cultural change from the community of the pious and, above all, from true membership in the nation. Fundamentalism's ideal order is a religious republicanism, the realization of divine law on earth, and the spread of this model throughout the world.

BASIC PATTERNS OF THE CARRIERS OF FUNDAMENTALISM

Despite all the social structural differences between the United States and Iran, surprising parallels exist between their carriers of fundamentalism, in particular the sociomoral integration of individuals in a milieu instead of socioeconomic integration into a class.

Fundamentalism as a Mobilized Sociomoral Milieu   The analysis of the composition of the carriers of both Protestant and Shi'ite fundamentalism has shown that they cannot be adequately characterized either objectively or subjectively by the conception of "class." Adherents came from the lower, middle, and upper classes, from among the unemployed, domestic personnel, blue-collar and white-collar workers, students, artisans and craftsmen, small and large merchants, and professionals. The composition of the adherents also corresponds to their self-perception, which was based not on economic interests but on common values and ideal ways of life. In terms of ideology and social composition, fundamentalist associations offer a countermodel to an industrial class society dramatizing material interest conflicts.

Accordingly, segments of various classes, strata, and groups are found within the fundamentalist milieu that are integrated on the basis of common sociomoral ideas. Four groups can be roughly distinguished: the clergy; the traditional middle class; urban migrants; and the "border crossers" between the traditionalist and the modern milieus. Each of these social groupings is further differentiated internally and characterized by specific experiences. In the following, I once again summarize these groups and their experiences of urbanization that are decisive for their mobilization as part of a fundamentalist movement.

The Clergy   The clergy, in both Protestant and Shi'ite fundamentalism, have the outstanding and leading roles as the organizers and intellectuals of the movement. A common characteristic in both cases is that the religious practitioners, rather than the leading theologians of the universities or *madrasas,* dominate the movement both in influence and because of their much greater numbers. In Iran the lower clergy, preachers, and theology students are the leaders; in the United States, the pastors, evangelists, and lay preachers. The inclusion of persons ranking high in the hierocracy, like Khomeini, or of respected theologians, like J. Gresham Machen (who, in many respects, is better characterized as conservative than as fundamentalist), is more the exception than the rule in both Shi'ite and Protestant fundamentalism.[12]

Fundamentalist intellectuals are strongly stamped by their education in traditional religious ideals, as well as by their practice-oriented mediation and application of these ideals. The ideology of fundamentalism is not the product of theological faculties within the modern universities but essentially represents the accumulated intellectual fruits, in politically radicalized form, of traditional educational institutions, the confessional colleges, Bible schools, and *madrasas.* From these places it is spread by religious practitioners to its predominantly urban followers.

Another common characteristic is the rural heritage of a large share of the fundamentalist clerics. Many of them come originally from the countryside or small towns. Similarly, a considerable portion of *madrasa* and Bible college students come from a rural milieu. Nevertheless, with its rigorous adherence to statutory thought, with its literalist rationalism and its statutory ethical regulation of life conduct, fundamentalism represents a typically urban form of religiosity. Although charismatic fundamentalism no doubt preserves the magical and ecstatic elements of rural religiosity in the city, rational fundamentalism represents an instance of socialization of urban migrants into their new environment.

Precisely among people with a rural or small-town heritage, the selection of a career in religion is particularly bound up with expectations of upward social mobility. These expectations are realized in various degrees. Religious practitioners have indeed attained their professional goals but have done so in a phase of social transformation in which their functions are relatively limited and their social prestige on a sharp downturn while that of other groups is markedly on the rise. For reasons of their education, ultimate values, and life conduct ideals, they are not willing to adapt or, as the case may be, not capable of adapting to a different clientele. They remain captives of the traditionalist milieu. Instead of the social betterment they had hoped for, they experience an enormous loss in prestige.

Students in the religious educational institutions, who are likewise predominantly practice oriented, are confronted with a fundamental change in educational values. Upward social mobility is now possible only through the acquisition of educational credentials in the secular sector. Few of them, however, have either the educational or financial resources requisite to gaining advanced degrees in the secular educational sector. Thus they find that the channels of upward mobility are closed off, the responsibility for which lies with the state or the church.

Urban Migrants   Urban migrants, in both Shi'ite and Protestant fundamentalism, are significant both in the leadership and among adherents. It is, to be sure, necessary to distinguish between members of the middle and lower-middle classes and the lower class; urban migrants do not all belong to the lower class. In both Iran and the United States parts of them belong to the traditional middle classes (merchants, artisans, professionals) and are employees in administration and industrial operations. Taken together, they make up an important and active component of fundamentalism. Like a career in religion, migration to the city is also bound up with hopes for upward social mobility, subject to various degrees of realization. Above all, the need to associate with others is particularly strong in foreign surroundings. Urban migrants tend either to found their own new (religious) associations or to join existing ones.

Those migrants in particular who are drawn to the big city because of their ambitions ("pull effect") have as their ideal an independent economic existence. Consequently, their positive reference group is the city-dwelling "middle class" of independent entrepreneurs and professionals. And this is the group from which they get oriented religiously, socially, and economically. This established middle class, however, has meanwhile lost prestige and significance and has been made economically insecure by the increase in modern, large-scale merchandising, warehouses, or supermarkets. Urban migrants from the middle class are plunged into this crisis, even if they are thoroughly successful in economic terms. The loss of prestige attached to the social location toward which they are striving or that of their positive reference group affects them as well and represents one of their critical experiences.

Urban migrants from the lower class who are seeking to escape bad living conditions in the countryside ("push effect") are put in an economically precarious position, which does not necessarily mean that they experience this as a worsening of their situation. Frequently faced with unemployment, they manage to get by with occasional jobs or as street vendors or peddlers. Women commonly work as domestic help. Their children are particularly subject to the temptations of criminality or prostitution. For this class, fundamentalism awakens the hope of rising from their slum or shanty milieu by their own efforts.

Protestant and Shi'ite fundamentalism are different in their integration of lower-class urban migrants. In Iran such persons made up a relatively inactive but still numerically significant part of the fundamentalist camp; in the rational fundamentalism of the United States they tended to be subordinate, turning in greater numbers to charismatic groups. There are a number of reasons for this difference.

The clergy's monopolization of sacred knowledge in Shi'ite Iran favored their control over all population groups and classes. The voluntarist and pluralistic organization of religion in the United States, however, tended more to encourage the formation of separate religious subcultures. In addition, the urban lower class in Iran, in comparison with that in the United States, was much more culturally and religiously homogeneous. Moreover, the notion common in ascetic Protestantism that poverty is "guilt," that is, the consequence of sin and immorality, may have encouraged a segregation of the lower classes; the obligation to support those in need in the form of the poor tax (zakat), which is deeply anchored in Islam in general, as well as the patrimonial political tradition might have favored in Iran an integration of the urban lower class on a clientelist basis.

The most important difference, however, is presumably the integration of rational and charismatic elements in the practice of Shi'ism as opposed to their separation in Protestantism. In Shi'ite Islam, rational, ritualistic, charismatic, ecstatic, and magical elements are woven together in religious practice. Religious legal judgments coexist with pilgrimages to saints' graves, self-flagellation in the Ashura processions, and magical belief in miracles. The traditional "heterodox" popular religion is integrated into "orthodoxy" and thus controlled by the hierocracy. In pluralist Protestantism in the United States, in contrast, differences in religious style and theological issues of dogma lead to institutional differentiation. Manifest in less institutionalized Sunni Islam as well is this tendency toward differentiation into a rational orthodoxy of the established urban middle classes and a charismatic heterodoxy among urban lower classes and the rural population.[13]

But this difference in the social composition of Shi'ite and Protestant fundamentalism refers only to the numerical representation of those categorized as lower-class urban migrants. Protestant fundamentalism also attempted to reach these people but required them to conform to its religious style. A larger share of them therefore were more strongly attracted by charismatic sects with ecstatic practices. Nevertheless, such people are also represented in rational fundamentalism emphasizing the ethical regulation of life conduct. It is true in general, however, that these lower classes are difficult to mobilize politically. The economic struggle for survival is their main priority, and they are most likely to be found in political action at bread riots or defending their usually illegally constructed settlements.

The Traditional Middle Class   Both in Shi'ite and Protestant fundamentalism the traditional urban middle class has a central role. In Iran the bazaar was the financial backbone of the Shi'ite clergy and the fundamentalist movement. And in the United States a significant portion of the movement's adherents were merchants, artisans, small traders, and professionals.

Moreover, "middle-class" ideals clearly predominate in fundamentalism, in reference to both values and the "rational" religious style. Even if charismatic, magical, and ecstatic elements were incorporated in Shi'ite Islam, their presence in fact represented a compromise with popular religious traditions and needs, which the clergy had always regarded as suspect but tolerated for reasons of power. Rational exegesis and rational discourse, legalistic ethics and a doctrine of virtue that emphasizes sobriety, modesty, and orderliness, characterize the practical orientation of the dominant forces within fundamentalism.

The traditionalist middle classes are made up above all of independent businesspeople, merchants, and artisans. The family business, not the large-scale enterprise, is typical, with a few employees if necessary. This settled urban grouping suffers a considerable loss of prestige and is reduced, at least subjectively, to precarious economic conditions. The nationalization and internationalization of the market forces the established middle class to adapt to the new competitive situation. But even if they continue to earn respectably during the growth phase associated with the change, the profits of newly ascending entrepreneurs and speculators are many times higher. Thus even their economic success loses its sheen in relation to that of others. Moreover, the changes inspire anxieties over their long-term prospects.

At the same time, their self-concept as the "healthy middle," as the representatives of a pious, morally exemplary way of life, is threatened.[14] New lifestyles spread through society, tempting even their own children. The criteria of moral and immoral, of good and evil, become confused. Still exemplary just a few years earlier, they are now regarded as unmodern and backward. The basic experiences of the traditional middle class are thus economic insecurity and an enormous loss in cultural prestige.

"Border Crossers" between the Milieus   As "border crossers" I have designated the younger generation from the traditionalist milieu who have received a (secular) university or college education. They come either from the traditional, settled urban middle class or from a small-town or rural-provincial milieu. The attainment of modern educational credentials, as always, is bound up with an expectation of considerable social betterment. In fact, however, the striving for upward mobility (especially, of course, in Iran) is either disappointing or denied altogether. Their values put them more in the traditional milieu, but their aspirations and their professional activities, for example as subordinate employees in the public or private sector, make them part of the modern milieu.

The "Uprooted"   In the interpretation of the Iranian revolution of 1979, as well as of other radical-right movements, the "dislocated" or the "uprooted" are often named the most important carriers.[15] This interpretation appears to me problematic for several reasons. First, it largely ignores the role of the traditional middle class. Even if it is no longer possible to maintain the interpretation of right radicalism as a movement of the "radical middle," from my point of view it is an overreaction to disregard this component of the carriers altogether.[16] In Shi'ite as well as Protestant fundamentalism the traditional middle class of merchants, artisans, and independent professionals are an important element.

Much also depends on what is meant by "dislocation." Does it mean a loss of social relationships because of a change of locale—as a rule, from small-town provincial or rural milieus to the big city? Or is the meaning more one of a change in social position? Or does it refer above all to an orientation crisis? For the first version it is possible to find evidence in the biographies of many representatives of fundamentalism. The argument loses some of its persuasive force, however, when one considers the demographic development of cities like Tehran or Chicago or the overall social data in the time periods relevant to the respective cases. Thus, 13.1 percent of the population in Iran in 1966 and 23.2 percent in 1976 were not born in the place where they were living at the time the data were collected.[17] Of these "dislocated" masses obviously only a fraction found their way into the fundamentalist camp. Fundamentalism did not take hold at all among industrial workers, and it scarcely mobilized the lower class.

Nor is it possible to delimit the carriers of fundamentalism more precisely by understanding "uprootedness" primarily as a dramatic change in social position. During rapid urbanization, the entire social structure changes so profoundly that, after a few years, even those who have changed neither location nor profession come to embody a different social status than they did previously, measured according to income, education, political influence, or the public prestige attached to their way of life. Only when "uprootedness" is conceived as the coincidence of "relative deprivation"—such as the experience or fear of downward social mobility or disappointed hopes of social betterment—and a profound crisis of orientation or meaning is it possible to arrive at a more precise understanding of the carriers of fundamentalism.[18]

BASIC PATTERNS OF THE CAUSES OF MOBILIZATION

Having named the most important characteristics of the ideology and carriers of fundamentalism in comparative perspective, I turn now in conclusion to the causes of mobilization. Both in Iran and in the United States three processes above all contributed to the transformation of traditionalism into fundamentalism: rapid urbanization and the socio-

cultural pluralization associated with it; the dramatic processes of transformation in the social structure, especially the rise of a new economic
elite and a new middle class; and the centralization and bureaucratization of the political institutions.

The transformative process attending rapid urbanization most significant for the mobilization of fundamentalism lies in the cultural sphere.
It, too, can be distinguished according to three aspects: sociocultural
differentiation of the urban population into modern and traditionalist
milieus; the role of the state in the conflict between the two milieus; and
the symptoms of dissolution within the traditionalist milieu brought
about by the penetration of modern tendencies.

Sociocultural Differentiation in Urbanization   Among the most significant causes of mobilization is the public loss of validity and prestige of
traditional values and life conduct ideals, as is manifest in the sociocultural differentiation inside cities. This process took place in different but
comparable ways in the United States and Iran.

Along with urbanization came the decline of the inner cities and the
formation of slums on the one hand and of new, modern business
centers, residential districts, and suburbs on the other. Considerable
numbers of the newly arriving lower class in the cities, the upper middle
and upper classes leaving it, and the expanding new middle class all
break with traditional values, ways of behaving, and consumer and
leisure-time habits.

Thus, in the process of rapid urbanization the traditionalist values
and behavior patterns that had been respected, if not practiced by all as
a standard, become the moral attitude of a partial culture. The sociocultural differentiation that leads to the formation of a modern competitive
milieu signifies to the traditionalist milieu the loss of its widely accepted
monopoly of a religiously and culturally exemplary way of life. In this
loss of public prestige and respect lies an important component contributing to the mobilization of the entire fundamentalist camp as a protest
movement.

The Withdrawal of Privileges by the State   The devaluation of traditionalist ideals is intensified by changing attitudes on the part of governments, legislative bodies, and parties. In the United States, political
parties had long provided an institutional anchor for the exemplary
status of traditionalist moral attitudes. In Iran following the period
from the initiation of drastic measures by Reza Pahlavi to his abdication

and after the anti-Mosaddeq putsch in 1953, a kind of truce ensued between Mohammed Reza Shah and the Shi'ite clerical elite. But the stance of the administrations changed after the death of the supreme religious leader, Ayatollah Borujerdi, and in the course of the "White Revolution." Now the shah undertook a conscious policy of humiliating the religious class.

In the United States the change in governmental support was less dramatic and not as onesided. Yet there as well administrations on the state and federal levels increasingly withdrew the privileged cultural status previously enjoyed by the traditionalist milieu. Thus, for example, they no longer enforced Sabbath restrictions, in some states prohibited Bible readings in the public schools, and allowed the teaching of evolutionary theory. In contrast to Iran the traditionalist camp in the United States also won partial victories, such as the passage of Prohibition legislation and a ban on the teaching of evolutionary theory in the public schools of some states.

Nevertheless, there can be no doubt that the governments in the United States and Iran considerably limited or even eliminated altogether the cultural privileges previously extended to traditionalist culture and life conduct. Thus, along with the public devaluation of the traditionalist milieu came its official degradation to the status of a subculture of equal or even inferior rights and prestige. This loss of its privileged status represents the second component in the process of cultural differentiation that leads to the mobilization of fundamentalism.[19]

The Problem of Cultural Reproduction and Generational Conflict
With the loss of its sociomoral monopoly, the value of traditionalism is also no longer self-evident. From now on it must reassert its legitimacy and organize to hold its ground. Yet the traditionalist milieu's chances to reproduce itself as one subculture among others are decreased and endangered by the multitude of transformative processes. Three aspects of the transformation are particularly prominent: changes in the educational system; the influence of the media of mass communication; and the mere existence of alternative subcultures.

In Iran as well as the United States, changes in the educational system had a central role. The modern milieu gained increasing influence over curricula and the control of educational institutions. Children from the traditionalist milieu were confronted with a body of thought that alienated them from their original milieu. In addition, many of them received a much better education than the generation of their parents. All of this contributed to alienation between the generations, to a weakening of parental authority, and to the threat to the cultural reproduction of the traditionalist milieu.

Alongside these difficulties, which are grounded in the unreliability or active hostility of the central institutions of socialization, the cultural reproduction of the traditionalist milieu is further complicated by general changes in sociomoral attitudes and in consumer and leisure-time habits. Just the circumstance that a large part of society no longer abides by traditional norms and orients its life conduct according to other values turns the raising of children in a pious traditionalist spirit, with the ascetic demands it entails, into an exceedingly difficult task, above all, of course, in the cities.

Modern consumer and leisure-time opportunities exert a powerful attraction on the youth of the traditionalist milieu. For they offer a loosening of self-restraint and emancipation from personalistic-patriarchal authority structures, symbolizing this emancipation and the upward social mobility frequently associated with it.

The reproduction of the traditionalist milieu confronts further difficulties in the spread of the media of mass communication, which are essentially dominated by the modern milieu and are influential as agents of the change in values. Alongside magazines, radio, television, and the cinema, advertising in particular propagates new definitions of social roles, uses female sexuality to stimulate consumption, and revolutionizes leisure-time and consumer behavior.

The effects of modernism, the problem of cultural reproduction, and the accompanying conflict between the generations are especially significant in the mobilization of fundamentalism. This is manifest not only in fundamentalism's critique of society but also in its attempts to maintain institutional stability. Fundamentalism distinguishes itself sharply from its environment both ideologically and socially, and establishes the infrastructure requisite to its cultural reproduction. This radicalization of traditionalism proves compulsory. To the extent that one does not want to give up one's place in society and withdraw from the world, it is not possible, given the change in the environment, to remain traditionalist without becoming fundamentalist.

Disappointed and Threatened Expectations of Upward Social Mobility   A further component of fundamentalist mobilization is thwarted upward social mobility. This applies above all to the students in traditional religious educational institutions and to parts of the new middle class. To a large number of students in the *madrasas* and Bible schools the career of a legal scholar or mullah, pastor or evangelist, signifies upward mobility. With the expansion of the modern educational sector and the change in curricula, social advancement is not easily attained by way of the traditionalist religious educational institutions.

Financially, career prospects are extremely modest. In Iran the secularization of education and jurisprudence eliminated a number of income possibilities. In the United States, fundamentalist clerics belonged among the most poorly paid professionals in their field. In regard to power and influence as well as social prestige the attractiveness of the clerical profession increasingly declines, especially once the exemplary function of religious education has shifted to secular education.

In both Iran and the United States, moreover, endeavors were under way to repeal the autonomy of the religious educational system and recast it academically in the context of the modern universities. A career in the clergy thus became impossible for the students in the *madrasas* and Bible schools, who lacked the formal prerequisites and, in part, the financial means for a university education. All of these factors make it understandable that the students and staff of the nonacademic (in a modern sense) religious educational institutions were among the most fiercely mobilized groups in the fundamentalist camp.

Yet the social expectations of the "border crossers," that is, students and members of the new middle class, were frequently disappointed as well. These disappointments could be economic or social, for example, failure in entering a desired profession or low wages. Frequently, however, the sensibilities of these "border crossers" were offended by the "modern world," by the anonymity of their working or educational conditions, or by the lack of social contact and communication. Because of their education and professional ambitions they were alienated from their original milieu but insufficiently integrated into the modern milieu, left isolated by their different sociomoral values. "Border crossers" are particularly receptive to associations that overcome their alienation and to ideologies that integrate modern and traditionalist elements, thus helping them to interpret and overcome their circumstances.

The Loss of Political Influence   The loss of direct access to political power in the mobilization of the traditionalist camp is less a factor than the cultural issues. For fundamentalism, political power serves above all to maintain a moral order in which its economic interests are embedded. As long as this order remains undisturbed, there is little occasion for direct political engagement. And even when this order is first threatened, the tendency is not to seek political office but to appeal to the government to remedy the situation. Fundamentalist protest is thus directed not so much against an exclusion from political office as it is against the dwindling of its influence over those in power.

In Iran the political influence of the traditionalist milieu was always limited. Only the top rungs of the hierocracy, to which the bazaar or clergy could bring their grievances for a hearing, were part of the political elite. Moreover, the *mujtahids* often came from influential large landholding or merchant families. The "White Revolution," however, introduced a radical change into the social composition of the political elite. For one thing, the large landholders were considerably stripped of their power and replaced by modern entrepreneurs and Western-trained civil servants at the peaks of state administration. Secondly, the shah used the transition period following Borujerdi's death to push the clergy out of politics. Their legal opinions were ignored and their institutions opposed. With that change the power of the clergy and the traditionalist milieu was restricted to closings of the bazaar and protest demonstrations. This closing of the vertical channels of interest articulation and mediation led necessarily to a radicalization of the protest.

It is also possible to identify a considerable loss in influence on the part of the traditionalist camp in the United States. On the one hand, organized interest groups increasingly translated their economic weight into political power. On the other, non-Protestant immigrants came increasingly to dominate party apparatuses, especially in the big cities. This loss of political power by the established middle class, as well as the traditionalist camp in general, found expression in their partial critique of democracy, and even in antidemocratic sentiment, which was frequently directed against Catholics, modern industrialists, and unions.

Economic Marginalization   In contrast with cultural and sociomoral issues, economic concerns were marginal in the ideology of fundamentalism. In the periods under investigation in both Iran and the United States no economic crisis can be identified in which the fundamentalist camp suffered to any particular extent. And, although the nationalization and internationalization of the market subjected both economies to dramatic changes, fundamentalists expressed hardly any direct fear of decline or dispossession. Nevertheless, a reflection of these processes of economic transformation is to be found in the fundamentalist protest against economic immorality and political repression and injustice.

In the United States, protest was directed against big industrialists, the nouveau riche, war profiteers, speculators, and occasionally, organized labor. In Iran fundamentalism protested against state support of foreign enterprises, banks, and supermarkets (when the bazaar was suffering new impediments); expanding state enterprises (which competed with the bazaar); and the ostentation and extravagance of the upper class and the court. Fundamentalism's primary target, however, was the decline in economic morality, manifest in the money that was being made off of immorality. Even if fears of economic marginalization contributed to mobilization, fundamentalists formulated them as sociomoral issues. Not material interest but moral implications of changes in the economic structure and economic ethics were in the foreground of fundamentalist mobilization.

FUNDAMENTALISM AS RADICAL PATRIARCHALISM

The comparisons undertaken here between Protestant fundamentalism in the United States in 1910–1928 and Shi'ite fundamentalism in Iran in 1961–1979 have shown that the two protest movements manifest clear parallels in ideology, carriers, and causes of mobilization despite all the admitted differences in the political and economic systems of the respective countries and in their religious-cultural traditions. Fundamentalism thus proves to be an independent type of social movement, which cannot be reduced to other types, such as fascism or populism, that are already familiar in the literature. Religion is not an arbitrary embellishment that can be easily dispensed with, but has an independent role, evident in the dramatization of the social critique in terms of a salvation history, in the universalistic features of the ideology, in the symbolism and rhythm of protests, and in the selection of its leadership.[20]

The theoretical approaches discussed at the outset, which interpret fundamentalism, for example, as a status movement, as "antimodernism," or as nativism, appropriately illuminate major aspects of the fundamentalist protest movement. Nevertheless, the interpretations narrow the perspective to one important characteristic, isolating the causes of mobilization or elements of the ideology arbitrarily, without their primacy having been systematically derived or justified. Other aspects of fundamentalism by no means of secondary significance are simply underestimated.

But, how can one avoid the shortcomings of eclectic interpretations? A satisfying explanation should accomplish two things. First, it should work out the basic patterns of the different traits of fundamentalism (ideology, constituency, and factors of mobilization). Second, it should integrate all relevant features into a coherent whole in which the social critique is adequately taken into account.

In our case, such a systematic coherence can be achieved, in my judgment, only when the conflict between fundamentalism and modernism is understood as a confrontation over principles of social organization and ideals of life conduct. Fundamentalism is not a "single-issue" movement, and it formulates its critique not of arbitrary phenomena but of quite specific social structural principles. Its idea of a legitimate order is bound up with patriarchal structural principles and values, and it raises its protest against their erosion and transformation into depersonalized structural principles.[21] Fundamentalism is a reaction to a transformation of epochal proportions of the foundations of interpersonal relationships in all social spheres. It is this aspect that I will bring to the fore of my concluding interpretation of fundamentalism, which simultaneously represents a systematic ordering of the various structural characteristics.

Mobilization: The Experience of Anomie as a Problem of Theodicy
Essentially, the transformation of traditionalism into fundamentalism is the result of different experiences of anomie: as a collapse of social order, that is, as chaos; as social injustice, in that the traditionalist milieu is intentionally subjected to disadvantageous conditions; as loss of legitimacy on the part of the state because of its inability to guarantee order and justice; and as the infiltration of foreign influences into state and society.

Anomie derives, first, from collapse of the general validity of received religious ideas of order. "Evil" and "immorality" exist in all times. Yet suddenly the meaning of these dissolves. Norms lose their obligatory quality and are no longer observed; transgresssions are no longer condemned, prosecuted, and penalized. Both social and state controls fail. In this sense, anomie is an orientation crisis, the experience of living in a chaotic and inverted world.

This aspect of anomie is related to the conception of cultural pluralism elaborated in modernization theory but remains distinct from it. For the problem of cultural pluralism is obviously not exhausted by reference to the formation of a multiplicity of lifestyles and subcultures, toward which the state behaves neutrally. For one thing, the state by no means behaves "neutrally" but withdraws privileges. For another, there yet remains an "anomic remnant" of criminality, prostitution, abuse and neglect of children, socioeconomic deterioration of cities, and mass poverty. Fundamentalism's critique of society is directed not the least against these phenomena, the cause of which it declares to be the turn away from faith and thus the direct responsibility of the "modernist milieu."

The second source of anomie is the subjection of the traditionalist camp to disadvantages by virtue of the willingness of others to violate hitherto established rules. The entirety of experiences of deprivation and of fears of social decline and disappointed hopes in upward social mobility in the context of the rapid rise of other social groups is explained as the fruit of unbelief and immorality. Those who continue to observe the customary rules legitimized by religious tradition will be disadvantaged compared with those who disdain them.

This aspect of anomie corresponds to modernization theory's concept of structural pluralism, that is, the formation of religiously disassociated partial ethics in the economic, political, legal, and cultural system. Furthermore, it corresponds to the conception of "relative deprivation." Yet, here as well, there remains an "anomic remnant" of corruption, structural discrimination, speculation, unregulated class conflict, exploitation, and impoverishment, that is, of phenomena again featured in the fundamentalist critique of society. Above all, the critique identifies a new type of elite that disregards religious morality both in the acquisition and expenditure of its wealth. With that, prosperity loses its religious legitimation.

Third, anomie results from a loss of the state's legitimacy. State institutions contribute both to the erosion of ideas of order and to the disadvantaging of the traditionalist camp, or, at least, prove themselves too weak to effectively counter these developments.

A fourth source of anomie is the increased influence of "foreigners" in the political, economic, and cultural sphere. "Foreigners" either enter the country themselves as advisers (Iran) or immigrants (United States), or they make use of indigenous accomplices. They import their culture and economic enterprises and increasingly take over political power. In extreme cases the state is even regarded as the instrument of such foreign powers, which have infiltrated it.

The anomie resulting from these four conditions **contributes to the mobilization and radicalization of the traditionalist camp and to its transformation into a fundamentalist movement. An important prerequisite to this process, however, is a reinterpretation of the quietistic-messianic** conception of the theodicy problem into a political-activist one. Anomie necessarily leads to a reconsideration of the religious premises of God's justice as well as the meaning of the current crisis and the tasks of the "pious" in response. It is not only true that people want their good fortune to be legitimate; the converse is also true: they want their misfortune to be illegitimate. And if a just settlement is not possible on earth, then it will at least be expected in the beyond.

The traditionalist camp finds itself in need of an explanation for why it is that the godless enjoy ever better fortune and the pious ever worse. The godless appear to hold power, to be luxuriating in wealth and abundance, while the pious are largely excluded from power, are humiliated and persecuted. Traditionalism tends to accept this situation passively, waiting for the messiah and the millennium, but fundamentalism politicizes the theodicy problem. Messianic expectations do not relieve believers of their duty to struggle against satanic powers. One must check the spread of evil, or, in other words, emulate Imam Hussein and battle to establish a just order. Only in this reinterpretation of the theodicy problem from a quietistic waiting for the messiah and millennium into an active struggle for the just order and against satanic powers does fundamentalism take form.

Legitimation: Religious Nativism as a Strategy of Exclusion   Anomie and the theodicy problem represent the foundations of the delegitimation of the government and the modernist milieu. Nativism, and the xenophobia and conspiracy consciousness associated with it, represents the basis of self-legitimation. Thus does fundamentalism justify its Manichaean dualism, which divides the world and the nation into representatives of the divine order and instruments of Satan. It claims exclusive authenticity for itself, a monopoly on the historical transmission and embodiment of divine law and the religious-national identity. Opponents are identified as the tools of Satan or as agents of the "foreigner" and excluded, regarded as wanting to destroy the nation (or, as the case may be, the transnational religious community) and robbing it of its religious-cultural heritage.

Although foreign or alien powers are represented here as the carriers of "evil," this argument also serves essentially to discredit domestic enemies and exclude them from the community of solidarity. As "agents" of foreigners they are stamped as traitors to their own nation or faith. What is interesting here is that this argument is not limited to Islamic fundamentalism in Iran, where, of course, it is correct to speak of the intervention of foreign powers, but appears to represent a universal characteristic of the fundamentalist mentality and rhetorical strategy. The most important function of nativism as a cognitive figuration thus lies in its monopolization of the claim to a divine mission and an authentic religious order, and thus to the timeless foundation of religious-national identity.

Dramatization: Millenarianism and Messianism Fundamentalist millenarianism and messianism lend this Manichaean image of the world the possibility of an additional dramatization. The conflict between modernists and fundamentalists is embedded in the universal drama of the struggle between God and Satan, the powers of light and darkness. The conflict thus far surpasses its contemporary historical significance. It is part of an overall salvation history directed toward the messiah's establishment of the millennium and thus of the kingdom of God on earth. Yet, in distinction to traditionalist quietism, which perseveres in passivity, awaiting the messiah's intervention, fundamentalism takes an active part in the struggle against satanic powers.

Fundamentalism transforms millenarianism into an ideological justification and motivation for political action. It offers a guarantee of victory over the long run, despite current defeats, and it offers the prospect of special compensation for injustice suffered and for the courage to make sacrifices. The pious will be rewarded and the unbelievers held in judgment, just as would be expected from the logic of a statutory ethics. But counted among the pious are not so much the religious quietists as the fundamentalist activists. It is this staging of the conflict between traditionalism and modernism as a universal eschatological drama, in which activism and a willingness to sacrifice are required, that transforms the quietistic or world-fleeing tendencies of traditionalism into a fundamentalist protest movement.

Countermodel: The Legitimate Order To counter the prevailing anomie, fundamentalism offers *nomos*, the eternally valid order of divine salvation, but now no longer as a distant historical ideal but as an immediate political program. The ideal order of the past in fundamentalist symbolism and rhetoric is primarily the original community of the founders of the respective religions, with the addition, in the American case, of the pilgrims and founding fathers. The ideal order in the future is the theocratic republic, the realization of divine law.

A common central characteristic is the restoration of the universal validity of traditional patriarchal social relationships and morals in the family, in consumer and leisure-time behavior, in politics, the economy, law, and culture. A religious conception of integration is juxtaposed against class conflict, ethical monism against ethical pluralism, and the universal claim to validity of the theocratic-patriarchal model against the expansion of "foreigners," injustice, and immorality.

The concrete institutional forms taken respectively by Shi'ite fundamentalism in Iran and Protestant fundamentalism in the United States are, naturally, distinct for reasons of evolved political structures. An essential difference between Iranian Shi'ite and American Protestant fundamentalism also lies in the methods selected to pursue their goals. For various reasons Protestant fundamentalism proceeds along the course of democratic reformism. It assumes that the American constitution provides for a Christian republic in its sense. Moreover, it is by no means hostile in principle to the political culture and democratic process in the United States, by which it has achieved some, if partial, reforms.

Shi'ite fundamentalism, in contrast, became revolutionary. First, the ruling order never possessed a high degree of religious legitimation, for the Iranian monarchy was never regarded as having been in agreement with the principles of the original community. Second, the government progressively delegitimized itself because it never respected the constitution of 1906–1907, which was officially in force until 1979 and provided for a kind of "Islamic supreme court." When, finally, the political system began to react to protest exclusively by intensifying repression, the only choice remaining was between traditionalist quietism and radical activism. That the latter ultimately ended in a successful revolution probably came as a surprise even to the bulk of the fundamentalist camp.

"Radical Traditionalism" as "Radical Patriarchalism"   At the beginning of this study I referred to Said Arjomand's concept of "revolutionary traditionalism," proposing the modification "radical traditionalism" for present purposes. It is now time to elaborate this concept further. Traditionalism, of course, in essence refers not only to the handing down of arbitrary ethical precepts and customs but also to ideas about the principles and forms of legitimate social relationships.[22] Thus it is possible to specify more precisely those concepts of an ideal and just, that is, religiously legitimate, social order.

In judging the fundamentalist protests of the 1920s in the United States and of the 1970s in Iran, two themes are dominant: the loss of religious identity, that is, of the Protestant character of the United States and the Shi'ite character of Iran; and—closely connected—general moral decay. Fundamentalist thinking is dominated, therefore, not by market or power opportunities on the part of economic or political interests but by sociomoral questions concerning the proper conduct of life and a just order. Even more prominent in the foreground than the moral dimension of politics and economics is the relationship between the sexes and thus the structure of the family.

If we assume that sociomoral questions do not always substitute for other "genuine" motivations or that their meaning does not always derive from their symbolic representation of other, "deeper" conflicts but that they are independent mobilizing factors, it becomes reasonable to interpret fundamentalism primarily as a protest against the assault on patriarchal structural principles in the family, economy, and politics brought on by official policy, public disdain, and general moral erosion.[23] If, following Max Weber, the tendency toward rationalization and depersonalization of social relationships in all social spheres is the central characteristic of Western modernity, fundamentalism can in that sense be termed "antimodern." Fundamentalism reacts to epochal structural and value transformations in central social institutions.

The erosion of patriarchal norms and structures takes place primarily in the sphere of the family and sexual morality. The progressive repeal of gender-specific distinctions in legal status and the diminishing need for a gender-based division of labor weakens paternal authority over women. This process also occurs through the public school system, which offers relatively large segments of the young the opportunity to acquire a higher educational status than their parents and exposes them to a changed and, as a rule, strongly secularized body of knowledge. Moreover, transformative processes in professional mobility, in opportunities for leisure-time and consumer activities, and in sexual morality make supervision of children more difficult. The younger generation's willingness to submit to paternal authority and family solidarity is diminished in favor of individual autonomy and the independent identification of goals.[24]

In the economic sphere a marginalization of patriarchally organized enterprises takes place. With the expansion of large-scale operations the patriarchal relationship between entrepreneur and worker is increasingly replaced by a depersonalized and codified relationship between capital and labor. The family operation with only a few employees is faced, first, with competition from large businesses and, second, with a gradual erosion of the nearly unlimited decision-making power of the entrepreneur as "master of the house."[25] Because of the newly arisen competitive environment, the defense of patriarchal economic structures by traditional businesspeople acquires the implicit character of a defense of market opportunities, even if the latter is of secondary significance and is formulated as a moral, rather than an economic, problem.

In politics, bureaucracies become increasingly powerful. Thus, for example, in the social sphere, patriarchal charity, coupled with social control, is supplanted by bureaucratically organized welfare. And in the educational system the state bureaucracy interferes in the organization and curricula of the schools. Even in areas where previously there had been no marked local autonomy, the centralizing and bureaucratizing tendencies of the modern state intensify the degree of control and intervention.

Fundamentalism protests first of all against this revolutionizing of patriarchal structural principles, which are stripped of all historical relativity by reference to divine law and the ideal order of the original community. The pluralization of culture and lifestyle, the depersonalization and codification of social relationships, the bureaucratization of politics and economics, and the removal of social phenomena from traditional moral regulation all represent a direct assault on fundamentalism's conceptions of the ideal ordering of collective social life. At the same time, fundamentalism distinguishes itself from illegitimate forms of patriarchalism. Thus, for example, Protestant fundamentalism in the United States opposed the Mormons' practice of polygamy and the political clientelism of Catholic and Jewish immigrants.

Moreover, fundamentalism succeeds in placing responsibility for the anomie of broad segments of the population, primarily their fear of social descent and disappointed hopes for social advancement, on modern institutions and the organizational principles underlying them. The frustration of the "border crossers" is thus channeled into a conflict of worldviews and cultures. Because it not only holds modernist innovations responsible for society's crises and abuses but also sees them as directly opposed to eternally valid divine law, the conflict takes on the character of a "holy war" or "crusade."

NEOPATRIARCHALISM: BETWEEN MODERNIZATION AND RESTORATION

There are a number of distinctions between the fundamentalist patriarchalism and traditionalist patriarchalism. First, the former represents a radicalization of the latter. Second, fundamentalism modifies the form of patriarchalism according to changes in society. For example, in order to preserve patriarchal morality under the conditions of the modern city, fundamentalism necessarily resorts to measures other than the ones used in traditionalist villages or small towns. Social control, the segregation of men and women, and behavioral and dress prescriptions have to be intensified to have the same effect.

In view of the increasing professional employment of women, higher population density, and big-city anonymity, not even fundamentalists are consistently able to realize strict gender separation. For precisely that reason, however, the multitude of opportunities for unsupervised meetings between the sexes forces them to intensify their efforts to control female sexuality in public. The attempt is made to compensate the loss of physical segregation of the sexes through greater symbolic segregation. In addition, the traditional order has been called into question, leading in response to an accentuation and symbolic overloading of such cultural features as alcohol consumption and women's dress, which had had much less symbolic significance under traditional conditions of daily life.

Juxtaposed against this radicalization are processes of adaptation to modern mass society. In order to be able to organize successfully, fundamentalism is forced to adopt the methods of its opponents, resort to technological aids, take into account the social ambitions of its adherents, and utilize its resources efficiently. Fundamentalism, like other comparable movements, readily employs the most modern technology and techniques. It sees in such aids the chance to spread its message effectively, and in reference to their social-structural implications, they are regarded as ethically "neutral." In the fundamentalist view modern technology in itself does not necessarily depersonalize social relationships. The unity between technicism and modernism breaks apart; or, in other words, fundamentalism is "reactionary modernism."[26] This proves, once again, that the formal and structural transformations of social relationships, rather than "modernity," are decisive for mobilization.

The adaptation of its patriarchal ideals to modern mass society poses a greater difficulty to fundamentalism. Here it seeks new forms within the patriarchal structural principle. What it cannot prevent in the way of structural transformation, it attempts at least to control sociomorally and to channel. Thus it gradually ceases (out of necessity) to reject professional employment for women out of hand but concentrates on preserving propriety in the workplace. Or it accepts better education for women but rejects coeducation. When that position can no longer be maintained, it takes aim against mixed physical education. In these cases fundamentalism combines adaptation with damage control.

Nor does fundamentalism by any means promote the complete removal of women from public life, at least, that is, as long as it remains a protest movement. Traditional conceptions of the role of women combine with their political mobilization. For fundamentalism recognizes and makes use of the fundamentally conservative attitude of a large number of women. Both in the campaign for Prohibition in the United States and in the fundamentalist movement to topple the shah in Iran, women had significant roles. Thus arises the paradox of fundamentalism's promotion of the political mobilization of women, in order thereby to maintain or recreate a patriarchal segregation of the sexes, division of labor, and morality that largely removes women from the political public sphere and attempts to limit their roles to the household. In efforts to maintain or recreate traditional roles, a radical reinterpretation of those roles emerges, at least temporarily.

The development of American fundamentalism in the 1970s and 1980s, in light of the change in its policy on alliances with other social groups, offers a good opportunity to observe the dominance of its neopatriarchal intentions. Catholic and Jewish immigrants, as well as sectarian Mormons, were still agents of Satan for the Protestant fundamentalism of the 1920s, because they undermined the religiously legitimate patriarchal order through alcohol consumption and prostitution (or polygamy), or even because they were seen as agents of a worldwide Catholic or Jewish conspiracy. This nativist view has lost ground in the fundamentalism of the 1980s in favor of a conservative alliance, as represented, for example, by the Moral Majority. The latter represents in essence a neopatriarchal alliance of conservative Protestants with Catholics, Jews, and Mormons, which, unhindered by their respective religious forms, opposes the erosion of the patriarchal family structure. Thus they have cooperated in the fight against the Equal Rights Amendment, the women's movement, the legalization of abortion, and the gay movement.

Fundamentalism represents an attempt, in times of intensifying rationalization, to preserve or recreate patriarchal structures and sociomorality to the greatest degree possible. In so doing, it is often thoroughly innovative, accomplishing radical although perhaps only partial change of the structural *form* in order to preserve the patriarchal structural *principle*. In many cases it is, of course, forced to construct a

206 Fundamentalism as Radical Patriarchalism

bureaucracy of its own to organize its institutions. It attempts to compensate for these tendencies by subordinating the bureaucratic to the personalistic. Bureaucratic institutions then stand in the service of charismatic leaders, thus prompting new, person-based dependencies.

Two clichés dominate the literature in reference to fundamentalism. One reduces it to its theological and mythical elements and asserts that it represents a "return to the Middle Ages." The other emphasizes its socialization function and sees it, because of its statutory ethical regulation of life conduct and its ascetic, "Puritan" attitude, as a force for modernization. Both interpretations, in my judgment, rather arbitrarily seek out one aspect in order to characterize fundamentalism either as reactionary or progressive. The consideration of the ideology and practices of fundamentalism in a larger context, however, makes it impossible to characterize it either as a "return to the Middle Ages" or as an agent of "modernization."

Fundamentalism is rather a retarding force within the general trend away from patriarchalism and toward depersonalization of social relationships. It offers an alternative vision that combines the technical side of Western modernity with, depending on the culture, quite various versions of partiarchal organizational forms and social morals. The inescapable need to conform to a changing social framework leads to innovations in the specific forms assumed by patriarchal social relationships. In reference to the organizational principles of social relationships and the ethical regulation of life conduct, fundamentalism is therefore most appropriately characterized as a patriarchal protest movement.

I have repeatedly pointed out that the results presented here refer exclusively to the comparison between Protestant fundamentalism in the United States in 1910–1928 and Shi'ite fundamentalism in Iran in 1961–1979. They make no claim to validity beyond this comparison but must be tested in other cases and, no doubt, modified accordingly. For that reason I resist the temptation to violate my good intentions by selectively identifying parallels between the movements investigated here and Sunni fundamentalism in Egypt and Turkey or fascist movements.[27] Instead, I will simply indicate, in conclusion, a few of the theoretical implications of the work by briefly contrasting them with feminist and Marxist perspectives.

Although my interpretation of fundamentalism as a radical patriarchal protest movement suggests considerable proximity to feminist interpretations, it distinguishes itself from the latter through its sociological perspective. A large part of the feminist literature is focused on the fact of male dominance and thus emphasizes its historical continuity; in my work this dominance is structurally qualified. The distinction between personalistic-patriarchal and male-dominated depersonalized structural principles and forms, however, is essential. Only when the personalistic principle of piety has been replaced by the depersonalized principle of performance are the foundations of legitimacy of social relationships transformed and does dramatic change become possible precisely in the relationship between the sexes as well. Those who think in terms of unstructured categories of male dominance fail to understand the drama of the transformation processes from which fundamentalism as an urban protest movement derives.

Approaches to the problem from within the Marxist tradition, in contrast, are possessed of a pronounced sense for such structural upheavals. They assume, however, even in their most elevated versions, the dominance of the economy in the structural formation of consciousness. Compared with this perspective, the Weberian conception of rationalization and depersonalization proves superior for an analysis of fundamentalism. The rationalization of the economy into modern industrial capitalism is, indeed, an essential aspect of this development but is by no means always the dominant one. And even within the economy, as is clearly manifest in fundamentalism, the quality of its social relationships can be an issue of greater importance than the quantitative distribution of goods.

Moreover, an essential factor in the rise of fundamentalism proves to be the institutional contexts in which the transformative processes are experienced most dramatically. Therefore, the "subjective" experiences and interpretations of fundamental historical change, not "objective" interests, define the conceptual framework of my study. This has the advantage of openness to the multitude of fundamentalist phenomena. In studying fundamentalist movements, as I hope I have now shown, it is not always necessary to assume that social upheaval is experienced most strongly in the realms of sexual morality and the family.

Yet the confirmation and qualification of this statement must be left to other comparative investigations. In reference to Protestant fundamentalism in the United States in 1910–1928 and Shi'ite fundamentalism in Iran in 1961–1979, however, it can be maintained that they are most appropriately designated radical patriarchal protest movements that counterpose to a modern society characterized by antagonistic

interests and class conflict the ideal of a religiously and morally integrated society. Fundamentalism's conceptions of order may not be
practical or even capable of garnering a democratic majority. Nevertheless, fundamentalism has succeeded in identifying certain structural
problems in modern societies that can by no means be characterized as
resolved.[28]

Notes

CHAPTER 1

1. On the events in Lebanon see Norton 1987 and Wright 1988; on Turkey see Alkan 1984; Heper 1981; Oehring 1984; and Werle and Kreile 1987. Overviews may be found in Dekmejian 1985; Dessouki 1982; Esposito 1980; S. Hunter 1988; Munson 1988; and Sivan 1985.

2. Berger 1981, 194.

3. Arjomand 1986; Caplan 1987; Marty 1988. On Jewish fundamentalism see Aran 1986; Friedman 1986; Hertzberg 1986; Lawrence 1989b, 120–52; Lustick 1988.

4. Arjomand 1986; Horowitz 1982; Caplan 1987; recently, Martin Marty's comparative fundamentalism project (1988) and Lawrence 1989b. With the exception of Arjomand, none of the authors apply a primarily sociological perspective.

5. On drawing parallels with fascist movements, see Afshar 1985b; Arjomand 1980, 161; 1984a; 1985a, 55; 1986; as a "typical Third World movement" or a reaction to imperialism, see S. Hunter 1986 and Gerami 1989.

6. See, for example, Meyer 1989.

7. Charles Tilly has kindly found further good arguments for this self-imposed modesty occasioned by the "shortage of resources"; see Tilly 1984, 76–79.

8. See Berger 1986, 22–23. A contrary estimation is offered by sociologically oriented experts on Islam, who emphasize precisely its "basic puritanical model" or its innovative character; for examples, see Arjomand 1984b; Dessouki 1982; Gellner 1981, 131–48; Waardenburg 1983.

9. In this connection one need only think of the conflict in Northern Ireland, in which, at least on the Protestant side, fundamentalists associated with the clergyman Ian Paisley have a dominant role. See Bruce 1986.

10. As, for example, Lawrence 1989b.

11. Arjomand 1984b. Arjomand's concept agrees with Ernst Troeltsch's descriptions of early Christianity, in which he likewise finds conservative-patriarchal as well as revolutionary elements. See Troeltsch 1931, 82–86.

12. See, in particular, the explanations by Charles Tilly 1984.

13. See Shepard 1987b.

14. See Sandeen 1970; Hofstadter 1963, 117–41; Lipset and Raab 1978, 113–16; Carter 1968; Niebuhr 1937.

15. McLoughlin 1978.

16. Wilson 1970.

17. Niebuhr 1937; Lipset and Raab 1978; McLoughlin 1978; Marsden 1980; Sandeen 1970.

18. Ryan 1984; Peters 1984, 91.

19. Alexander 1985.

20. Keddie 1980b. As a further alternative the concept of conservatism is sometimes proposed. But it should not be applied to millenarian movements, to which a number of fundamentalist groups belong.

21. See S. Hunter 1986; Youssef 1985; Gholamasad 1985.

22. This applies above all to terrorist fundamentalist groups in Egypt; see Ansari 1984; E. Davis 1984; Ibrahim 1980 and 1983; Kepel 1985.

23. See Humphreys 1979 and 1983. Lawrence 1987 follows Humphreys on essential features.

24. William Shepard pushes Humphreys's typology further and distinguishes between secularism, Islamic modernism, radical Islam, traditionalism, and neotraditionalism. His conception of the "modern" as well as his substantive designation of the types, however, lack precision and clarity. Presumably, his intention is to provide less a typology with its strict emphasis on structural distinctions than a complex model with fluid interchanges. See Shepard 1987a, 321, and 1987b; for a critique see Lawrence 1989a.

25. See Berger 1981. Berger demonstrated his sense of irony when he wrote, some years later, about such comparisons: "A number of commentators (usually hostile ones) have compared the Protestant and the Muslim versions of what they often call 'fundamentalism' (usually a pejorative term). There may be certain parallels . . . but there are also decisive differences." See Berger 1986, 22–23.

26. The book by James Barr (1978), misleadingly titled *Fundamentalism*, is limited to more moderate evangelical groups in Great Britain. For an evaluation see Marty 1988, 16.

27. Caplan 1987, 22.

28. Marty 1988, 20–23.

29. Lawrence 1989b.

30. Cf. Duran 1983.

31. Arjomand 1984b.

32. The modernist Chicago theologian Shailer Mathews formulated a similar thought when he criticized the premillenarian fundamentalists: "Premillenarians miss the spirit by emphasizing the letter." See Mathews 1917, 10. The distinction between myth and utopia proves more expedient here than Mann-

heim's famous, and otherwise intended, distinction between ideology and utopia. See Mannheim 1936, 36 and 173.

33. See Marty 1988 as well as Arjomand 1986, 92–97.

34. See Weber 1951: 173–225; Gellner 1981, 114–30. On charismatic fundamentalism of the lower classes see Bourdieu 1977; Crapanzano 1972 and 1973. Within Islamic mysticism as well a distinction is made between rational and charismatic striving after salvation. Thus does Tirmidhi, an Arab Sufi of the ninth century, distinguish between two types of saints, "one reaching the state of saintship through faithful adherence to every detail of the shari'a and the tariqa, . . . one by God's grace through the act of loving." See Schimmel 1975, 203.

35. Tibi 1990; Gellner 1981, 131–48; Waardenburg 1983.

36. Tilly 1978, 12–51. Other systematizations of approaches within historical-comparative sociology can be found in Skocpol 1984 and Skocpol, ed., 1984; Tilly 1984; Roth 1987.

37. Thus, for example, does Mancour Olson declare his approach as little suited to an interpretation of "philanthropic and religious lobbies," referring instead to psychology. See Olson 1965, 159–61. And Marxist authors continue to work with the concept of "false consciousness," explaining fundamentalism as "petit bourgeois chiliasm" and thus as an irrational reaction to the disintegration of the traditional mode of production. See Gholamasad 1985, 441–500.

38. Gusfield 1963.

39. Kornhauser 1959, 13–17.

40. Durkheim 1951, 252–53; Hofstadter 1955a, 131–73; 1955b, 84; Lipset 1955, 308–9. Theodor Geiger also developed similar thoughts in his analysis of the "old middle classes"; see Geiger 1932, 87–89.

41. Parsons 1969, 115; see also Lipset 1985, 253.

42. Gusfield 1963, 166–88.

43. See, for example, Ash 1972; Useem 1975. The literature on new social movements also neglects reactionaries or conservatives.

44. Berger 1967; Berger et al. 1974; J. Hunter 1983.

45. J. Hunter 1983, 12–13.

46. Berger 1981; J. Hunter 1983, 107–19.

47. Shils 1968.

48. Mannheim 1986, 72–77. Applied to Islam, see Enayat 1983a and Hudson 1980.

49. Arjomand 1984b.

50. Kippenberg 1981.

51. Thus the sense of Sandeen 1967, 66–67.

52. See Gholamasad 1985.

53. See Hofstadter 1963, 123; Lipset 1964, 116; Lipset and Raab 1978, 121. They follow earlier interpretations, such as Mecklin 1924; Niebuhr 1929, 181–87, and 1937.

54. Kornhauser 1959, 223. This view of mass society and life in large cities as complete disintegration and atomization of social relationships is obviously influenced by Ferdinand Tönnies's dichotomy between "community" (*Gemeinschaft*) and "society" (*Gesellschaft*) as well as by Louis Wirth's *Urbanism as a Way of Life* (1938, 60–83). As early as 1962, Gusfield emphasized the new

mechanisms of integration in mass society in his critique (Gusfield 1962), and more recent investigations of urban life in the Third World have shown that urbanization does not necessarily lead to anomie, marginality, or atomization, although in doing so they have overlooked the significance of religious associations (Arjomand 1986, 92).

55. Arjomand 1984b; 1986; and 1988a; 100–101, 206–7.

56. Despite his partial agreement with Lipset, Arjomand comes to the opposite conclusion on the origin of fundamentalist religiosity. See Arjomand 1986, 92–97. His interpretation corresponds with Germani's phase model of mobilization and reintegration. See Germani 1978, 13–41. Of interest here is the discrepancy between system integration and social integration. See Lockwood 1964.

57. Arjomand 1988a, 197–99 and 201–2.

58. Olson 1965.

59. Lepsius 1966, 383. The milieu concept also occurs in analyses of Islamic revitalization movements; see Humphreys 1983, 75–76.

60. Geiger 1932; Merton 1968.

61. Gusfield 1963.

62. Weber already commented on this, Weber 1978, 468–80. See also Gellner 1981, 114–30; Arjomand 1986, 92–97.

CHAPTER 2

1. On this issue see the penetrating analysis by Allan Silver 1990.

2. On American religious history see, above all, Ahlstrom 1975; Gaustad 1974; Marty 1977 and 1984; Mead 1963 and 1975; Noll et al. 1983; Reichley 1985; as well as the relevant articles in Lippy and Williams, eds. 1988. On the relation between the state and religion see, especially, Pfeffer 1967; Stokes 1950; and the collection of documents in Wilson and Drakeman 1987. An excellent depiction of institutionalized religious values is found in Lipset 1979, 140–69.

3. Reichley 1985, 56–57.

4. Reichley 1985, 57.

5. Ahlstrom 1975, 1:210; Reichley 1985, 60.

6. Reichley 1985, 111; in general, Lipset 1964, and 1979, 140–69. On the relation between the state and religion in the Constitution and the decisions of the Supreme Court see Morgan 1972; Oaks 1963; Pfeffer 1975; and the literature cited in note 2.

7. For the most suggestive treatment see Mead 1954.

8. On the influence of industrialization and urbanization on Protestantism see Cross 1967; Abell 1943; May 1967. On the Social Gospel and the Settlement Movement see A. Davis 1984; Hopkins 1940.

9. On the educational system see Cremin 1988 and Liebersohn 1985.

10. Cf. Sandeen 1967, 1970, and 1971; Szasz 1982; Marsden 1971 and 1980; Moore 1968; Furniss 1954; S. Cole 1931; Niebuhr 1937; Lipset and Raab 1978, 12. On opposition to evolutionary theory and the Scopes trial see, among others, Allen 1925; Gatewood 1966 and 1969. For a fundamentalist perspective see Dollar 1973, 85ff.; Falwell et al. 1981, 78–108.

11. A precise delimitation of social movements in this sense is found in Raschke 1987, 76–78.

12. Thus, for example, Mecklin 1924; Lake 1925, 69; Lippmann 1929; Niebuhr 1937; and Lipset and Raab 1978; but also Hofstadter (1955b, 1963, 1965, 1979), whose writings nevertheless represent a storehouse of sensitive observations on fundamentalism.

13. *Fundamentals* 1910–1915; *God Hath Spoken* 1919, 12.

14. See Holmes 1921; Macartney 1925, 179–80; Sandeen 1967, 1970, and 1971. On the history of premillenarianism in the United States see T. Weber 1987.

15. *King's Business*, October 1926; Harry Emerson Fosdick, perhaps the most prominent representative of liberal theology, also understood fundamentalism as the alliance of predominantly premillenarian Baptists and orthodox Presbyterians; see Fosdick 1922, 172.

16. *King's Business* 1919, 396–97; Lumpkin 1969; Delnay 1963. Yet there were also postmillenarians among the fundamentalist Baptists in the North; see, for example, B. Bustard 1920, 143–44.

17. See Marsden 1980, 125–27.

18. Biographical sketches of the most important fundamentalists can be found in Russell 1976.

19. On Bryan see Levine 1965 and Gould 1987; on Presbyterian orthodoxy and its struggle against modernism see, in particular, Smith 1985.

20. Thus Mecklin 1924, 21, 51, 95ff.

21. Sandeen (1970) does not mention the Ku Klux Klan at all; Marsden does in only two places (1980, 189, 191), without taking a position on its relationship to fundamentalism.

22. Miller 1956, 356.

23. Jackson 1967, 18; Wade 1987, 167–85.

24. Furniss 1954, 38; Miller 1956, 366; Bradley 1962.

25. See the advertisements of the Ku Klux Klan in *Searchlight* 11 April 1924, 4; 7 November 1924, 3.

26. Goldberg 1981, 188.

27. Jackson 1967, 237, 239.

28. On the history of the Pentecostals in the United States see, especially, R. Anderson 1979 as well as Brumback 1961; Hollenweger (1972) offers a worldwide overview.

29. The following representation is based almost exclusively on my own evaluation of popular periodicals with a broad distribution and central importance for the fundamentalist movement, such as the *King's Business* from the Bible Institute of Los Angeles and *Searchlight,* published by J. Frank Norris. From the *King's Business* I analyzed volumes 1915–1928; from *Searchlight,* which appeared as *Fencerail* prior to 2 March 1917 and in 1927 was renamed, first, the *Fundamentalist* (April 15) and then the *Baptist Fundamentalist of Texas* (April 29), I have used the volumes 1917–1927. I have also drawn from pamphlets by the leading fundamentalist clerics, such as William B. Riley and John R. Straton. A general overview of fundamentalist social criticism is offered by the article by Greene (1919).

30. Cf. the periodization in Riesebrodt 1988, 113. The transition from a religious to a social movement is documented in the annual conferences from 1918 to 1920; see, among others, *Light on Prophecy* 1918; *God Hath Spoken* 1919; *Baptist Fundamentals* 1920.

31. Thus, among other sources, *King's Business* 1918, 741–50; 1919, 100 and 899; 1920, 17, 43, 550; 1921, 1186; 1922, 987–89; *Searchlight* 5 June 1924, 1–4; 3 July 1925, 1–2; 9 April 1926, 4 and 8. And see Gray 1922 and Torrey 1918.

32. Thus, for example, in Lyman 1918.

33. Machen 1923. On the significance of Machen see Lippmann 1929; for biographical information see Russell 1976, 135–61. On the development of liberal theology see Hutchinson 1982.

34. Thus, for example, *King's Business* 1916, 772; 1917, 197; 1919, 394–96, 590–91.

35. Cf. Torrey in *King's Business* 1919, 499–500. On the emphasis on voluntarism and orthodoxy see Massee 1920, 4–5.

36. *King's Business* 1919, 491. The analogy between liberal ecclesiastical and industrial capital organizational forms was emphasized in particular by William B. Riley, who opposed the voluntary cooperation in fundamentalism to the trend toward a monopolistic corporation in liberalism. See Riley 1917, 154–81; 1919, 41.

37. Cf. *King's Business* 1915, 103–12; 1919, 394–96; 1920, 734; 1923, 773; Straton 1920, 150–59; Marsden 1980, 156–57.

38. *King's Business* March 1925, title page.

39. This attitude was already evident in *Fundamentals* (1910–1915). See also the caricatures in *King's Business* 1919, 594; 1921, 1184; 1923, 228.

40. Cf. *King's Business* 1917, 100–101, 873–74, 968; 1918, 5–7, 548–49; 1919, 202–4, 588, 799. J. Frank Norris fought the Catholics much more aggressively; see *Searchlight* 11 January 1924, 1–3; 1 August 1924, 1–4; 8 August 1924, 1–4. The attacks became sharper once the Catholic Alfred E. Smith began seeking the Democratic presidential nomination in 1927; see the following 1927 issues of *Searchlight*: 22 April, 4–6; 20 May, 1–7; 28 October, 3; 11 November, 1–2; 18 November, 1–2, 4–6. On Smith see especially Handlin 1987.

41. See Marsden 1980, 146–47.

42. See *King's Business* 1915, 943; 1918, 95–100, 276–77, 365–66, 837; 1919, 110–15, 902–4; Dixon 1920, 134. In reference to Bryan see Gould 1987.

43. *King's Business* 1919, 205.

44. Higham 1955, 222–33.

45. *King's Business* 1919, 933.

46. *King's Business* 1919, 593. On a "Zionist" position on the role of Jews in the premillenarian, prophetic literature see Rausch 1980.

47. This changed after the world economic crisis, above all, on the part of William B. Riley; see Marsden 1980, 210, and, more generally, Roy 1953.

48. Straton 1920; 1929; n.d.a.; n.d.b. On the change in social morality in the 1920s see Leuchtenburg 1958, 158–77; Ostrander 1968; Haller 1972, 299.

49. *King's Business* 1919, 1103.

50. *King's Business* 1917, 99–100, 869–72.

51. *King's Business* 1920, 1015. On the populist character of fundamentalism see also Riley 1916, 210; Bryan 1922, 243.

52. *King's Business* 1916, 1059.

53. *King's Business* 1971, 964.

54. *King's Business* 1915, 106–7; 1917, 874; 1918, 187–88, 456–58, 929–31.

55. For example, Reuben Torrey was explicit in naming the United States a "Protestant nation"; see *King's Business* 1919, 202.

56. *King's Business* 1915, 944; 1916, 387, 485–88; 1917, 390–91; 1918, 186–87. Quite unabashedly in favor of the war, in contrast, was *Searchlight* 15 June 1917.

57. Bryan 1922, 240.

58. *King's Business* 1917, 581, 1059–60.

59. *King's Business* 1917, 389; 1918, 932–33; 1919, 402–5, 799–800; Marsden 1980, 154–55.

60. Keesecker 1930, 1–5.

61. On the Scopes trial see, among others, Allen 1925; Marsden 1980, 184–87.

62. This is best exemplified by the caricatures of teachers and professors that frequently appeared in *King's Business;* for example, *King's Business* 1926, 254 and 557. Another important contribution to this image was made by a study by James Leuba (1916) that established empirically the decline of religious faith among college students and professors.

63. *King's Business* 1919, 701.

64. *King's Business* August 1925, title page; for comments in the same sense see Greene 1919, 346–47.

65. *King's Business* 1923, 675.

66. *King's Business* 1918, 2.

67. *King's Business* 1918, 188–89, 546–47, 1026–27.

68. *King's Business* 1919, 397.

69. For fundamentalists, heaven and hell, like God and Satan, are real, not metaphorical or symbolic. Just as real is the anticipation of the return of Christ to earth. See Reuben Torrey in *King's Business* 1918, 194–203, and Torrey 1913 and 1918. The fundamental differences were also apparent in the numerous public debates between fundamentalists and modernists; see, for example, Straton 1925.

70. *King's Business* 1919, 100 and 899.

71. *King's Business* 1918, 837. See also Higham 1955, 222–23.

72. *King's Business* 1920, 243; *Presbyterian* 4 November 1920, 10 and 30.

73. *Presbyterian* 1 January 1920, 16.

74. *King's Business* 1917, 100–101, 968; 1918, 5–6, 548–49; 1919, 202–4.

75. *King's Business* 1917, 874 and 873; similarly in *Searchlight* 1 August 1924, 1–4.

76. *King's Business* 1919, 588 and 799–800. Nor, however, should it be overlooked that parts of the liberal camp were no less vulnerable to paranoid impulses. Thus fundamentalists were charged with being in the pay of the Germans (according to the Chicago theologian Shirley Jackson Case; see

Marsden 1980, 147); being used (or financed) by the capitalists (Lake 1925, 161; *Christian Century* 14 April 1921, 1); and being akin (or comparable) to the Bolsheviks ideologically (Taylor 1919, 16–17).

77. Straton 1920, 38–50, 87–105.
78. Straton 1920, 57.
79. *King's Business* 1923, 233 and 317.
80. Straton 1920, 49.
81. Straton 1920, 49–50. On the inclinations toward uniform dress in Islam aside from the veil see Pipes 1983, 126.
82. *King's Business* 1920, 926.
83. *King's Business* 1916, 387; 1921, 217; as well as 1919, 5, 202, 508. On the universalist view on an individual foundation see Brougher 1920, 195. On the Calvinist view of a Protestant America see Smith 1985, 53–73.
84. *King's Business* 1920, 265–66; Marsden 1980, 126.
85. *King's Business* 1920, 928.
86. *King's Business* 1921, 859–60.
87. *King's Business* 1919, 697.
88. Haldeman in *King's Business* 1920, 265; Vogelsonger in *Presbyterian* 6 May 1920, 9–10 and 29.
89. *Presbyterian* 13 May 1920.
90. Bryan 1922, 243.
91. Bryan 1922, 244–45.
92. Eells 1923, 443.
93. Thus Russell 1976, 92, concerning William B. Riley.
94. *King's Business* 1917, 99–100, 870–71; Norris in *Searchlight* 21 September 1923, 2; Riley 1916, 210.
95. *King's Business* 1923, 675 and 26.
96. *Searchlight* 5 June 1919, 1.
97. *Searchlight* 5 June 1919, 4.
98. Thus a headline in *Searchlight* 12 June 1919, 2: "Organized Labor Capital's Best Ally."
99. Clow 1922, 647.
100. Clow 1922, 656.
101. Clow 1922, 657.
102. Bryan 1922, 229–32; "Report of the Board of Home Missions to the Assembly of the Presbyterian Church in the USA," quoted in Eells 1923, 453–55.
103. *King's Business* 1915, 654–55; Eells 1923, 444–47; Porter 1920, 112.
104. See notes 64 and 65.
105. Mecklin 1924; Niebuhr 1929, 181–87, and 1937; Lipset 1964, 116; Lipset and Raab 1978.
106. Rogin 1967; Jackson 1967; Sandeen 1970.
107. Lipset and Raab 1978, 121; see also Marsden 1980, 202, note 16.
108. Caldwell 1980.
109. Nichols 1925, 14; Ashworth 1924.
110. Bailey 1964, 48–49, shows that there were isolated fundamentalist endeavors also among the Baptists of the South. In my definition, however, these represent separate movements, which, with the exception of Norris, were not part of the main movement. Norris, however, was extensively iso-

lated among the Baptists of the South. This is also confirmed indirectly by the fact that Ashworth, in his contemporary depiction of the fundamentalist movement among the Baptists, treats only the Baptists of the North; see Ashworth 1924.

111. Betts 1929, 31–49.

112. Wenger 1973, 74.

113. Wenger 1973, 54–75.

114. Douglass and Brunner 1935, 145.

115. Gill and Pinchot 1913, 15.

116. Gill and Pinchot 1913, 19.

117. *Christian Century* 7 February 1918, 4–5. This tendency was also confirmed by the later studies of the Interchurch World Movement (1920a, 63–69, and 1920b, 26) and by Brunner 1921 and 1923, 45.

118. Athearn et al. 1923, 281.

119. Douglass and Brunner 1935, 37–40.

120. *King's Business* 1916, 1060.

121. Ellis 1974, 192ff. On the diffusion of urban culture and institutions in small towns see, among others, Atherton 1972.

122. Delnay 1963, 22.

123. Wenger 1973, 81.

124. Lynd and Lynd 1929, 320, 324, 329.

125. Lynd and Lynd 1929, 359, note 23.

126. Lynd and Lynd 1929, 360–66, 376–77; Douglass and Brunner 1935, 291.

127. On the fundamentalist character of the Pentecostals see Hollenweger 1972, 291ff., and R. Anderson 1979, 147ff.; on the social composition see R. Anderson 1979, 151ff. An interesting interpretation of the function of their faith is found in Wacker 1984.

128. Ellis 1974; Hallenbeck 1929.

129. Perry 1959, 323–24.

130. Ellis 1974, 132–78.

131. Ellis 1974, 117.

132. Ellis 1974, 119.

133. Ellis 1974, 132–78.

134. The split took place in 1922. Unfortunately, the corresponding archival documents are not available. Ellis (1974, 162, 166), however, has reconstructed the basic features of the social composition of the congregation for the year 1913 from the membership as it was later, following the split. The calculation is based on Ellis 1974, 162, and 166, and the identification of 448 congregation members.

If one defines occupational groupings as professional, clerical, and workers, the following tabulation results:

	Total	Liberal	Fundamentalist
Professional	29.3%	52.4%	22.0%
Clerical	42.6%	33.7%	45.5%
Worker	28.1%	14.0%	32.6%

135. Hallenbeck 1929, 108.
136. Sanderson 1932, 64.
137. Hallenbeck 1929, 20.
138. Hallenbeck 1929, 81. The resulting sum is 105.6 percent and must, therefore, contain an error. The listing is nevertheless useful, because of interest here is only a rough classification.
139. Hallenbeck 1929, 70, 75, 80.
140. Hallenbeck 1929, 24.
141. Neither of Hallenbeck's sums adds up to 100 percent. See note 138 above.
142. Hallenbeck 1929, 64–82.
143. Marsden 1980, 202. On qualifications in reference to Northern European workers, see note 150 below. Sanderson expressed the facts simply but accurately when he wrote: "Rich fundamentalists and poor fundamentalists agree in their fundamentalism." See Sanderson 1932, 229.
144. The tendencies of the Protestant establishment in the United States toward caste formation and compartmentalization in reaction to social ascent, symbolized in country clubs and the suburbs, have been brilliantly worked out by E. Digby Baltzell (1964, 197–225). On intraurban segregation see, among others, Glaab 1968; Haller 1972; Tuttle 1972; Winter 1961, 39. On the effect on the school system see Katznelson and Weir 1985, 214–20.
145. Ellis 1974, 122.
146. Ellis 1974, 118.
147. Allen 1925; Marsden 1980, 184–88.
148. Wenger 1973, 81.
149. Marsden, to be sure, refers to a portion of Northern European labor with an orientation toward upward mobility into the middle class (1980, 202). The Northern European components are primarily due to his reliance on Ellis (1974), whose case study of Minneapolis with its high percentage of Scandinavian inhabitants he generalizes.
150. See S. Cole 1931; Niebuhr 1929 and 1937; Furniss 1954; McLoughlin 1978.
151. For an analysis of the transformation of worldviews as a change of paradigms see T. Weber 1982, 101–4.
152. Marsden 1982, 79–81; Wacker 1982, 133–34; Kniker 1982.
153. Wacker very correctly describes this aspect in reference to the Pentecostals; see Wacker 1984, 363.
154. This institutional side of the conflict is not usually accorded much attention. See, for example, Marsden 1980; Sandeen 1970; Szasz 1982; Vanderlaan 1925. It had, however, a demonstrably important role in the mobilization of fundamentalism; see, for example, *God Hath Spoken* 1919, 12–14; Riley 1920; Dixon 1920.
155. Delnay 1963, 156.
156. The analogy to the market was already made in the contemporary literature (cf. Leete 1915) and was later taken up by Berger (1963).
157. Leach 1922; Lee 1967; Winter 1961; Kincheloe 1928.
158. Douglass 1926a, 90.

159. Douglass 1926a, 56.

160. Sanderson 1932, 190.

161. For a vivid polemical depiction of a liberal cleric of this type see Caldwell 1980, 80–85.

162. On financial problems in reference to functional expansion, using the example of the Interchurch Movement, see Delnay 1963, 24–26.

163. Douglass 1926a, 166.

164. On the fear of a "Protestant papacy" see G. E. Moorehouse in *Presbyterian* 1 April 1920, 9–10.

165. For a typical representation of social segregation in the modern big city see Burgess 1925 and 1928; for a contemporary analysis of the attendant problems see Brown 1922, especially 42–45. According to Sanderson 1932, 173, note 23, the share of "fundamentalists" in the inner cities amounted to approximately 17 percent; of conservatives, 49 percent; and liberals, 34 percent. If one distinguishes within the inner cities between the immediate city center and contiguous residential districts, the proportions are: "fundamentalists" 19 percent versus 13 percent; conservatives 52 percent versus 40 percent; and liberals 29 percent versus 47 percent. The figures show the relatively concentrated distribution of "fundamentalists" and conservatives in the city centers, that is, the first point of arrival for urban migrants. Since Sanderson did not explain his concept of fundamentalism, his data presumably refer more to charismatic groups, and "rational" fundamentalism would probably be subsumed under conservatism. On the evangelism and social work of religious groups in the slums see, among others, N. Anderson 1923, 250–63. On the adaptation of pastors to the various situations in the big city see M. May 1933, 302–39.

166. Leete 1915; Strong 1915; Douglass 1924, 1926a, 1926b, 1927; Douglass and Brunner 1935; Sanderson 1932; Hallenbeck 1934.

167. Sanderson 1932, 182–97; Hallenbeck 1929; Douglass 1929.

168. On the fundamentalist critique see Mark A. Matthews in *Presbyterian* 29 April 1920, 8–9.

169. On the ethnic, cultural, religious, and political composition of a typical big city see Interchurch World Movement 1920a, 32.

170. On the old and new middle classes in the United States, C. Wright Mills's study remains worthwhile reading; see Mills 1951.

171. Connelly 1980, 48–66; Harring 1983.

172. See Gusfield 1963 as well as Hofstadter 1955a, 292, note 4. The problem of children's upbringing was key in this; see Haller 1972, 290–301.

173. Schlesinger 1951, 113–16; Flexner 1979, 235–303. Generational conflict within families was also significant; see, among others, *Presbyterian* 15 April 1920, 1.

174. Hays 1957, 152–54; Baltzell 1964, 206–8; Wiebe 1967, 293–94; and, especially, Buenker 1973.

175. Corresponding to the usual overemphasis on the controversy over evolutionary theory is the neglect of the conflict on Bible readings in public schools. On the conflict from a contemporary Jewish perspective see, among others, Newman 1925.

176. Keesecker 1930, 1–5.

177. It took nearly sixty years for parts of the fundamentalist camp to move beyond this narrow construction and, with the conception of a "Judeo-Christian tradition," recognize religious pluralism at least to the extent of being able to form a conservative alliance of Protestants, Catholics, Jews, and Mormons as formulated in the program of the "Moral Majority."

178. On the development of these structures see, among others, Hofstadter 1963 and 1955a, 215–71; Leuchtenberg 1958, 178–203.

179. Young men were transformed above all through the experience of war as soldiers. Moreover, many of them returned from Europe with venereal diseases. Women were drawn into the labor force with a new intensity and then did not want to give up their new status. See Ostrander 1968, 340.

180. See Lawrence 1989b, 170–88; Gatewood 1969.

181. Bryan's view was influenced by Vernon Kellogg's reports from the headquarters of the German general staff. Kellogg had spoken there with German officers, many of whom were professors of the natural sciences, who also justified the war with Social Darwinian arguments. See Gould 1987; on the Scopes trial see Allen 1925.

CHAPTER 3

1. On variety in Islam and the different structural conditions see Geertz 1968; Tibi 1990, 160–77.

2. On the historical background of the power of the Shi'ite clergy in contrast with that of Sunni Islam see Keddie 1972; on "Puritanism," see Gellner 1981, 131–48; Waardenburg 1983.

3. On Twelver Shi'ism in general in Iran, see Nagel 1981; Momen 1985; Tabataba'i 1977; Ende 1984; Richard 1983a. On Shi'ite messianism see in particular Sachedina 1981; still worth reading as well, however, is Sarkisyanz 1955. On the relation between religion and politics see Algar 1969; Arjomand 1984c; Bayat 1982; Sachedina 1988. Although the bulk of the literature focuses on the tension between the clergy and the monarch, Bayat emphasizes that between orthodoxy and heterodoxy.

4. Arjomand 1984c, 107.

5. Arjomand 1984c, 146; Algar 1969, 34–36.

6. Gellner 1981, 114–39.

7. Arjomand 1984c, 156, 138, 165.

8. Arjomand 1984c, 161.

9. Max Weber 1978, 519.

10. Arjomand 1984c, 181.

11. On the Qajar period see especially, in addition to Arjomand 1984c, Algar 1969.

12. Arjomand 1984c, 217; Algar 1969, 33–40.

13. Arjomand 1984c, 230–31; Lambton 1964, 132.

14. Lambton 1956, 144.

15. Arjomand 1984c, 223–29.

16. Arjomand 1984c, 245–48; Calmard 1989; Momen 1985, 205; J. Cole 1983.

17. On the structure of the Shi'ite hierocracy see Algar 1969, 1–25; Momen 1985, 203–5; Binder 1965.

18. Algar 1969, 19.

19. The *mujtahids* were connected in particular to rich wholesalers but also to large landholders. Their relations with the mass of petty merchants, artisans, and workers in the bazaar were not so much direct as mediated through the mullahs, who had clientelist ties with them. See Algar 1969, 17; on familial relations see especially Thaiss 1971, 199, as well as Keddie 1980a, 96–97.

20. Algar 1969, 24–25.

21. The tobacco protest was a national embargo on the use of tobacco directed against the monopolistic concession granted to a British company by the shah. This first modern mass protest in Iran was organized by an alliance of the hierocracy and the bazaar. See Keddie 1966.

22. Akhavi 1980, 32–37; Arjomand 1981a. On the processes of economic transformation in the nineteenth century as the precondition for the mobilization of the bazaar see Nashat 1981.

23. Abrahamian 1968, 1979, 1983, 50–101; Keddie 1980a, 53–65.

24. See Amanat 1968, 122; Arjomand 1981a, 1988a, 34–58; Lahidji 1988; Hairi 1977a, 236–41, and 1976/1977; as well as the statements of Na'ini, a leading proponent of the constitution, and his understanding of freedom and equality, in Hairi 1977a, 217–34.

25. Translations of excerpts of Nuri's critique may be found in Hairi 1977b, reprinted in Esposito 1983, 292–96, and in Arjomand 1988a, 354–70. On Nuri see also Arjomand 1981a; 1988a, 48–58; 1988c, 180–81; Hairi 1977a, 209–34.

26. Lahidji 1988.

27. On the electoral procedure see Browne 1910, 372–73; Nuri criticized precisely this aspect of democratization; see Hairi 1977b.

28. Akhavi 1980, 35.

29. Faghfoory 1987, 423; on Reza Khan's rise to power and rule see further Abrahamian 1983, 102–65; Banani 1961; Elwell-Sutton 1978.

30. Faghfoory 1987, 419.

31. A few years later, for example, he compelled the sale of alcoholic beverages in Qum. On the tactical character of Reza Shah's religious policy see Arjomand 1988a, 81–82; Faghfoory 1987, 424; Banani 1961, 42, 50–51. On Reza's inaugural address and its religious references see Elwell-Sutton 1978, 28–29.

32. Faghfoory 1987, 425.

33. Akhavi 1980, 61.

34. Keddie 1981, 95–96.

35. Seger 1975, 1978, 1979.

36. Faghfoory 1987, 427.

37. Arjomand 1988a, 84.

38. Abrahamian 1983, 152–53; Arjomand 1988a, 82; Avery 1965, 290–91; Wilber 1975, 166–67.

39. Faghfoory 1987, 427.

40. Faghfoory 1987, 427.

41. Keddie 1981, 115; Abrahamian 1983.

42. On the Fedayan-i Islam see Adele Ferdows 1967; Amir Ferdows 1983; Kazemi 1984, 1985.

43. Akhavi 1980, 63, 65; Keddie 1980a, 135–36.

44. Akhavi 1980, 63–64.

45. Keddie 1980a, 140; on Kashani see Faghfoory 1978; Richard 1983c; Akhavi 1988.

46. Akhavi 1980, 63, 65, 91–95; Keddie 1980a, 135–36.

47. Lambton 1964, 119.

48. Amuzegar and Fekrat 1971, 114–25; Pahlavi 1967; *Revolution of the Shah* 1967; Denman 1978.

49. Lambton 1964, 120; Avery 1965, 505–6.

50. Quoted in Farmayan 1971, 105; see further Algar in Khomeini 1981, 309, note 26; Zonis 1971, 75.

51. Zonis 1971, 45.

52. See Keddie 1981, 157–58. Lambton (1969, 112) points out explicitly that Khomeini did not oppose land reform; likewise, Cottam 1979, 308, and Algar 1972, 246. Lenczowski (1978, 459) argues the contrary. Ashraf distinguishes two factions within the clergy. He claims that one represented the interests of the bazaar, the other the interests of large landholders. He puts Khomeini in the first group (following Fischer 1980a, 179). Representative Mahmudi-Golpagani, in contrast, recently confirmed in a debate in the Iranian parliament that nearly all clerics rejected the land reform plan of 1963; see Bakhash 1989. On the importance of the extension of suffrage to women see Farmayan 1971, 107; Savory 1978, 115–16; Abrahamian 1983, 425, note 10.

53. Khomeini's address may be found in Khomeini 1981, 177–80. The estimates of the number of demonstrators killed range from 56 to 20,000, with the opposition claiming 15,000–20,000, the government admitting 56 on one occasion, another time 86, yet another 200. Moderate estimates put the number at several thousand dead. See Zonis 1971, 45, 63; Algar 1981, 17; Irfani 1983, 82–84; Abrahamian 1980, 24; 1989, 21. On the guerrilla movement as a reaction to the events see Abrahamian 1981 and 1989, 85–87.

54. Arjomand 1984b, 216; Najmabadi 1987, 210, note 8; Green 1982, 40.

55. Fischer 1980a, 195.

56. Fischer 1980a, 193. A listing of mysterious deaths from 1966 to 1977, from Gholam Reza Takhti to Samad Behrangi, Jalal Al-e Ahmad, Nasser Amiri, and Ali Shariati to Mustapha Khomeini, may be found in Zonis 1980, 86.

57. Abrahamian 1983, 505; Keddie 1981, 242–43.

58. Fischer 1980a, 194.

59. Keddie 1981, 244.

60. The most important analyses of the causes of the revolution may be found in Abrahamian 1980; Arjomand 1985a; 1986; 1988a, 189–210; Ashraf and Banuazizi 1985; Cottam 1986; Green 1982; Greussing 1981; Halliday 1979; Jabbari and Olson 1981; Keddie 1988; Parsa 1989; Skocpol 1982 with commentary by Keddie (1982), Ahmad 1982, and Goldfrank 1982. For the perspective of adherents within the revolutionary coalition see Algar 1983; Irfani 1983; Mutahhari 1985b; 1986. From a Marxist or socialist perspective

see Afshar 1983; Jazani 1980. On the politics of the Islamic republic see Akhavi 1986; Bakhash 1986; Beeman 1986; Bill 1982; Hooglund 1986a. On the formation of factions within the clergy see Akhavi 1983b; 1987; Hooglund 1986b; Richard 1983b.

61. McLoughlin 1978, 2.

62. Homa Katouzian (1981) speaks of a "pseudo-modernism," which, given the legal insecurity and political repression, seems appropriate to me, if one does not want to reduce Western modernity to economic growth and technology. See also the juxtaposition of traditionalism and technicism in Pfaff 1966.

63. On the reform movement and its composition see Lambton 1964; Akhavi 1980, 117–29 and 229, note 31; Fischer 1980a, 164–65. On Musa Sadr see Ajami 1986.

64. Lambton 1964, 121–35; Akhavi 1980, 119–20.

65. On Shariati, see Abrahamian 1988; Akhavi 1980, 143–58; 1981; Algar 1979; Bayat 1980a; Irfani 1983, 116–37; Richard 1981, 218–20; Sachedina 1983. On the intellectual and political relationship between Shariati and the Mojahedin see Abrahamian 1989, 92–125.

66. Shariati 1980, 6–7; Al-e Ahmad 1984. For a comparison of the two see Hanson 1983.

67. Shariati 1981, 150. Adele Ferdows effaces these distinctions to a considerable degree; see Ferdows 1983, 1986. On the difference between Khomeini and Shariati see especially Bayat 1980b.

68. Mottahedeh 1985, 16.

69. On the Fedayan-i Islam see note 42 above. On their ties with Mutahhari and Taleghani see Algar 1982, 12; 1985, 17–18. On the thoroughgoing agreement between their ideology and that of Khomeini see Amir Ferdows 1983.

70. Khomeini 1981, 31, 33, 58.

71. Fedayan-i Islam 1967, 9; similarly, Khomeini 1981, 171–72, 222.

72. Fedayan-i Islam 1967, 11; similarly, Khomeini 1981, 33–34.

73. Fedayan-i Islam 1967, 14–15, 12; Khomeini 1981, 257–58, 183.

74. Fedayan-i Islam 1967, 9.

75. Fedayan-i Islam 1967, 18–19; on the historical background see Azari 1983b, 119–24.

76. See note 52 above and Floor 1983, 84–85.

77. Khomeini 1981, 175; 193; 310, note 37; 442; and 223.

78. Khomeini 1981, 31, 33, 58, 258; cf. Beeman 1983, 210.

79. Fedayan-i Islam 1967, 12–17; Khomeini 1981, 118, 171; Beeman 1983, 210.

80. Naficy 1981; Azari 1983b, 125.

81. Azari 1983b, 135–36.

82. Khomeini 1981, 200–208.

83. Khomeini 1981, 217–18.

84. Khomeini 1981, 175–76, 197; Floor 1983, 84–85.

85. Khomeini 1981, 174–76; Fischer 1980a, 194.

86. Khomeini 1981, 309, note 26.

87. Abrahamian 1983, 505; Keddie 1981, 243.

88. Khomeini 1981, 177.

89. Khomeini 1981, 175–80; 440; 193; 201; 243; 308, note 14.

90. Khomeini 1981, 182.

91. Fedayan-i Islam 1967, 6.

92. Fedayan-i Islam 1967, 18.

93. Khomeini 1981, 223.

94. Khomeini 1981, 34, 58, 86. Such statements have led many to consider Khomeini socially engaged or even "progressive" on this point, but that view represents a misunderstanding of hierocratic interests and strategies. Hierocrats have always included the "protection of the weak" among their slogans to preserve their power interests against rivals; see Weber 1978, 1165.

95. Khomeini 1981, 190.

96. Khomeini 1981, 58–59.

97. Arjomand 1981b; 1984b; 1988a, 177–88; 1988c.

98. Kippenberg 1981; Fischer 1980a, 181–231; on the transformation of the interpretation of Hussein in the countryside see Hegland 1983a and 1983b.

99. See note 3 above.

100. Duran 1983.

101. Khomeini 1981, 30–31, 47, 200.

102. Arjomand 1984c, 233–34.

103. Khomeini 1981, 169–73, quotation on 169.

104. Fischer 1980a, 194.

105. The literature on Khomeini's concept of the *velayat-i faqih*, the guardianship of the jurisconsult, is constantly growing. Of particular importance are Arjomand 1988b; Enayat 1983b; Göbel 1984; Rajaee 1983; Rose 1983.

106. Khomeini 1981, 79.

107. Khomeini 1981, 79.

108. Algar 1972, 232, note 3.

109. Khomeini 1981, 60–65; cf. Enayat 1983a, 201.

110. Khomeini 1981, 64–65.

111. Khomeini 1981, 62.

112. Khomeini 1981, 76.

113. On popular religious traditions see Momen 1985, 233–45. On *ta'zieh* see Chelkowski, ed. 1979, especially the contribution by Peterson 1979; also Kippenberg 1981, where additional relevant literature may be found. On the religious readings devoted to Hussein's passion, in particular during Muharram, see Thaiss 1972; 1973, 299–340. On the Ashura processions cf. Haidari 1975. On the relationship between suffering and redemption in these institutions see Ayoub 1978.

114. Kippenberg 1981, 241–42.

115. Thaiss 1972, 357.

116. Khomeini 1981, 131.

117. Kippenberg 1981, 243–48; Fischer 1980a, 183.

118. Khomeini 1981, 127.

119. Khomeini 1981, 139.

120. Khomeini 1981, 47.

121. Khomeini 1981, 89.

122. Khomeini 1981, 27.

123. Fedayan-i Islam 1967, 12.

124. Fedayan-i Islam 1967, 9. On Ghazali see Mernissi 1987, 28; Azari 1983b, 92–95; on the parallelism with the Fedayan-i Islam see Fedayan-i Islam 1967, 9–11. Also see Fischer 1978, 193–97.

125. Mernissi 1987, 27–45, especially 31; Azari 1983b, 95. On the issue complex of the "Eve myth" see also Keddie and Beck 1978, 19; Pipes 1983, 176–82.

126. Khomeini 1981, 27–166. After the referendum of 30 March 1979, in which a 98 percent majority voted for the Islamic Republic, Khomeini declared 1 April 1979 to be the first day of the rule of God; see Göbel 1984, 228.

127. Constitution [1980], 22.

128. Constitution [1980], 22. This is also unambiguously evident from an interview with Khomeini conducted by Said Arjomand before the former's return to Iran. Khomeini stated that it was self-evident that only such areas as were not already covered by religious law and were beneath the dignity of consideration by legal scholars could be subject to parliamentary legislation. See Arjomand 1980, 155–56.

129. Constitution [1980], 11, 15; Khomeini 1981, 48–49.

130. Khomeini thus prepared a legal decision in October 1979 in which he reproached many Shi'ites for refusing to accept Sunni prayer leaders. See Enayat 1982, 51.

131. Even if the oppositions are less marked then they were about 120 years ago (cf. Vámbéry 1867, 123), they continue nevertheless to be significant today, for example, in the conflict between Iran and Saudi Arabia or within the Afghani resistance. See Cole and Keddie 1986; Halliday 1986.

132. Fedayan-i Islam 1967, 47–48; Taleghani 1982, 41, 45.

133. Fedayan-i Islam 1967, 49, 53; see also Khomeini 1981, 190. Taleghani generally stresses the individual producer and to such an extent that he praises the peasant life, and its connection to nature, over the conditions of modern industry, which is directly contrary to the traditional Islamic disdain for rural life and valorization of the city. See Taleghani 1982, 34–35. On the populist implications of this perspective see Bakhash 1989; on the traditional valuation and functional separation between the city and countryside see, among others, English 1966a; Gulick 1969; E. Wirth 1966a, 1973.

134. Fedayan-i Islam 1967, 5.

135. Constitution [1980], 11; in the same sense, Taleghani 1982, 47–53.

136. Taleghani 1982, 28–29. On the general hostility to bureaucracy see Constitution [1980], 16; H. Afshar 1985a, 224–25.

137. See, among other sources, Fedayan-i Islam 1967, 48–49; Khomeini 1981, 190; Abrahamian 1989, 73; H. Afshar 1985a, 225ff. Afshar correctly and emphatically points out that Shi'ite fundamentalism is not egalitarian but hierocratic and patrimonial.

138. Bourdieu 1977, 37, 39. The existence of a patriarchal ideal in working conditions in postrevolutionary Iran is verified in a statement by a labor minister in which he rejected legal regulation of wages and conditions with the argument, "employers, as good Muslims, know best how to take care of their employees" (Abrahamian 1989, 73).

139. Sivers 1981, 365; see also Seger 1978, 67–68.

140. Seger 1978, 67–68; Sivers 1981, 365; Taleghani 1982, 28–30 and 34–35; Taleqani 1983, 112–17.

141. E. Wirth 1974/1975, 216; Sivers 1981; Taleghani 1982, 43–44. For a general discussion of modern Islamic economic doctrines see Cummings et al. 1980; Ishaque 1983; Katouzian 1983.

142. Momen 1985, 235–36; Thaiss 1973, 45–48, 378–79.

143. Constitution [1980], 14; H. Afshar 1982, 79; Khomeini in Tabari and Yeganeh 1982, 98–103. On the acceptance of this view see Pakizegi 1978, 224.

144. Although, earlier, separation was possible with the veil because of Islamic architecture, modern architecture required other, in some cases, strengthened measures of symbolic or physical separation to achieve the same effect. On the functional change of veiling see Keddie and Beck 1978, 8; Williams 1980; on the problem of separation within urban strata see Bauer 1985; Gulick and Gulick 1978, 508–17. A noteworthy interpretation of veiling from a feminist perspective, as a result of insufficient ethical rationalization in the early phase of Islam, is offered by Mernissi (1989, 240–52).

145. Seger 1975, 146.

146. Seger 1978, 56–65; Touba 1985, 136–37, 142–43.

147. Nashat 1983b, 212–15; Touba 1985, 136–44.

148. See Fischer 1980a, 80 and 94; Akhavi 1980, 97; Hooglund 1986b, 79–82.

149. Binder 1965; Momen 1985, 204–6; Mottahedeh 1985, 233 and 240–41.

150. Hooglund 1986b, 75–77. The following figures are either taken directly from Hooglund or calculated on the basis of his data.

151. Ashraf according to Fischer 1980a, 179; Akhavi 1980, 100–103; Thaiss 1973, 116. Thaiss reports here that he attempted to ascertain the strength of the followings among the bazaar merchants of the various *mujtahid*. But he always got the response, "If you are interested in religion, why do you ask political questions?"

152. Abrahamian 1983, 505; Keddie 1981, 156–58; Hooglund 1986b, 76, 81–82.

153. Hooglund 1986a, 77–82; Bakhash 1984, 180–82.

154. Algar 1972; Floor 1981; Tabari 1983; Keddie 1986.

155. On the question of the extent to which Max Weber represented such a position, see Riesebrodt 1980.

156. Akhavi 1980, 23–59; Algar 1972, 241.

157. Abrahamian 1983, 432–33; Fischer 1982; Keddie 1981, 244.

158. Ehlers 1980, 286–87; on the bazaar see also Fischer 1977, 180–83.

159. Thaiss 1973, 37.

160. Bill 1972, 6–15; Keddie 1981, 244; Thaiss 1973, 38.

161. Zonis 1971, 173; Thaiss 1973, 53–55, 85–88.

162. Zonis 1971, 174.

163. On urbanization and urban migration in Iran see especially Kazemi 1980a (in particular 2–3) and 1980b; further, see Brown 1981; Danesh 1985; Mojtahed 1980.

164. Kazemi 1980a, 94–96; Bauer 1983; Munson 1988, 100–102. The low level of fundamentalist religiosity in the countryside is apparent from Hooglund 1982 and Loeffler 1988.

165. Khomeini 1981, 131–32; on the practical application see Kippenberg 1981. With his demand that "every day should be Ashura, every grave Kerbala," Khomeini, in Kippenberg's view, recast Ashura as a "completely ethical principle"; see Kippenberg 1981, 227.

166. Thaiss 1973, 53–55, 85–88; see also Tibi 1988, 95–112.

167. Thaiss 1973, 69–70. M. Rainer Lepsius has repeatedly referred to the significance of association processes for the constitution of classes, strata, or milieus; see, among other works, Lepsius 1974, 1987.

168. Thaiss 1972, 352–53; Kazemi 1980a, 63.

169. Thaiss 1972, 354; Kazemi 1980a, 63.

170. Kippenberg 1981, 223; E. Wirth 1974/1975, 215.

171. Kippenberg 1981, 225–27; Fischer 1980a, 133.

172. Thaiss 1972, 352; E. Wirth 1974/1975, 215.

173. Thaiss 1972, 353.

174. E. Wirth 1974/1975, 240–41.

175. Seger 1978.

176. Thaiss 1972, 353.

177. E. Wirth 1974/1975, 218.

178. Thaiss 1973, 107–8, 209.

179. Fischer 1980a, 94.

180. Hooglund 1986b, 77–82; Thaiss 1973, 207.

181. Thaiss 1971, 199; 1973, 45.

182. Zonis 1971, 173.

183. Zonis 1971, 171–87.

184. Najmabadi 1986.

185. See Ashraf 1988.

186. The following analysis of Tehran's development is based essentially on the outstanding studies by Martin Seger; see Seger 1978 and also 1975 and 1979.

187. E. Wirth 1968, 110–12.

188. For Kirman see English 1966a and 1966b; for the Persian provincial city Maragheh see Good 1978, 484–93. Among the works on the structure of the city and bazaar in the Middle East, those by Eugen Wirth stand out; see E. Wirth 1966a, 1966b, 1968, 1973, and 1974/1975; Gaube and Wirth 1978. On oriental and Islamic cities in general, see Abu-Lughod 1969, 1987; C. Brown 1973; Hourani and Stern, eds., 1970; Lapidus, ed., 1969; Lapidus 1969, 1973a, 1973b, 1984; Saqqaf 1987. The dual modern development of cities has a precursor in the divided city under colonial rule; see Abu-Lughod 1980.

189. Seger 1978, 73–74.

190. Seger 1978, 102–13.

191. Thaiss 1973, 53–55. On the compulsory reintroduction after the revolution of gender-segregated wedding parties with no alcoholic beverages and no music or dancing see Schuckar 1983, 90.

192. Cf. Sivers 1981.

193. Pahlavi 1980, 156; see also Keddie 1981, 169–74; Abrahamian 1980, 25.

194. Abrahamian 1983, 496–98; Pahlavi 1980, 155–56; Green 1982, 42.

195. Thaiss 1973, 86.

196. Thaiss 1973, 85.

197. Arjomand 1988a, 59–74. On the analysis of the Iranian elite in the 1960s and 1970s see Bill 1975 and Zonis 1975.

198. On the function of the guilds see, among others, Thaiss 1971; 1973, 26–37; Bonine 1981, 204. On their dissolution in 1975 see Abrahamian 1983, 443; 1989, 25.

199. Binder 1962, 172.

200. Moreover, he attempted, in vain, to preserve his Islamic legitimacy as well. On the mix of Islamic, monarchical, and national identity see Binder 1962, 280–86; Filippani-Ronconi 1978.

201. Thaiss 1973, 29.

202. Abrahamian 1983, 439–46; 1989, 25–27.

203. Abrahamian 1983, 445.

204. Keddie 1981, 242–43.

205. Kippenberg 1981.

206. Abrahamian 1989, 73. On politics regarding women and the control of sexual morality under Pahlavi and the Islamic Republic see Azari 1983a; 1983b; 1983c; Fathi 1985; Haeri 1983; Mossavar-Rahmani 1983; Nashat 1983a and 1983b; Schuckar 1983; Tabari 1982; Touba 1985; Vatandoust 1985; Yeganeh 1982; Yeganeh and Keddie 1986; and the documents in Tabari and Yeganeh, eds. 1982. For a comparison between pre- and postrevolutionary economic policy see Issawi 1978; Katouzian 1983; Pesaran 1982; Hooglund 1986a; Karimi 1986. An excellent overview of postrevolutionary politics is available in Bakhash 1986.

CHAPTER 4

1. This process corresponds to the transition from traditionalism to conservatism as Karl Mannheim has described it. See Mannheim 1986 as well as Arjomand 1984b.

2. Max Weber 1978, 471–72; Arjomand 1986, 92–93; Geertz 1968, 60; Gellner 1981, 24.

3. In reference to its preservation of structural *principles* fundamentalism is patriarchalism; in reference to its partial "modernization" of structural *forms* it is neopatriarchalism. On the distinction between structural principles and structural forms see Schluchter 1981, 1. An application of the patriarchalism concept to political circumstances in the Middle East may be found in Bill and Leiden 1984, 148–76. They correctly emphasize the dominance of a patriarchal foundation for the establishment of patrimonial rule.

4. On the effect of the form of leisure-time practices on the patriarchal family structure in postrevolutionary Iran see Touba 1985, 133–34.

5. I will deal later with the political ideal of a religious republicanism.

6. A good example of this may be found in Taleqani 1983, 141.

7. On the significance of such an ethical differentiation see Lepsius 1977.

8. This is revealed above all in the more recent development of Protestant fundamentalism. Thus Jerry Falwell occasionally speaks of democracy as "mob rule" (Falwell 1980, 51), and "reconstructionism" quite clearly upholds a theocratic regime; see Shupe 1989.

9. See S. Hunter 1986; Tibi 1990.

10. Something similar can be found in Germany as well around the turn of the century, when processes of socioeconomic transformation were attributed either to the Jews or to Roman law. There, too, the evil came from without, was disseminated by foreigners, and was regarded as destructive to the bonds of German solidarity. And there, too, the "special path" for Germany was propagated as a remedy.

11. Algar 1972, 232.

12. Michael Fischer has pointed out that, in many respects, Khomeini possessed atypical characteristics for a Shi'ite legal scholar. See Fischer 1980b, 1983. On Khomeini see also Algar 1988.

13. Thus sources as early as Ibn Khaldun; see Gellner 1981, 1–85, and 114–30; Crapanzano 1973.

14. On this see Lepsius 1966.

15. Said Arjomand (1988a, 197–200) in particular emphasizes this aspect without, admittedly, reducing the phenomenon to it. However, this is one of the few points in which I find his interpretation of the phenomenon not persuasive.

16. Lipset 1960, 131–76.

17. Danesh 1985, 62.

18. Peter Berger in particular emphasizes this dimension; see Berger 1967, 1980; Berger et al. 1974.

19. Joseph Gusfield, in particular, has drawn attention to this aspect; see Gusfield 1963, 166–88.

20. In much of the literature the impression is made that religion represents only an embellishment with no independent significance or consequences for the specific form taken by the movement. See, for example, S. Hunter 1986.

21. I distinguish between structural principles and structural forms (see note 3 above). The institutions and ideals of Shi'ite and Protestant fundamentalism incorporate, according to the different social conditions and cultural traditions in Iran and the United States, different forms within a patriarchal principle based on piety.

22. It is also in this sense that I understand Craig Calhoun's analysis of "radicalism of tradition"; see Calhoun 1983. His emphasis on communitarian cohesiveness as the foundation of political radicalism corresponds to my emphasis on the reproduction of the traditional milieu under conditions of rapid urbanization.

23. The central significance of the family, the role of women, the relationship between the sexes, and sexual morality serving to distinguish Islam from the "decadent West" is also to be found in the writings of the most important Egyptian theoretician of fundamentalism, Sayyid Qutb. See, for example, Benard and Khalilzad 1984, 95–102; on Qutb's worldview see Haddad

1983. That these concerns are not a result of contact between Islam and the West but are structurally conditioned is evidenced by their dominance within contemporary Protestant fundamentalism in the United States as well.

24. Hofstadter (1963, 119) has brought attention to the sexual aspect, as well as a conception of masculinity that was projected onto Jesus.

25. The transformation from personalistic-patriarchal to depersonalized economic relationships and their economic as well as sociopsychological implications were elaborated with particular clarity by Max Weber in his early work; see Riesebrodt 1986.

26. See Pfaff 1966, Herf 1984.

27. On the parallelism between the cases studied here and other fundamentalist movements on issues such as sexual morality, women's rights, the family, and consumer and leisure-time behavior see, among others, Hoffmann-Ladd 1987; Mitchell 1969, 223–24, 254–59; Toprak 1984; Williams 1980; Yadlin 1983; Zubaida 1987. A comparison with populism and fascism fails if only because those concepts are themselves insufficiently differentiated. Cf. Ionescu and Gellner 1969; Canovan 1981; and Laqueur 1983, in particular the essay by Linz.

28. Aspects of the "new religious movements" represent reactions comparable to the structural transformation of the family; see Robbins 1985, 11.

References

Abel, Wilhelm et al., eds. 1966. Wirtschaft, Geschichte, und Wirtschaftsge-schichte. Stuttgart: Gustav Fischer.

Abell, Aaron Ignatius. 1943. The Urban Impact on American Protestantism, 1865–1900. Reprint. Hamden and London: Archon, 1962.

Abrahamian, Ervand. 1968. The Crowd in Iranian Politics, 1905–1953. In: Past and Present 41: 184–210.

———. 1979. The Causes of the Constitutional Revolution in Iran. In: International Journal of Middle East Studies 10: 381–414.

———. 1980. Structural Causes of the Iranian Revolution. In: MERIP Reports, no. 87, May: 21–26.

———. 1981. Die Guerilla-Bewegung im Iran von 1963 bis 1977. In: Berliner Institut, ed. 1981: 337–60.

———. 1983. Iran between Two Revolutions. 2d printing, with corrections. Princeton: Princeton University Press.

———. 1988. Ali Shariati: Ideologue of the Iranian Revolution. In: Burke and Lapidus, eds. 1988: 289–97.

———. 1989. The Iranian Mojahedin. New Haven: Yale University Press.

Abu-Lughod, Janet. 1969. Varieties of Urban Experience: Contrast, Coexistence, and Coalescence in Cairo. In: Lapidus, ed. 1969: 159–87.

———. 1980. Rabat: Urban Apartheid in Morocco. Princeton: Princeton University Press.

———. 1987. The Islamic City—Historic Myth, Islamic Essence, and Contemporary Relevance. In: International Journal of Middle East Studies 19, 2: 155–76.

Afshar, Haleh. 1982. Khomeini's Teachings and Their Implications for Iranian Women. In: Tabari and Yeganeh, eds. 1982: 75–90.

———. 1985a. The Iranian Theocracy. In: Afshar, ed. 1985: 220–43.

———. 1985b. Epilogue. In: Afshar, ed. 1985: 244–53.

Afshar, Haleh, ed. 1985. Iran: A Revolution in Turmoil. Albany: SUNY Press.

Afshar, Soraya. 1983. The Economic Base for the Revival of Islam in Iran. In: Azari, ed. 1983: 72–89.

Ahlstrom, Sydney E. 1975. A Religious History of the American People. 2 vols. Garden City, N.Y.: Doubleday.

Ahmad, Eqbal. 1982. Comment on Skocpol (1982). In: Theory and Society 11: 293–300.

Ajami, Fouad. 1986. The Vanished Imam: Musa Al Sadr and the Shia of Lebanon. Ithaca: Cornell University Press.

Akhavi, Shahrough. 1980. Religion and Politics in Contemporary Iran: Clergy-State Relations in the Pahlavi Period. Albany: SUNY Press.

———. 1983a. Shariati's Social Thought. In: Keddie, ed. 1983: 125–44.

———. 1983b. The Ideology and Praxis of Shi'ism in the Iranian Revolution. In: Comparative Studies in Society and History 25: 195–221.

———. 1986. Clerical Politics in Iran since 1979. In: Keddie and Hooglund, eds. 1986: 57–73.

———. 1987. Elite Factionalism in the Islamic Republic of Iran. In: Middle East Journal 41, 2: 181–201.

———. 1988. The Role of the Clergy in Iranian Politics, 1949–1954. In: Bill and Louis, eds. 1988: 91–117.

Al-e Ahmad, Jalal. 1982. Iranian Society. Compiled and edited by Michael C. Hillmann. Lexington: Mazda Publishers.

———. 1984. Occidentosis: A Plague from the West. Introduction by Hamid Algar. Berkeley: Mizan Press.

Alexander, Daniel. 1985. Is Fundamentalism an Integrism? In: Social Compass 32, 3: 373–92.

Algar, Hamid. 1969. Religion and State in Iran, 1785–1906: The Role of the Ulama in the Qajar Period. Berkeley and Los Angeles: University of California Press.

———. 1972. The Oppositional Role of the Ulama in Twentieth-Century Iran. In: Keddie, ed. 1972: 231–55.

———. 1979. Introduction. In: Shariati 1979: 5–38.

———. 1981. Introduction. In: Khomeini 1981: 13–23.

———. 1982. Introduction. In: Taleghani 1982: 9–21.

———. 1983. The Roots of the Islamic Revolution. London: Open Press.

———. 1985. Introduction. In: Mutahhari 1985: 9–22.

———. 1988. Imam Khomeini, 1902–1962: The Pre-Revolutionary Years. In: Burke and Lapidus, eds. 1988: 263–88.

Alkan, Türker. 1984. The National Salvation Party. In: Heper and Israeli, eds. 1984: 79–102.

Allen, Leslie H., ed. 1925. Bryan and Darrow at Dayton. New York: Russell and Russell.

Amanat, Abbas. 1988. Inbetween the Madrasa and the Marketplace: The Designation of Clerical Leadership in Modern Shi'ism. In: Arjomand, ed. 1988: 98–132.

Amirsadeghi, Hossein, and Ferrier, R. W., eds. 1977. Twentieth-Century Iran. London: Heinemann.

Amuzegar, Jahangir, and Fekrat, M. Ali. 1971. Iran: Economic Development under Dualistic Conditions. Chicago and London: University of Chicago Press.

Anderson, Nels. 1923. The Hobo: The Sociology of the Homeless Man. Chicago: University of Chicago Press.

Anderson, Robert Mapes. 1979. Vision of the Disinherited: The Making of American Pentecostalism. New York: Oxford University Press.

Ansari, Hamied N. 1984. The Islamic Militants in Egyptian Politics. In: International Journal of Middle East Studies 16: 123–44.

Aran, Gideon. 1986. From Religious Zionism to Zionist Religion: The Roots of Gush Emunim. In: Medding, ed. 1986: 116–43.

Arjomand, Said Amir. 1980. The State and Khomeini's Islamic Order. In: Iranian Studies 13: 1–4, 147–64.

———. 1981a. The Ulama's Traditionalist Opposition to Parliamentarianism, 1907–1909. In: Middle Eastern Studies 17, 2: 174–90.

———. 1981b. Shi'ite Islam and the Revolution in Iran. In: Government and Opposition 16, 3: 293–316.

———. 1984a. Introduction: Social Movements in the Contemporary Near and Middle East. In: Arjomand, ed. 1984: 1–27.

———. 1984b. Traditionalism in Twentieth-Century Iran. In: Arjomand, ed. 1984: 195–232.

———. 1984c. The Shadow of God and the Hidden Imam: Religion, Political Order, and Societal Change in Shi'ite Iran from the Beginning to 1890. Chicago: University of Chicago Press.

———. 1985a. The Causes and Significance of the Iranian Revolution. In: State, Culture, and Society 1, 3: 41–66.

———. 1985b. Religion, Political Order, and Societal Change: With Special Reference to Shi'ite Islam. In: Current Perspectives in Social Theory 6: 1–15.

———. 1986. Iran's Islamic Revolution in Comparative Perspective. In: World Politics 38: 383–414.

———. 1988a. The Turban for the Crown: The Islamic Revolution in Iran. New York and Oxford: Oxford University Press.

———. 1988b. Introduction: Shi'ism, Authority, and Political Culture. In: Arjomand, ed. 1988: 1–22.

———. 1988c. Ideological Revolution in Shi'ism. In: Arjomand, ed. 1988: 178–209.

———. 1989. The Rule of God in Iran. In: Social Compass 36, 4: 539–48.

Arjomand, Said Amir, ed. 1984. From Nationalism to Revolutionary Islam. Albany: SUNY Press.

———. 1988. Authority and Political Culture in Shi'ism. Albany: SUNY Press.

Aronoff, Myron J., ed. 1983. Culture and Political Change. New Brunswick and London: Transaction Books.

Ash, Roberta. 1972. Social Movements in America. Chicago: Markham.

Ashraf, Ahmad. 1988. Bazaar-Mosque Alliance: The Social Basis of Revolts and Revolutions. In: Politics, Culture, and Society 1, 4: 538–67.

Ashraf, Ahmad, and Banuazizi, Ali. 1985. The State, Classes, and Modes of

Mobilization in the Iranian Revolution. In: State, Culture, and Society 1, 3: 3–40.

Ashworth, Robert A. 1924. The Fundamentalist Movement among the Baptists. In: Journal of Religion 4, 6: 611–31.

Athearn, Walter S., et al. 1923. The Religious Education of Protestants in an American Commonwealth. New York: George H. Doran.

Atherton, Lewis. 1972. The City Comes to Main Street. In: Jackson and Schultz, eds. 1972: 429–41.

Avery, Peter. 1965. Modern Iran. New York and Washington, D.C.: Praeger.

Ayoub, Mahmoud. 1978. Redemptive Suffering in Islam: A Study of the Devotional Aspects of Ashura in Twelver Shi'ism. The Hague: Mouton.

Azari, Farah. 1983a. Islam's Appeal to Women in Iran: Illusions and Reality. In: Azari, ed. 1983: 1–71.

———. 1983b. Sexuality and Women's Oppression in Iran. In: Azari, ed. 1983: 90–156.

———. 1983c. The Post-Revolutionary Women's Movement in Iran. In: Azari, ed. 1983: 190–225.

Azari, Farah, ed. 1983. Women of Iran: The Conflict with Fundamentalist Islam. London: Ithaca Press.

Bahar, Sima. 1983. A Historical Background to the Women's Movement in Iran. In: Azari, ed. 1983: 170–89.

Bailey, Kenneth K. 1964. Southern White Protestantism in the Twentieth Century. New York: Harper and Row.

Bakhash, Shaul. 1984. Sermons, Revolutionary Pamphleteering, and Mobilisation: Iran, 1978. In: Arjomand, ed. 1984: 177–94.

———. 1986. The Reign of the Ayatollahs. London: Unwin.

———. 1989. The Politics of Land, Law, and Social Justice in Iran's Islamic Republic. Paper presented at the Conference on the Transmission of Religious Culture in Islam, Princeton, 27–29 April.

Baltzell, E. Digby. 1964. The Protestant Establishment: Aristocracy and Caste in America. Reprint. New Haven: Yale University Press, 1987.

Banani, Amin. 1961. The Modernization of Iran, 1921–1941. Stanford: Stanford University Press.

Baptist Fundamentals. 1920. Being Addresses Delivered at the Pre-Convention Conference at Buffalo, June 21–22, 1920. Philadelphia: Judson Press.

Barr, David L., and Piediscalzi, Nicholas, eds. 1982. The Bible in American Education: From Source Book to Text Book. Philadelphia: Fortress Press.

Barr, James. 1978. Fundamentalism. Philadelphia: Westminster Press.

Bauer, Janet. 1983. Poor Women and Social Consciousness in Revolutionary Iran. In: Nashat, ed. 1983: 141–69.

———. 1985. Demographic Change, Women and the Family in a Migrant Neighborhood of Teheran. In: Fathi, ed. 1985: 158–86.

Bayat, Mangol. 1980a. Shi'ism in Contemporary Iranian Politics: The Case of Ali Shari'ati. In: Kedourie and Haim, eds. 1980: 155–68.

———. 1980b. Islam in Pahlavi and Post-Pahlavi Iran: A Cultural Revolution? In: Esposito, ed. 1980: 87–106.

————. 1982. Mysticism and Dissent: Socioreligious Thought in Qajar Iran. Syracuse: Syracuse University Press.

Beck, Lois, and Keddie, Nikki R., eds. 1978. Women in the Muslim World. Cambridge and London: Harvard University Press.

Beeman, William O. 1983. Images of the Great Satan: Representations of the United States in the Iranian Revolution. In: Keddie, ed. 1983: 191–217.

————. 1986. Iran's Religious Regime: What Makes It Tick? Will It Ever Run Down? In: Annals, AAPSS 483: 73–83.

Bell, Daniel, ed. 1963. The Radical Right. Garden City, N.Y.: Doubleday.

Benard, Cheryl, and Khalilzad, Zalmay. 1984. "The Government of God": Iran's Islamic Republic. New York: Columbia University Press.

Berger, Peter L. 1963. A Market Model for the Analysis of Ecumenicity. In: Social Research 30: 77–93.

————. 1967. The Sacred Canopy: Elements of a Sociological Theory of Religion. New York: Doubleday.

————. 1980. The Heretical Imperative: Contemporary Possibilities of Religious Affirmations. Garden City, N.Y.: Anchor Books.

————. 1981. The Class Struggle in American Religion. In: Christian Century, 25 February: 194–99.

————. 1986. American Religion: Conservative Upsurge, Liberal Prospects. In: Michaelsen and Roof, eds. 1986: 19–36.

Berger, Peter L., et al. 1974. The Homeless Mind: Modernization and Consciousness. New York: Vintage Books.

Berliner Institut für Vergleichende Sozialforschung, ed. 1980. Revolution in Iran und Afghanistan. Frankfurt: Syndikat.

————. 1981. Religion und Politik im Iran. Frankfurt: Syndikat.

Betts, George H. 1929. The Beliefs of Seven Hundred Ministers and Their Meaning for Religious Education. New York: Abingdon Press.

Bill, James A. 1972. The Politics of Iran: Groups, Classes, and Modernization. Columbus, Ohio: Charles E. Merrill.

————. 1975. The Patterns of Elite Politics in Iran. In: Lenczowski, ed. 1975: 17–40.

————. 1982. Power and Religion in Revolutionary Iran. In: Middle East Journal 36: 22–47.

Bill, James A., and Leiden, Carl. 1984. Politics in the Middle East. 2d ed. Boston: Little, Brown.

Bill, James A., and Louis, Wm. Roger, eds. 1988. Musaddiq, Iranian Nationalism, and Oil. Austin: University of Texas Press.

Binder, Leonard. 1962. Iran: Political Development in a Changing Society. Berkeley and Los Angeles: University of California Press.

————. 1965. The Proofs of Islam: Religion and Politics in Iran. In: Makdisi, ed. 1965: 118–40.

Bonine, Michael E. 1981. Shops and Shopkeepers: Dynamics of an Iranian Provincial Bazaar. In: Bonine and Keddie, eds. 1981: 203–28.

Bonine, Michael E., and Keddie, Nikki R., eds. 1981. Continuity and Change in Modern Iran. (Corrected Edition.) Albany: SUNY Press.

Bourdieu, Pierre. 1977. Algeria 1960. Cambridge: Cambridge University Press.

Bradley, Laura L. 1962. Protestant Churches and the Ku Klux Klan in Mississippi during the 1920s: Study of an Unsuccessful Courtship. M. A. thesis, University of Mississippi.

Braeman, John, et al., eds. 1968. Change and Continuity in Twentieth-Century America: The 1920s. Cleveland: Ohio State University Press.

Brougher, J. Whitcomb. 1920. Baptists and World-Wide Missions. In: Baptist Fundamentals 1920: 191–202.

Brown, Carl L., ed. 1973. From Madina to Metropolis. Princeton: Darwin Press.

Brown, Melvin R. 1981. Migrant Adjustment in Teheran, Iran. Ph.D. diss., Brown University.

Brown, William Adams. 1922. The Church in America. New York: Macmillan.

Browne, Edward G. 1910. The Persian Revolution, 1905–1909. Cambridge: Cambridge University Press. (Reprint. London: Frank Cass, 1966).

Bruce, Steve. 1986. God Save Ulster: The Religion and Politics of Paisleyism. New York: Oxford University Press.

Brumback, Carl. 1961. Suddenly . . . from Heaven: A History of the Assemblies of God. Springfield, Mo.: Gospel Publishing House.

Brunner, Edmund de S. 1921. The Country Church. In: Christian Century, 28 April: 13–15.

———. 1923. Church Life in the Rural South. New York: George H. Doran.

Bryan, William J. 1922. In His Image. New York: Fleming H. Revell.

Buenker, John D. 1973. Urban Liberalism and Progressive Reform. New York: Charles Scribner's Sons.

Burgess, Ernest W. 1925. The Growth of the City: An Introduction to a Research Project. In: Park et al., eds. 1925: 47–62.

———. 1928. Residential Segregation in American Cities. In: Annals 40: 105–15.

Burke, Edmund III, and Lapidus, Ira, eds. 1988. Islam, Politics, and Social Movements. Berkeley and Los Angeles: University of California Press.

Bustard, W. W. 1920. The Baptist Program of Evangelism. In Baptist Fundamentals 1920: 143–47.

Caldwell, Erskine. 1980. Deep South. Athens: University of Georgia Press.

Calhoun, Craig J. 1983. The Radicalism of Tradition: Community Strength or Venerable Disguise and Borrowed Language. In: American Journal of Sociology 88, 5: 886–914.

Calmard, J. 1989. Mardja-i taqlid. In: Encyclopaedia of Islam, New Edition, vol. 6: 548–56.

Canovan, Margaret. 1981. Populism. New York: Harcourt Brace Jovanovich.

Caplan, Lionel. 1987. Introduction. In: Caplan, ed. 1987: 1–24.

Caplan, Lionel, ed. 1987. Studies in Religious Fundamentalism. Albany: SUNY Press.

Carter, Paul A. 1968. The Fundamentalist Defense of the Faith. In: Braeman et al., eds. 1968: 179–214.

Chelkowski, Peter J., ed. 1979. Ta'ziyeh: Ritual and Drama in Iran. New York: New York University Press.

Clow, W. M. 1922. The Justification of Capitalism. In: Princeton Theological Review 20: 647–60.

Cole, Juan R. 1983. Imami Jurisprudence and the Role of the Ulama: Mortaza Ansari on Emulating the Supreme Exemplar. In: Keddie, ed. 1983: 33–46.

Cole, Juan R. J., and Keddie, Nikki R., eds. 1986. Shi'ism and Social Protest. New Haven: Yale University Press.

Cole, Stewart G. 1931. The History of Fundamentalism. New York: Harper and Row.

Connelly, Mark Thomas. 1980. The Response to Prostitution in the Progressive Era. Chapel Hill: University of North Carolina Press.

Constitution. 1980. The Constitution of the Islamic Republic of Iran. Tehran: Islamic Propagation Organization.

Conze, Werner, and Kocka, Jürgen, eds. 1985. Bildungsbürgertum im 19. Jahrhundert. Part 1: Bildungssystem and Professionalisierung im internationalen Vergleich. Stuttgart: Klett-Cotta.

Cottam, Richard W. 1979. Nationalism in Iran. Updated Edition. University of Pittsburgh Press.

———. 1986. The Iranian Revolution. In: Cole and Keddie, eds. 1986: 55–87.

Coulson, Noel, and Hinchcliffe, Doreen. 1978. Women and Law Reform in Contemporary Islam. In: Beck and Keddie, eds. 1978: 37–51.

Crapanzano, Vincent. 1972. The Hamadsha. In: Keddie, ed. 1972: 327–48.

———. 1973. The Hamadsha: A Study in Moroccan Ethnopsychiatry. Berkeley and Los Angeles: University of California Press.

Cremin, Lawrence A. 1988. American Education: The Metropolitan Experience, 1876–1980. New York: Harper and Row.

Cross, Robert D., ed. 1967. The Church and the City, 1865–1910. Indianapolis and New York: Bobbs-Merrill.

Cummings, John Thomas, et al. 1980. Islam and Modern Economic Change. In: Esposito, ed. 1980: 25–47.

Dabashi, Hamid. 1989. By What Authority? The Formation of Khomeini's Revolutionary Discourse, 1964–1977. In: Social Compass 36, 4: 511–38.

Danesh, Abol Hassan. 1985. Rural-Urban Migration, Urbanization, and Squatter Settlements in the Developing Countries: A Case Study in Iran. Ph.D. diss., University of California, Riverside.

Davis, Allen F. 1984. Spearheads for Reform: The Social Settlements and the Progressive Movement, 1890–1914. New Brunswick, N.J.: Rutgers University Press.

Davis, Eric. 1984. Ideology, Social Class, and Islamic Radicalism in Modern Egypt. In: Arjomand, ed. 1984: 134–57.

Dekmejian, R. Hrair. 1985. Islam in Revolution: Fundamentalism in the Arab World. Syracuse: Syracuse University Press.

———. 1988. Islamic Revival: Catalysts, Categories, and Consequences. In: S. Hunter, ed. 1988: 3–19.

Delnay, Robert G. 1963. A History of the Baptist Bible Union. Th.D. diss., Dallas Theological Seminary.

Denman, D. R. 1978. Land Reforms of Shah and People. In: Lenczowski, ed. 1978: 253–301.

Dessouki, Ali E. Hillal. 1982. The Islamic Resurgence: Sources, Dynamics, and Implications. In: Dessouki, ed. 1982: 3–31.

Dessouki, Ali E. Hillal, ed. 1982. Islamic Resurgence in the Arab World. New York: Praeger.

Dixon, A. C. 1920. The Bible at the Center of the Modern University. In: Baptist Fundamentals 1920: 119–40.

Dollar, George W. 1973. A History of Fundamentalism in America. Greenville, S.C.: Bob Jones University Press.

Douglass, H. Paul. 1924. The Saint Louis Church Survey. A Religious Investigation with a Social Background. New York: George H. Doran.

———. 1926a. One Thousand City Churches: Phases of Adaptation to an Urban Environment. New York: George H. Doran.

———. 1926b. The Springfield Church Survey: A Study of Organized Religion with its Social Background. New York: George H. Doran.

———. 1927. The Church in the Changing City. New York: George H. Doran.

———. 1929. Church Comity: A Study of Cooperative Church Extension in American Cities. New York: George H. Doran.

Douglass, H. Paul, and Brunner, Edmund de S. 1935. The Protestant Church as a Social Institution. New York: Harper and Brothers.

Duran, Khalid. 1983. The "Golden Age" Syndrome: Islamist Medina and Other Historical Models of Contemporary Muslim Thought. In: Schweizerische Zeitschrift für Soziologie 3: 703–16.

Durkheim, Emile. 1951. Suicide: A Study in Sociology. Glencoe, Ill.: Free Press.

Eells, Earnest E. 1923. Protestantism and Property (3). In: Princeton Theological Review 21: 430–57.

Ehlers, Eckart. 1980. Iran: Grundzüge einer geographischen Landeskunde. Darmstadt: Wissenschaftliche Buchgesellschaft.

Ellis, Walter Edmund Warren. 1974. Social and Religious Factors in the Fundamentalist-Modernist Schism among Baptists in North America, 1895–1934. Ph.D. diss., University of Pittsburgh.

Elwell-Sutton, L. P. 1978. Reza Shah the Great: Founder of the Pahlavi Dynasty. In: Lenczowski, ed. 1987: 1–50.

Enayat, Hamid. 1982. Modern Islamic Political Thought. London: Macmillan.

———. 1983a. Revolution in Iran 1979: Religion as Political Ideology. In: O'Sullivan, ed. 1983: 191–205.

———. 1983b. Iran: Khumayni's Concept of the "Guardianship of the Jurisconsult." In: Piscatori, ed. 1983: 160–80.

Ende, Werner. 1984. Der schiitische Islam. In: Ende and Steinbach, eds. 1984: 70–90.

Ende, Werner, and Steinbach, Udo, eds. 1984. Der Islam der Gegenwart. Munich: C. H. Beck.

English, Paul Ward. 1966a. City and Village in Iran: Settlement and Economy in the Kirman Basin. Madison: University of Wisconsin Press.

———. 1966b. Culture Change and the Structure of a Persian City. In: Leiden, ed. 1966: 32–48.

Esposito, John L., ed. 1980. Islam and Development: Religion and Sociopolitical Change. Syracuse: Syracuse University Press.

———, ed. 1983. Voices of Resurgent Islam. New York and Oxford: Oxford University Press.

Faghfoory, Mohammad H. 1978. The Role of the Ulama in Twentienth-Century Iran with Particular Reference to Ayatullah Haj Sayyid Abul-Qasim Kashani. Ph.D. diss., University of Wisconsin, Madison.

———. 1987. The Ulama-State Relations in Iran: 1921–1941. In: International Journal of Middle East Studies 19: 413–32.

Falwell, Jerry. 1980. Listen America! New York: Doubleday.

Falwell, Jerry, et al. 1981. The Fundamentalist Phenomenon. Garden City, N.Y.: Doubleday.

Farmayan, Hafez F. 1971. Politics during the Sixties: A Historical Analysis. In: Yar-Shater, ed. 1971: 88–116.

Fathi, Asghar, ed. 1985. Women and the Family in Iran. Leiden: E. J. Brill.

Fedayan-I Islam. 1967. Rahnema-yi Haqa'iq. Translated by Adele Ferdows as "The Book of Ideology by the Fadyan Islam." Published as Appendix in Ferdows 1967.

Ferdows, Adele K. 1967. Religion in Iranian Nationalism: The Study of the Fedayan-I Islam. Ph.D. diss., Indiana University.

———. 1983. Women and the Islamic Revolution. In: International Journal of Middle East Studies 15: 283–98.

———. 1986. Shariati and Khomeini on Women. In: Keddie and Hooglund, eds. 1986: 127–38.

Ferdows, Amir H. 1983. Khomaini and Fadayan's Society and Politics. In: International Journal of Middle East Studies 15: 241–57.

Filippani-Ronconi, Pio. 1978. The Tradition of Sacred Kingship in Iran. In: Lenczowski, ed. 1978: 51–83.

Fischer, Michael M. J. 1977. Persian Society: Transformation and Strain. In: Amirsadeghi and Ferrier, eds. 1977: 171–95.

———. 1978. On Changing the Concept and Position of Persian Women. In: Beck and Keddie, eds. 1978: 189–215.

———. 1980a. Iran: From Religious Dispute to Revolution. Cambridge and London: Harvard University Press.

———. 1980b. Becoming Mollah: Reflections on Iranian Clerics in a Revolutionary Age. In: Iranian Studies 13: 83–117.

———. 1982. Islam and the Revolt of the Petite Bourgeoisie. In: Daedalus 111, 1: 101–25.

———. 1983. Imam Khomeini: Four Levels of Understanding. In: Esposito, ed. 1983: 150–74.

Flexner, Eleanor. 1979. Century of Struggle: The Women's Rights Movement in the United States. Revised edition. Cambridge, Mass.: Belknap Press.

Floor, Willem. 1983. The Revolutionary Character of the Ulama: Wishful Thinking or Reality? In: Keddie, ed. 1983: 73–97.

Fosdick, Harry Emerson. 1922. Shall the Fundamentalists Win? Reprinted in: Hutchison, ed. 1968: 170–82.

Friedman, Menachem. 1986. Haredim Confront the Modern City. In: Medding, ed. 1986: 74–96.

The Fundamentals. 1910–1915. A Testimony to the Truth. Chicago: Testimony Publishing.

Furniss, Norman F. 1954. The Fundamentalist Controversy, 1918–1931. New Haven: Yale University Press.

Gatewood, Willard B. 1966. Preachers, Pedagogues, and Politicians: The Evolution Controversy in North Carolina, 1920–1927. Chapel Hill: University of North Carolina Press.

Gatewood, Willard B., ed. 1969. Controversy in the Twenties: Fundamentalism, Modernism, and Evolution. Nashville: Vanderbilt University Press.

Gaube, Heinz, and Wirth, Eugen. 1978. Der Bazar von Isfahan. Wiesbaden: Dr. Ludwig Reichert.

Gaustad, Edwin S. 1974. A Religious History of America. 2d ed. New York: Harper and Row.

Geertz, Clifford. 1968. Islam Observed: Religious Development in Morocco and Indonesia. Chicago and London: University of Chicago Press.

———. 1973. The Interpretation of Cultures. New York: Basic Books.

Geiger, Theodor. 1932. Die soziale Schichtung des deutschen Volkes. Reprint. Darmstadt: Wissenschaftliche Buchgesellschaft, 1972.

Gellner, Ernest. 1981. Muslim Society. Cambridge: Cambridge University Press.

Gellner, Ernest, and Vatin, Jean-Claude, eds. 1981. Islam et politique au Maghreb. Paris: CRESM.

Gerami, Shahin. 1989. Religious Fundamentalism as a Response to Foreign Dependency: The Case of the Iranian Revolution. In: Social Compass 36, 4: 451–67.

Germani, Gino. 1978. Authoritarianism, Fascism, and National Populism. New Brunswick, N.J.: Transaction Books.

Gholamasad, Dawud. 1985. Iran: Die Entstehung der "Islamischen Revolution." Hamburg: Junius.

Gill, Charles Otis, and Pinchot, Gifford. 1913. The Country Church: The Decline of Its Influence and the Remedy. New York: Macmillan.

Glaab, Charles N. 1968. Metropolis and Suburb: The Changing American City. In: Braeman et al., eds. 1968: 399–437.

Göbel, Karl-Heinrich. 1984. Moderne schiitische Politik und Staatsidee nach Taufiq al-Fukaiki, Muhammad Gawad Mugniya, Ruhullah Humaini (Khomeyni). Opladen: Leske and Budrich.

God Hath Spoken. 1919. Twenty-five Addresses Delivered at the World Conference on Christian Fundamentals, May 25 to June 1, 1919. Philadelphia: Bible Conference Committee.

Goldberg, Robert Alan. 1981. Hooded Empire: The Ku Klux Klan in Colorado. Urbana: University of Illinois Press.

Goldfrank, Walter L. 1982. Comment on Skocpol (1982). In: Theory and Society 11: 301–4.

Good, Mary-Jo Del Vecchio. 1978. A Comparative Perspective on Women in Provincial Iran and Turkey. In: Beck and Keddie, eds. 1978: 482–500.

Gould, Stephen J. 1987. William Jennings Bryan's Last Campaign. In: Natural History 11: 16–26.

Gray, James M. 1922. The Deadline of Doctrine around the Church. Chicago: Moody Bible Institute.

Green, Jerrold D. 1982. Revolution in Iran: The Politics of Countermobilization. New York: Praeger.

Greene, William B. 1919. The Crises of Christianity and Their Significance. In: Princeton Theological Review 17: 345–64.

Greussing, Kurt. 1981. Neue Politik, alter Despotismus: Perspektiven der islamischen Revolution im Iran. In: Berliner Institut, ed. 1981: 18–44.

Gulick, John. 1969. Village and City: Cultural Continuities in Twentieth-Century Middle Eastern Cultures. In: Lapidus, ed. 1969: 122–58

Gulick, John, and Gulick, Margaret E. 1978. The Domestic Social Environment of Women and Girls in Isfahan, Iran. In: Beck and Keddie, eds. 1978: 501–21.

Gusfield, Joseph. 1962. Mass Society and Extremist Politics. In: American Sociological Review 27, 1: 19–30.

———. 1963. Symbolic Crusade: Status Politics and the American Temperance Movement. Urbana: University of Illinois Press.

Haddad, Yvonne Y. 1983. Sayyid Qutb: Ideologue of Islamic Revival. In: Esposito, ed. 1983: 67–98.

Haeri, Shala. 1983. The Institution of Mut'a Marriage in Iran: A Formal and Historical Perspective. In: Nashat, ed. 1983: 231–51.

Haidari, Ibrahim. 1975. Zur Soziologie des schiitischen Chiliasmus: Ein Beitrag zur Erforschung des irakischen Passionsspiels. Freiburg: Klaus Schwarz.

Hairi, Abdul-Hadi. 1976/1977. Why Did the Ulama Participate in the Persian Constitutional Revolution of 1905–1909? In: Die Welt des Islams 17: 127–54.

———. 1977a. Shi'ism and Constitutionalism in Iran. Leiden: E. J. Brill.

———. 1977b. Shaykh Fazl Allah Nuri's Refutation of the Idea of Constitutionalism. In: Middle Eastern Studies 13: 327–39.

Hallenbeck, Wilbur C. 1929. Minneapolis Churches and Their Comity Problems. New York: Institute of Social and Religious Research.

———. 1934. Urban Organization of Protestantism. New York: Harper and Brothers.

Haller, Mark. 1972. Urban Vice and Civic Reform: Chicago in the Early Twentieth Century. In: Jackson and Schultz, eds. 1972: 290–305.

Halliday, Fred. 1979. Theses on the Iranian Revolution. In: Race and Class 21: 81–90.

———. 1986. Iranian Foreign Policy since 1979: Internationalism and Nationalism in the Islamic Revolution. In: Cole and Keddie, eds. 1986: 88–107.

Halliday, Fred, and Alavi, Hamza, eds. 1988. State and Ideology in the Middle East and Pakistan. New York: Monthly Review Press.

Handlin, Oscar. 1987. Al Smith and His America. New Edition. Boston: Northeastern University Press.

Hanson, Brad. 1983. The "Westoxication" of Iran: Depictions and Reactions of Behrangi, Al-e Ahmad, and Shari'ati. In: International Journal of Middle East Studies 15: 1–23.

Harring, Sidney L. 1983. Policing a Class Society: The Experience of American Cities, 1865–1915. New Brunswick, N.J.: Rutgers University Press.

Hatch, Nathan O., and Noll, Mark A., eds. 1982. The Bible in America. New York: Oxford University Press.

Hays, Samuel P. 1957. The Response to Industrialism, 1885–1914. Chicago: University of Chicago Press.

Hegland, Mary. 1983a. Two Images of Husain: Accommodation and Revolution in an Iranian Village. In: Keddie, ed. 1983: 218–35.

———. 1983b. Ritual and Revolution in Iran. In: Aronoff, ed. 1983: 75–100.

Heper, Metin. 1981. Islam, Polity, and Society in Turkey: A Middle Eastern Perspective. In: Middle East Journal 35: 345–63.

Heper, Metin, and Israeli, Raphael, eds. 1984. Islam and Politics in the Modern Middle East. London and Sydney: Croom Helm.

Herf, Jeffrey. 1984. Reactionary Modernism: Technology, Culture, and Politics in Weimar and the Third Reich. Cambridge: Cambridge University Press.

Hertzberg, Arthur. 1986. The Religious Right in the State of Israel. In: Annals, AAPSS, January: 84–92.

Higham, John. 1955. Strangers in the Land: Patterns of American Nativism, 1860–1925. New Brunswick, N.J.: Rutgers University Press.

Hoffmann-Ladd, Valerie J. 1987. Polemics on the Modesty and Segregation of Women in Contemporary Egypt. In: International Journal of Middle East Studies 19, 1: 23–50.

Hofstadter, Richard. 1955a. The Age of Reform. New York: Vintage.

———. 1955b. The Pseudo-Conservative Revolt. In: Bell, ed. 1963: 75–95.

———. 1963. Anti-Intellectualism in American Life. New York: Vintage.

———. 1965. Fundamentalism and Status Politics on the Right. In: Columbia University Forum 8, 3: 18–24.

———. 1979. The Paranoid Style in American Politics. Chicago: University of Chicago Press.

Hofstadter, Richard, ed. 1963. The Progressive Movement, 1900–1915. Englewood Cliffs, N.J.: Prentice-Hall.

Hollenweger, Walter J. 1972. The Pentecostals. Minneapolis: Augsburg Publishing House.

Holmes, Obadiah. 1921. The Threat of Millenialism. In: Christian Century, 28 April: 10–13; 5 May: 15–18.

Hooglund, Eric. 1982. Land and Revolution in Iran, 1960–1980. Austin: University of Texas Press.

———. 1986a. Iran, 1980–1985: Political and Economic Trends. In: Keddie and Hooglund, eds. 1986: 17–31.

———. 1986b. Social Origins of the Revolutionary Clergy. In: Keddie and Hooglund, eds. 1986: 74–83.

Hooglund, Eric, and Royce, William. 1985. The Shi'i Clergy of Iran and the Conception of an Islamic State. In: State, Culture, and Society 1, 3: 102–17.

Hopkins, Charles H. 1940. The Rise of the Social Gospel in American Protestantism, 1865–1915. New Haven: Yale University Press.

Horowitz, Irving L. 1982. The New Fundamentalism. In: Society 20: 40–47.

Hourani, Albert, and Stern, S. M., eds. 1970. The Islamic City. Oxford: Oxford University Press.

Hudson, Michael C. 1980. Islam and Political Development. In: Esposito, ed. 1980: 1–24.

Humphreys, R. Stephen. 1979. Islam and Political Values in Saudi Arabia, Egypt, and Syria. In: Middle East Journal 33, 1: 1–19.

———. 1983. The Contemporary Resurgence in the Context of Modern Islam. In: Dessouki, ed. 1983: 67–83.

Hunter, James D. 1983. American Evangelicalism: Conservative Religion and the Quandary of Modernity. New Brunswick, N.J.: Rutgers University Press.

Hunter, Shireen T. 1986. Islamic Fundamentalism: What It Really Is and Why It Frightens the West. In: SAIS Review 6/1: 189–200.

Hunter, Shireen T., ed. 1988. The Politics of Islamic Revivalism: Diversity and Unity. Bloomington and Indianapolis: Indiana University Press.

Hutchison, William R. 1982. The Modernist Impulse in American Protestantism. New York: Oxford University Press.

Hutchison, William R., ed. 1968. American Protestant Thought: The Liberal Era. New York: Harper and Row.

Hyman, Anthony. 1985. Muslim Fundamentalism. In: Conflict Studies 174: 3–27.

Ibrahim, Saad Eddin. 1980. Anatomy of Egypt's Militant Islamic Groups: Methodological Note and Preliminary Findings. In: International Journal of Middle East Studies 12, 4: 423–53.

———. 1983. Islamic Militancy as a Social Movement: The Case of Two Groups in Egypt. In: Dessouki, ed. 1983: 117–37.

Interchurch World Movement. 1920a. World Survey. Vol. 1: American Volume. New York: Interchurch Press.

———. 1920b. Susquehanna County Survey: Fieldwork Done by F. E. Cholerton. New York: Interchurch Press.

Ionescu, Ghita, and Gellner, Ernest, eds. 1969. Populism: Its Meaning and National Characteristics. London: Weidenfeld and Nicolson.

Irfani, Suroosh. 1983. Revolutionary Islam in Iran: Popular Liberation or Religious Dictatorship? London: Zed Books.

Ishaque, Khalid M. 1983. The Islamic Approach to Economic Development. In: Esposito, ed. 1983: 268–76.

Issawi, Charles. 1978. The Iranian Economy, 1925–1975: Fifty Years of Economic Development. In: Lenczowski, ed. 1978: 129–66.

Jabbari, Ahmad. 1981. Economic Factors in Iran's Revolution: Poverty, Inequality, and Inflation. In: Jabbari and Olson, eds. 1981: 163–214.

Jabbari, Ahmad, and Olson, Robert, eds. 1981. Iran: Essays on a Revolution in the Making. Lexington: Mazda Publishers.

Jackson, Kenneth T. 1967. The Ku Klux Klan in the City, 1915–1930. New York: Oxford University Press.

Jackson, Kenneth T., and Schultz, Stanley K., eds. 1972. Cities in American History. New York: A. Knopf.

Jazani, Bizhan. 1980. Capitalism and Revolution in Iran. London: Zed Press.

Karimi, Setareh. 1986. Economic Policies and Structural Changes since the Revolution. In: Keddie and Hooglund, eds. 1986: 32–54.

Katouzian, Homa. 1981. The Political Economy of Modern Iran: Despotism and Pseudo-Modernism, 1926–1979. New York and London: New York University Press.

———. 1983. Shi'ism and Islamic Economics: Sadr and Bani Sadr. In: Keddie, ed. 1983: 145–65.

Katznelson, Ira, and Weir, Margaret. 1985. Schooling for All: Class, Race, and the Decline of the Democratic Ideal. New York: Basic Books.

Kazemi, Farhad. 1980a. Poverty and Revolution in Iran: The Migrant Poor, Urban Marginality, and Politics. New York: New York University Press.

———. 1980b. Urban Migrants and the Revolution. In: Iranian Studies 13: 257–77.

———. 1984. The Feda'iyan-e Islam: Fanaticism, Politics, and Terror. In: Arjomand, ed. 1984: 158–76.

———. 1985. State and Society in the Ideology of the Devotees of Islam. In: State, Culture, and Society 1, 3: 118–35.

Keddie, Nikki R. 1966. Religion and Rebellion in Iran: The Tobacco Protest of 1891–1892. London: Frank Cass.

———. 1972. The Roots of Ulama's Power in Modern Iran. In: Keddie, ed. 1972: 211–29.

———. 1980a. Iran: Religion, Politics, and Society. London: Frank Cass.

———. 1980b. L'ayatollah est-il un integriste? In: Le Monde, 22 August: 2.

———. 1981. Roots of Revolution: An Interpretive History of Modern Iran. New Haven and London: Yale University Press.

———. 1982. Comment on Skocpol (1982). In: Theory and Society 11: 285–92.

———. 1986. Is Shi'ism Revolutionary? In: Keddie and Hooglund, eds. 1986: 113–26.

———. 1988. Iranian Revolutions in Comparative Perspective. In: Burke and Lapidus, eds. 1988: 298–313.

Keddie, Nikki R., ed. 1972. Scholars, Saints, and Sufis: Muslim Religious Institutions in the Middle East since 1500. Berkeley and Los Angeles: University of California Press.

———, ed. 1983. Religion and Politics in Iran: Shi'ism from Quietism to Revolution. New Haven and London: Yale University Press.

Keddie, Nikki R., and Beck, Lois. 1978. Introduction. In: Beck and Keddie, eds. 1978: 1–34.

Keddie, Nikki R., and Hooglund, Eric, eds. 1986. The Iranian Revolution and the Islamic Republic. Syracuse: Syracuse University Press.

Kedourie, Elie, and Haim, Sylvia, eds. 1980. Towards a Modern Iran: Studies in Thought, Politics, and Society. London: Frank Cass.

Keesecker, Ward W. 1930. Legal Status of Bible Reading and Religious Instruction in Public Schools. U.S. Dept. of the Interior, Bulletin, 1930, no. 14, Washington, D.C.

Kepel, Gilles. 1985. Muslim Extremism in Egypt: The Prophet and Pharaoh. Berkeley and Los Angeles: University of California Press.

Khomeini, Sayyed Ruhollah. 1981. Islam and Revolution: Writings and Declarations of Imam Khomeini. Translated and annotated by Hamid Algar. Berkeley: Mizan Press.

Kincheloe, Samule C. 1928. Major Reactions to City Churches. Reprinted in: Lee, ed. 1967: 102–15.

Kippenberg, Hans G. 1981. Jeder Tag 'Ashura, jedes Grab Kerbala: Zur Ritualisierung der Straßenkämpfe im Iran. In: Berliner Institut, ed. 1981: 217–56.

Kniker, Charles R. 1982. New Attitudes, New Curricula: The Changing Role of the Bible in Protestant Education, 1880–1920. In: Barr and Piediscalzi, eds. 1982: 121–42.

Kocka, Jürgen, ed. 1987. Bürger und Bürgerlichkeit im 19. Jahrhundert. Göttingen: Vandenhoeck and Ruprecht.

Kodalle, Klaus-M., ed. 1988. Gott und Politik in USA. Frankfurt: Athenäum.

Kornhauser, William. 1959. The Politics of Mass Society. Glencoe, Ill.: Free Press.

Lahidji, Abdol Karim. 1988. Constitutionalism and Clerical Authority. In: Arjomand, ed. 1988: 133–58.

Lake, Kirsopp. 1925. The Religion of Yesterday and To-morrow. Boston: Houghton Mifflin.

Lambton, Ann K. S. 1956. Quis custodiet custodes? Some Reflections on the Persian Theory of Government (Conclusion). In: Studia Islamica 6: 125–46.

———. 1964. A Reconsideration of the Position of the Marja' Al-Taqlid and the Religious Institution. In: Studia Islamica 20: 115–35.

———. 1969. The Persian Land Reform, 1962–1966. Oxford: Clarendon Press.

Lapidus, Ira M. 1969. Muslim Cities and Islamic Societies. In: Lapidus, ed. 1969: 47–79.

———. 1973a. Traditional Muslim Cities: Structure and Change. In: Brown, ed. 1973: 51–69.

———. 1973b. The Evolution of Muslim Urban Society. In: Comparative Studies in Society and History 15: 21–50.

———. 1984. Muslim Cities in the Later Middle Ages. New York: Cambridge University Press.

Lapidus, Ira M., ed. 1969. Middle Eastern Cities. Berkeley and Los Angeles: University of California Press.

Laqueur, Walter, ed. 1983. Fascism: A Reader's Guide. Berkeley and Los Angeles: University of California Press.

Lawrence, Bruce B. 1987. Muslim Fundamentalist Movements: Reflections toward a New Approach. In: Stowasser, ed. 1987: 15–36.

———. 1989a. Critique of William Shepard "Fundamentalism, Christian and Islamic." In: Religion 19: 275–80.

———. 1989b. Defenders of God: The Fundamentalist Revolt against the Modern Age. San Francisco: Harper and Row.

Leach, William H. 1922. The Weakness of Protestantism in American Cities. In: Journal of Religion 2, 6: 616–23.

Lee, Robert, ed. 1967. Cities and Churches: Readings on the Urban Church. Philadelphia: Westminster Press.

Lee, Robert, and Marty, Martin E., eds. 1964. Religion and Social Conflict. New York: Oxford University Press.

Leete, Frederick DeLand. 1915. The Church in the City. New York: Abingdon Press.

Leiden, Carl, ed. 1966. The Conflict of Traditionalism and Modernism in the Muslim Middle East. Austin: University of Texas Press.

Lenczowski, George, ed. 1975. Political Elites in the Middle East. Washington, D.C.: American Enterprise Institute.

———, ed. 1978. Iran under the Pahlavis. Stanford: Hoover Institution Press.

Lepsius, M. Rainer. 1966. Parteiensystem und Sozialstruktur: Zum Problem der Demokratisierung der deutschen Gesellschaft. In· Abel et al., eds. 1966. 371–93.

———. 1974. Sozialstruktur und soziale Schichtung in der Bundesrepublik Deutschland. In: Löwenthal and Schwarz, eds. 1974: 263–88.

———. 1977. Modernisierungspolitik als Institutionenbildung: Kriterien institutioneller Differenzierung. In: Zapf, ed. 1977: 17–28.

———. 1987. Zur Soziologie des Bürgertums und der Bürgerlichkeit. In: Kocka, ed. 1987: 79–100.

Leuba, James H. 1916. The Belief in God and Immortality. Boston: Sherman, French.

Leuchtenburg, William E. 1958. The Perils of Prosperity, 1914–1932. Chicago: University of Chicago Press.

Levine, Lawrence W. 1965. Defender of the Faith, William Jennings Bryan: The Last Decade, 1915–1925. New York: Oxford University Press.

Liebersohn, Harry. 1985. The American Academic Community before the First World War. In: Conze and Kocka, eds. 1985: 163–85.

Light on Prophecy. 1918. Proceedings and addresses at the Philadelphia Prophetic Conference, 28–30 May 1918. New York: Christian Herald.

Lippmann, Walter. 1929. A Preface to Morals. New York: Macmillan.

Lippy, Charles H., and Williams, Peter W., eds. 1988. Encyclopedia of the American Religious Experience. 3 vols. New York: Charles Scribner's Sons.

Lipset, Seymour M. 1955. The Sources of the "Radical Right." In: Bell, ed. 1963: 307–71.

———. 1960. Political Man: The Social Base of Politics. New York: Doubleday.

———. 1964. Religion and Politics in American Past and Present. In: Lee and Marty, eds. 1964: 69–126.

———. 1979. The First New Nation. New York: W.W. Norton.

———. 1985. Consensus and Conflict: Essays in Political Sociology. New Brunswick, N.J.: Transaction Books.

Lipset, Seymour M., and Raab, Earl. 1978. The Politics of Unreason. 2d ed. Chicago: University of Chicago Press.

Lockwood, David. Social Integration and System Integration. In: Zollschan and Hirsch, eds. 1964: 244–57.

Loeffler, Reinhold. 1988. Islam in Practice: Religious Beliefs in a Persian Village. Albany: SUNY Press.

Löwenthal, Richard, and Schwarz, Hans-Peter, eds. 1974. Die Zweite Republik. Stuttgart: Seewald.

Lumpkin, William L. 1969. Baptist Confessions of Faith. Revised Edition. Valley Forge: Judson Press.

Lustick, Ian S. 1988. For the Land and the Lord: Jewish Fundamentalism in Israel. New York: Council on Foreign Relations.

Lyman, Eugene. 1918. The Religion of Democracy. In: Union Theological Seminary Bulletin, 2: 30–54.

Lynd, Robert S., and Lynd, Helen Merrell. 1929. Middletown: A Study in Modern American Culture. Reprint. New York: Harcourt Brace Jovanovich, 1956.

Macartney, Clarence E. 1925. The State of the Church. In: Princeton Theological Review 23: 177–92.

Machen, J. Gresham. 1923. Christianity and Liberalism. New York: Macmillan.

Makdisi, George, ed. 1965. Arabic and Islamic Studies in Honor of Hamilton A.R. Gibb. Cambridge: Harvard University Press.

Mannheim, Karl. 1936. Ideology and Utopia: An Introduction to the Sociology of Knowledge. Translated by Louis Wirth and Edward Shils. New York: Harcourt, Brace and World.

———. 1986. Conservatism: A Contribution to the Sociology of Knowledge. Translated by D. Ketteler, V. Meja, and N. Stehr. London: Routledge and Kegan Paul.

Marsden, George. 1971. Defining Fundamentalism. In: Christian Scholar's Review 1, 2: 141–51.

———. 1980. Fundamentalism and American Culture. New York: Oxford University Press.

———. 1982. Every One's Own Interpreter? The Bible, Science, and Authority in Mid-Nineteenth-Century America. In: Hatch and Noll, eds. 1982: 79–100.

Marty, Martin E. 1977. Righteous Empire: The Protestant Experience in America. New York: Harper and Row.

———. 1984. Pilgrims in Their Own Land. Boston: Little, Brown.

———. 1988. Fundamentalism as a Social Phenomenon. In: Bulletin of the American Academy of Arts and Sciences 42, 2: 15–29.

Massee, J.C. 1920. Opening Address. In: Baptist Fundamentals 1920: 3–11.

Mathews, Shailer. 1917. Will Christ Come Again? Pamphlet. Chicago.

May, Henry. 1967. Protestant Churches and Industrial America. New York: Harper and Row.

May, Mark A., et al. 1933. The Education of American Ministers. Vol. 2. The Profession of the Ministry: Its Status and Problems. New York: Institute of Social and Religious Research.

McLoughlin, William G. 1978. Revivals, Awakenings, and Reform. Chicago: University of Chicago Press.

Mead, Sidney E. 1954. Denominationalism: The Shape of Protestantism in America. In: Church History 23, 4: 291–320.

———. 1963. The Lively Experiment: The Shaping of Christianity in America. New York: Harper and Row.

———. 1975. The Nation with the Soul of a Church. New York: Harper and Row.

Mecklin, John M. 1924. The Ku Klux Klan: A Study of the American Mind. New York: Harcourt, Brace.

Medding, Peter, ed. 1986. Studies in Contemporary Jewry (2). Bloomington: Indiana University Press.

Mernissi, Fatima. 1987. Beyond the Veil: Male-Female Dynamics in Modern Muslim Society. Revised Edition. Bloomington and Indianapolis: Indiana University Press.

———. 1991. The Veil and the Male Elite. Translated by Mary Jo Lakeland. Reading, Mass.: Addison Wesley.

Merton, Robert K. 1968. Social Theory and Social Structure. Enlarged Edition. New York: Free Press.

Meyer, Thomas. 1989. Fundamentalismus: Aufstand gegen die Moderne. Hamburg: Rowohlt.

Meynen, Emil, ed. 1973. Geographie Heute. Wiesbaden: Steiner.

Michaelsen, Robert S., and Roof, Wade Clarke, eds. 1986. Liberal Protestantism. New York: Pilgrim Press.

Miller, Robert M. 1956. A Note on the Relationship between the Protestant Churches and the Revived Ku Klux Klan. In: Journal of Southern History 22: 355–68.

Mills, C. Wright. 1951. White Collar: The American Middle Classes. Reprint. New York: Oxford University Press, 1979.

Mitchell, Richard P. 1969. The Society of the Muslim Brothers. London: Oxford University Press.

Mojtahed, Davoud. 1980. Rural-Urban Migration in Iran, 1966–1976. Ph.D. diss., United States International University.

Momen, Moojan. 1985. An Introduction to Shi'i Islam: The History and Doctrines of Twelver Shi'ism. New Haven: Yale University Press.

Moore, LeRoy. 1968. Another Look at Fundamentalism: A Response to Ernest R. Sandeen. In: Church History 37, 2: 195–202.

Morgan, Richard E. 1972. The Supreme Court and Religion. New York: Free Press.

Mossavar-Rahmani, Yasmin L. 1983. Family Planning in Post-Revolutionary Iran. In: Nashat, ed. 1983: 253–62.

Mottahedeh, Roy. 1985. The Mantle of the Prophet: Religion and Politics in Iran. New York: Pantheon.

Munson, Henry. 1988. Islam and Revolution in the Middle East. New Haven and London: Yale University Press.

Mutahhari, Murtaza. 1985a. Fundamentals of Islamic Thought. With annotations and an introduction by Hamid Algar. Berkeley: Mizan Press.

———. 1985b. Die Geistlichkeit und die Islamische Revolution. Ed. by the Embassy of the Islamic Republic of Iran. Bonn.

———. 1986. Wesen und Faktoren der Islamischen Revolution in Iran. Ed. by the Embassy of the Islamic Republic of Iran. Bonn.

Naficy, Hamid. 1981. Cinema as a Political Instrument. In: Bonine and Keddie, eds. 1981: 265–83.

Nagel, Tilman. 1981. Staat und Glaubensgemeinschaft im Islam. 2 vols. Zurich and Munich: Artemis.

Najmabadi, Afsaneh. 1986. Mystifications of the Past and Illusions of the Future. In: Keddie and Hooglund, eds. 1986: 147–62.

———. 1987. Iran's Turn to Islam: From Modernism to a Moral Order. In: Middle East Journal 41, 2: 202–17.

Nashat, Guity. 1981. From Bazaar to Market: Foreign Trade and Economic Development in Nineteenth-Century Iran. In: Iranian Studies 14, 1: 53–85.

———. 1983a. Women in Pre-Revolutionary Iran: A Historical Overview. In: Nashat, ed. 1983: 5–35.

———. 1983b. Women in the Ideology of the Islamic Republic. In: Nashat, ed. 1983: 195–216.

———, ed. 1983. Women and Revolution in Iran. Boulder: Westview Press.

Newman, Louis I. 1925. The Sectarian Invasion of Our Public Schools. San Francisco.

Nichols, Robert H. 1925. Fundamentalism in the Presbyterian Church. In: Journal of Religion 5, 1: 14–36.

Niebuhr, H. Richard. 1929. The Social Sources of Denominationalism. Reprint. New York: Peter Smith, 1975.

———. 1937. Fundamentalism. In: Encyclopaedia of the Social Sciences, vol. 5: 526–27.

Noll, Mark A., et al., eds. 1983. Eerdman's Handbook to Christianity in America. Grand Rapids: W. B. Eerdman's.

Norton, August Richard. 1987. Amal and the Shi'a: Struggle for the Soul of Lebanon. Austin: University of Texas Press.

Oaks, Dallin H., ed. 1963. The Wall between Church and State. Chicago: University of Chicago Press.

Oehring, Otmar. 1984. Die Türkei im Spannungsfeld extremer Ideologien, 1973–1980. Berlin: Klaus Schwarz.

Olson, Mancur. 1965. The Logic of Collected Action: Public Goods and the Theory of Groups. Cambridge: Harvard University Press.

Ostrander, Gilman M. 1968. The Revolution in Morals. In: Braeman et al., eds. 1968: 323–49.

O'Sullivan, Noel, ed. 1983. Revolutionary Theory and Political Reality. New York: St. Martin's Press.

Pahlavi, Mohammed Reza. 1961. Mission for My Country. London: Hutchinson.

———. 1967. The White Revolution. 2d ed. Tehran: Kayhan Press.

———. 1980. Answer to History. New York: Stein and Day.

Pakizegi, Behnaz. 1978. Legal and Social Position of Iranian Women. In: Beck and Keddie, eds. 1978: 216–26.

Park, Robert, et al., eds. 1925. The City. Chicago: University of Chicago Press.

Parsa, Misagh. 1989. Social Origins of the Iranian Revolution. New Brunswick, N.J.: Rutgers University Press.

Parsons, Talcott. 1969. Politics and Social Structure. New York: Free Press.

Perry, Everett L. 1959. The Role of Socio-Economic Factors in the Rise and Development of American Fundamentalism. Ph.D. diss., University of Chicago.

Pesaran, M.H. 1982. The System of Dependent Capitalism in Pre- and Post-Revolutionary Iran. In: International Journal of Middle East Studies 14: 501–22.

Peters, Rudolph. 1984. Erneuerungsbewegungen im Islam vom 18. bis zum 20. Jahrhundert und die Rolle des Islams in der neueren Geschichte: Antikolonialismus und Nationalismus. In: Ende and Steinbach, eds. 1984: 91–131.

Peterson, Samuel R. 1979. The Ta'ziyeh and Related Arts. In: Chelkowski, ed. 1979: 64–87.

Pfaff, Richard H. 1966. Technicism versus Traditionalism: The Developmental Dialectic in the Middle East. In: Leiden, ed. 1966: 101–16.

Pfeffer, Leo. 1967. Church, State, and Freedom. Revised edition. Boston: Beacon Press.

———. 1975. God, Caesar, and the Constitution: The Court as Referee of Church-State Confrontation. Boston: Beacon Press.

Pipes, Daniel. 1983. In the Path of God: Islam and Political Power. New York: Basic Books.

Piscatori, James P., ed. 1983. Islam in the Political Process. Cambridge: Cambridge University Press.

Porter, J. W. 1920. An Unexpected Message. In: Baptist Fundamentals 1920: 109–15.

Rajaee, Farhang. 1983. Islamic Values and World View: Khomeyni on Man, the State, and International Politics. New York: University Press of America.

Ranulf, Svend. 1964. Moral Indignation and Middle-Class Psychology. 2d ed. New York: Schocken Books.

Raschke, Joachim. 1987. Soziale Bewegungen: Ein historisch-systematischer Abriß. Frankfurt: Campus.

Rausch, David A. 1980. Zionism within Early American Fundamentalism, 1878–1918. Lewiston, N.Y: Edwin Mellen.

Reichley, A. James. 1985. Religion in American Public Life. Washington, D.C.: Brookings Institution.

The Revolution of the Shah and the People. 1967. 10 vols. London: Transorient.

Richard, Yann. 1981. Contemporary Shi'i Thought. In: Keddie, ed. 1981: 202–28.

———. 1983a. Der verborgene Imam: Die Geschichte des Schiismus in Iran. Berlin: Klaus Wagenbach.

———. 1983b. Le rôle du clergé: tendances contradictoires du Chi'isme iranien contemporain. In: ASSR 55, 1: 5–27.

———. 1983c. Ayatollah Kashani: Precursor of the Islamic Republic? In: Keddie, ed., 1985: 101–24.

Riesebrodt, Martin. 1980. Ideen, Interessen, Rationalisierung: Kritische Anmerkungen zu F. H. Tenbrucks Interpretation des Werkes Max Webers. In: Kölner Zeitschrift für Soziologie und Sozialpsychologie 32: 111–29.

———. 1986. From Patriarchalism to Capitalism: The Theoretical Context of Max Weber's Agrarian Studies, 1892–1893. In: Economy and Society 15: 476–502.

———. 1988. Fundamentalismus und "Modernisierung": Zur Soziologie protestantisch-fundamentalistischer Bewegungen in den USA im 20. Jahrhundert. In: Kodalle, ed. 1988: 112–25.

Riley, William B. 1916. The Perennial Revival: A Plea for Evangelism. Revised edition. Philadelphia: American Baptist Publication Society.

———. 1917. The Menace of Modernism. New York: Christian Alliance Publishing.

———. 1919. The Great Divide, or Christ and the Present Crisis. In: God Hath Spoken 1919: 27–45.

———. 1920. Modernism in Baptist Schools. In: Baptist Fundamentals 1920: 165–87.

Robbins, Thomas. 1985. New Religious Movements on the Frontier of Church and State. In: Robbins et al., eds. 1985: 7–27.

Robbins, Thomas, et al., eds. 1985. Cults, Culture, and the Law: Perspectives on New Religious Movements. Chico, Calif.: Scholars Press.

Rogin, Michael Paul. 1967. The Intellectuals and McCarthy: The Radical Specter. Cambridge: MIT Press.

Rose, Gregory. 1983. Velayat-e Faqih and the Recovery of Islamic Identity in the Thought of Ayatollah Khomeini. In: Keddie, ed. 1983: 166–88.

Roth, Günther. 1987. Politische Herrschaft und persönliche Freiheit. Frankfurt: Suhrkamp TW.

Roy, Ralph Lord. 1953. Apostles of Discord. Boston: Beacon Press.

Russell, C. Allyn. 1976. Voices of American Fundamentalism: Seven Biographical Studies. Philadelphia: Westminster Press.

Ryan, Patrick J. 1984. Islamic Fundamentalism: A Questionable Category. In: America: 437–40.

Sachedina, Abdulaziz. 1981. Islamic Messianism: The Idea of the Mahdi in Twelver Shi'ism. Albany: SUNY Press.

———. 1983. Ali Shariati: Ideologue of the Iranian Revolution. In: Esposito, ed. 1983: 191–214.

———. 1988. The Just Ruler in Shi'ite Islam: The Comprehensive Authority of the Jurist in Imamite Jurisprudence. New York: Oxford University Press.

Sandeen, Ernest R. 1967. Towards a Historical Interpretation of the Origins of Fundamentalism. In: Church History 36, 1: 66–83.

———. 1970. The Roots of Fundamentalism. Chicago: University of Chicago Press.

———. 1971. Defining Fundamentalism: A Reply to Professor Marsden. In: Christian Scholar's Review 1, 3: 227–32.

Sanderson, Ross W. 1932. The Strategy of City Church Planning. New York: Institute of Social and Religious Research.

Saqqaf, Abdulaziz Y., ed. 1987. The Middle East City. New York: Paragon House.

Sarkisyanz, Emanuel. 1955. Russland und der Messianismus des Orients: Sendungsbewußtsein und politischer Chiliasmus des Ostens. Tübingen: J. C. B. Mohr (Paul Siebeck).

Savory, Roger M. 1978. Social Development in Iran during the Pahlavi Era. In: Lenczowski, ed. 1978: 85–127.

Schimmel, Annemarie. 1975. Mystical Dimensions of Islam. Chapel Hill: University of North Carolina Press.

Schlesinger, Arthur M. 1951. The Rise of Modern America, 1865–1951. New York: Macmillan.

Schluchter, Wolfgang. 1981. The Rise of Western Rationalism. Berkeley and Los Angeles: University of California Press.

Schuckar, Monika. 1983. Der Kampf gegen die Sünde: Frauenbild und Moralpolitik in der Islamischen Republik Iran. Reihe Internationalismus Informationen, no. 10. Gießen.

Seger, Martin. 1975. Strukturelemente der Stadt Teheran und das Modell der modernen orientalischen Stadt. In: Erdkunde 29: 21–38.

———. 1978. Teheran: Eine stadtgeographische Studie. Wien: Springer.

———. 1979. Zum Dualismus der Struktur orientalischer Städte: Das Beispiel Teheran. In: Mitteilungen der Österreichischen Geographischen Gesellschaft 121: 129–58.

Shariati, Ali. 1979. On the Sociology of Islam. Translated by Hamid Algar. Berkeley: Mizan Press.

———. 1980. From Where Shall We Begin? Translated by F. Marjani. Houston: Free Islamic Literature.

———. 1981. Fatima is Fatima. Translated by L. Bakhtiar. Tehran: Shariati Foundation.

Shepard, William E. 1987a. Islam and Ideology: Towards a Typology. In: International Journal of Middle East Studies 19: 307–36.

———. 1987b. Fundamentalism, Christian and Islamic. In: Religion 17: 355–78.

Shils, Edward. 1968. The Concept and Function of Ideology. In: International Encyclopedia of the Social Sciences, vol. 7: 66–76.

Shupe, Anson. 1989. Prophets of a Biblical America. In: Wall Street Journal, 12 April: A18.

Silver, Allan. 1990. The Curious Centrality of the Small Group in American Sociology. In: Sociology in America, Herbert Gans, ed. Newbury Park, Calif.: Sage.

Sivan, Emmanuel. 1985. Radical Islam: Medieval Theology and Modern Politics. New Haven: Yale University Press.

Sivers, Peter von. 1981. Work, Leisure, and Religion: The Social Roots of the Revival of Fundamentalist Islam in North Africa. In: Gellner and Vatin, eds. 1981: 355–72.

Skocpol, Theda. 1982. Rentier State and Shi'a Islam in the Iranian Revolution. In: Theory and Society 11: 265–83.

———. 1984. Emerging Agendas and Recurrent Strategies in Historical Sociology. In: Skocpol, ed. 1984: 356–91.

Skocpol, Theda, ed. 1984. Vision and Method in Historical Sociology. Cambridge: Cambridge University Press.

Smith, Gary S. 1985. The Seeds of Secularization: Calvinism, Culture, and Pluralism in America, 1870–1915. St. Paul: Christian University Press.

Stokes, Anson Phelps. 1950. Church and State in the United States. 3 vols. New York: Harper Brothers.

Stowasser, Barbara F., ed. 1987. The Islamic Impulse. London and Sydney: Croom Helm.

Straton, John R. 1920. The Menace of Immorality in Church and State. New York: George H. Doran.

————. 1925. The Famous New York Fundamentalist-Modernist Debates: The Orthodox Side. New York: George H. Doran.

————. 1929. Fighting the Devil in Modern Babylon. Boston: Stratford.

————. n.d.a. Church versus Stage. New York: Calvary Baptist Church.

————. n.d.b. Religious Democracy. New York: Calvary Baptist Church.

Strong, Josiah. 1915. The Challenge of the Church in the Twentieth-Century City. Boston.

Szasz, Ferenc Morton. 1982. The Divided Mind of Protestant America, 1880–1930. University of Alabama Press.

Tabari, Azar. 1982. Islam and the Struggle for Emancipation of Iranian Women. In: Tabari and Yeganeh, eds. 1982: 5–25.

————. 1983. The Role of the Clergy in Modern Iranian Politics. In: Keddie, ed. 1983: 47–72.

Tabari, Azar, and Yeganeh, Nahid, eds. 1982. In the Shadow of Islam: The Women's Movement in Iran. London: Zed Press.

Tabataba'i, Muhammad Husayn. 1977. Shi'ite Islam. Albany: SUNY Press.

Tachau, Frank, ed. 1975. Political Elites and Political Development in the Middle East. New York: Schenkman.

Taleghani, Mahmud. 1982. Society and Economics in Islam. With annotations and an introduction by Hamid Algar. Berkeley: Mizan Press.

Taleqani, Mahmood [Taleghani, Mahmud]. 1983. Islam and Ownership. Translated by Ahmad Jabbari and Farhang Rajaee. Lexington: Mazda Publishers.

Taylor, Alva W. 1919. Millenarians and Bolsheviks. In: Christian Century, 24 April: 16–17.

Thaiss, Gustav E. 1971. The Bazaar as a Case Study of Religion and Social Change. In: Yar-Shater, ed. 1971: 189–216.

————. 1972. Religious Symbolism and Social Change: The Drama of Husain. In: Keddie, ed. 1972: 349–66.

————. 1973. Religious Symbolism and Social Change: The Drama of Husain. Ph.D. diss., Washington University.

Tibi, Bassam. 1988. The Crisis of Modern Islam. Translated by J. von Sivers. Salt Lake City: University of Utah Press.

————. 1990. Islam and the Cultural Accommodation of Social Change. Translated by Clare Krojzl. Boulder: Westview Press.

Tilly, Charles. 1978. From Mobilization to Revolution. Reading, Mass.: Addison-Wesley.

————. 1984. Big Structures, Large Processes, Huge Comparisons. New York: Russel Sage Foundation.

Toprak, Binnaz. 1984. Politicisation of Islam in a Secular State: The National Salvation Party in Turkey. In: Arjomand, ed. 1984: 119–33.

Torrey, Reuben A. 1913. The Return of the Lord Jesus. Los Angeles: Bible Institute of Los Angeles.

―――. 1918. Will Christ Come Again? Los Angeles: Bible Institute of Los Angeles.

Touba, Jacquiline Rudolph. 1985. Effects of the Islamic Revolution on Women and the Family in Iran. In: Fathi, ed. 1985: 131–47.

Troeltsch, Ernst. 1931. The Social Teaching of the Christian Churches. 2 vols. Translated by Olive Wyan. New York: Macmillan. (Also a 1981 University of Chicago edition.)

Tuttle, William M. 1972. Contested Neighborhoods and Racial Violence: Chicago 1919, a Case Study. In: Jackson and Schultz, eds. 1972: 232–48.

Useem, Michael. 1975. Protest Movements in America. Indianapolis: Bobbs Merrill.

Vámbéry, Hermann. 1867. Meine Wanderungen und Erlebnisse in Persien. Reprint. Nuremberg: Nomad Press, 1979.

Vanderlaan, Eldred C., ed. 1925. Fundamentalism versus Modernism. New York: H.W. Wilson.

Vatandoust, Gholam-Reza. 1985. The Status of Iranian Women during the Pahlavi Regime. In: Fathi, ed. 1985: 107–30.

Waardenburg, Jacques. 1983. The Puritan Pattern in Islamic Revival Movements. In: Schweizerische Zeitschrift für Soziologie 3: 687–702.

Wacker, Grant. 1982. The Demise of Biblical Civilization. In: Hatch and Noll, eds. 1982: 121–38.

―――. 1984. The Function of Faith in Primitive Pentecostalism. In: Harvard Theological Review 77: 353–75.

Wade, Wyn Craig. 1987. The Fiery Cross: The Ku Klux Klan in America. New York: Simon and Schuster.

Warburg, Gabriel R., and Kupferschmidt, Uri M., eds. 1983. Islam, Nationalism, and Radicalism in Egypt and Sudan. New York: Praeger.

Weber, Max. 1951. The Religion of China. Translated by H. Gerth. New York: Free Press.

―――. 1978. Economy and Society. 2 vols. G. Roth and C. Wittich, eds. Berkeley and Los Angeles: University of California Press.

Weber, Timothy P. 1982. The Fundamentalist Use of the Bible. In: Hatch and Noll, eds. 1982: 101–20.

―――. 1987. Living in the Shadow of the Second Coming: American Premillenialism, 1875–1982. Chicago: University of Chicago Press.

Wenger, Robert E. 1973. Social Thought in American Fundamentalism, 1918–1933. Ph.D. diss., University of Nebraska.

Werle, Rainer, and Kreile, Renate. 1987. Renaissance des Islam—Das Beispiel der Türkei. Hamburg: Junius.

Wiebe, Robert H. 1967. The Search for Order, 1877–1920. New York: Hill and Wang.

Wilber, Donald N. 1975. Riza Shah Pahlavi: The Resurrection and Reconstruction of Iran. Hicksville: Exposition Press.

Williams, John A. 1980. Veiling in Egypt as a Political and Social Phenomenon. In: Esposito, ed. 1980: 71–85.

Wilson, Bryan R. 1970. Religious Sects. London: Weidenfeld and Nicolson.

Wilson, John F., and Drakeman, Donald L., eds. 1987. Church and State in
American History. 2d ed. Boston: Beacon Press.
Winter, Gibson. 1961. The Suburban Captivity of the Churches: An Analysis of
Protestant Responsibility in the Expanding Metropolis. Garden City, N.Y.:
Doubleday.
Wirth, Eugen. 1966a. Die soziale Stellung und Gliederung der Stadt im Os-
manischen Reich des 19. Jahrhunderts. In: Untersuchungen zur gesellschaft-
lichen Struktur der mittelalterlichen Städte in Europa, 403–27. Konstanz:
Jan Thorbecke.
————. 1966b. Damaskus-Aleppo-Beirut: Ein geographischer Vergleich dreier
nahöstlicher Städte im Spiegel ihrer sozial und wirtschaftlich tonangebenden
Schichten. In: Die Erde 97, 2: 96–137; 97, 3: 166–202.
————. 1968. Strukturwandlungen und Entwicklungstendenzen der orientalischen Stadt. In: Erdkunde 22: 101–28.
————. 1973. Die Beziehung der orientalisch-islamischen Stadt zum umgeben-
den Lande. In: Meynen, ed. 1973: 323–33.
————. 1974/1975. Zum Problem des Basars (Suq, Carsi): Versuch einer
Begriffsbestimmung und Theorie des traditionellen Wirtschaftszentrums der
orientalisch-islamischen Stadt. In: Der Islam 51, 2: 203–60; 52, 1: 6–45.
Wirth, Louis. 1938. Urbanism as a Way of Life. In: On Cities and Social Life.
Chicago: University of Chicago Press. 1964: 60–83.
Wright, Robin. 1988. Sacred Rage: The Wrath of Militant Islam. New York:
Simon and Schuster.
Yadlin, Rivka. 1983. Militant Islam in Egypt: Some Sociocultural Aspects. In:
Warburg and Kupferschmidt, eds. 1983: 159–82.
Yar-Shater, Ehsan, ed. 1971. Iran Faces the Seventies. New York: Praeger.
Yeganeh, Nahid. 1982. Women's Struggles in the Islamic Republic of Iran. In:
Tabari and Yeganeh, ed. 1982: 26–74.
Yeganeh, Nahid, and Keddie, Nikki R. 1986. Sexuality and Shi'i Social Protest
in Iran. In: Cole and Keddie, eds. 1986: 108–36.
Youssef, Michael. 1985. Revolt against Modernity: Muslim Zealots and the
West. Leiden: E. J. Brill.
Zapf, Wolfgang, ed. 1977. Probleme der Modernisierungspolitik. Meisenheim:
A. Hain.
Zollschan, George K., and Hirsch, Walter, eds. 1964. Explorations in Social
Change. Boston: Houghton Mifflin.
Zonis, Marvin. 1971. The Political Elite of Iran. Princeton: Princeton University
Press.
————. 1975. The Political Elite of Iran: A Second Stratum? In: Tachau, ed.
1975: 193–216.
————. 1980. The Pahlavi Political System of the 1970s. In: Friedrich-Ebert-
Stiftung 1980: 79–91.
Zubaida, Sami. 1987. The Quest for the Islamic State: Islamic Fundamentalism
in Egypt and Iran. In: Caplan, ed. 1987: 25–50.

Index